CONTENTS AT A GLANCE

MW00907687

Joomla!® Start to Finish

Joomla!® Start to Finish

HOW TO PLAN, EXECUTE, AND MAINTAIN YOUR WEB SITE

Jen Kramer

Wiley Publishing, Inc.

Joomla!® Start to Finish

Published by
Wiley Publishing, Inc.
10475 Crosspoint Boulevard
Indianapolis, IN 46256
www.wiley.com

For general information on our other products and services please contact our Customer Care Department within the United States at (877) 762-2974, outside the United States at (317) 572-3993 or fax (317) 572-4002.

Wiley also publishes its books in a variety of electronic formats. Some content that appears in print may not be available in electronic books.

Library of Congress Control Number: 2009940877

For all my students:

It depends.

Done is better than perfect.

Just because you can, doesn't mean you should.

You know more than you think you do.

ABOUT THE AUTHOR

JEN KRAMER has been educating clients, colleagues, friends, and students about the meaning of a "quality web site" for more than nine years. She is the president of 4Web, Inc., a web design and development firm creating highly customized Joomla web sites.

Jen is a senior faculty member at the Marlboro College Graduate School, teaching courses and workshops in web site design and management, including Joomla. She is the Program Director for the Master's of Science in Internet Technologies program (MSIT), advising students and overseeing courses and faculty pertaining to the degree. She also teaches Joomla at the Center for Digital Imaging Arts at Boston University. She has also previously taught at Champlain College and the Community College of Vermont.

Jen is a Lynda.com author for the titles *Joomla! Creating and Editing Custom Templates*, *Joomla! Advanced CSS, Website Strategy and Planning*, and *Preparing CMS Web Graphics and Layouts Using Open Source Tools*.

Jen earned a BS in biology at University of North Carolina at Chapel Hill and an MS in Internet Strategy Management at the Marlboro College Graduate School. She is the manager for the Joomla! User Group New England and a past manager of the New England Adobe User Group.

ABOUT THE TECHNICAL EDITOR

BILL TOMCZAK wrote his first FORTRAN program in 1970. Since then, he has worked with computers and technology in a wide-ranging variety of roles. He was introduced to Joomla in 2006, and now works almost entirely on writing custom extensions and providing technical support for Joomla.

CREDITS

EXECUTIVE EDITOR
Carol Long

PROJECT EDITOR
John Sleeva

TECHNICAL EDITOR
Bill Tomczak

PRODUCTION EDITOR
Rebecca Anderson

COPY EDITOR
Paula Lowell

EDITORIAL DIRECTOR
Robyn B. Siesky

EDITORIAL MANAGER
Mary Beth Wakefield

ASSOCIATE DIRECTOR OF MARKETING
David Mayhew

PRODUCTION MANAGER
Tim Tate

**VICE PRESIDENT AND
EXECUTIVE GROUP PUBLISHER**
Richard Swadley

**VICE PRESIDENT AND
EXECUTIVE PUBLISHER**
Barry Pruett

ASSOCIATE PUBLISHER
Jim Minatel

PROJECT COORDINATOR, COVER
Lynsey Stanford

COMPOSITOR
Craig J. Woods,
Happenstance Type-O-Rama

PROOFREADERS
Sheilah Ledwidge and Jen Larsen,
Word One

INDEXER
Robert Swanson

COVER IMAGE
© Allan Baxter/Photographer's Choice
RF/Getty

COVER DESIGNER
Michael E. Trent

ACKNOWLEDGMENTS

Thank you to John Sleeva and Paula Lowell for their tireless editing of the manuscript. You did so much to improve it!

Thanks to Carol Long and everyone at Wrox and Wiley for giving me the opportunity to write the book I wanted.

Thanks to the Marlboro College Graduate School in Brattleboro, Vermont, for teaching me to think strategically about web sites and teaching how to learn new technologies effectively.

Thanks to the Joomla! User Group New England for all their support. We now have two authors in our group! How cool is that?

Most of all, many thanks to my longtime friend and engineer Bill Tomczak, for technically editing the book, learning Joomla with me over these last four years, and for generally putting up with my need to be in charge. Designers and developers can indeed be friends!

CONTENTS

INTRODUCTION

I ENTERED THE WEB WORLD IN 2000, back when we built web sites in Macromedia Dreamweaver 3, made our navigation buttons as JavaScript-based image rollovers, used tables for layout, and used the font tag and spacer GIF images quite liberally throughout our sites.

In those days, "weekend web masters" would buy a copy of Microsoft FrontPage on a Friday night, spend the weekend learning the software and configuring their web host, and by Monday morning, they were hanging out their shingle as a web professional.

In 2009, our weekend web masters are now Saturday web masters. Call up a hosting company, get them to buy a domain name for you and set up an open source content management system like Joomla, click a few buttons, and you've got a web site up in a day or less. What's more, you don't need to know any HTML, CSS, PHP, MySQL, what a web application is, or even what FTP is.

Many of my fellow web designer and web developer friends are shocked by this. What differentiates their years of experience from those who just installed Joomla for the first time yesterday? What justifies your higher hourly rate?

Actually, those of us who have been in the business for a while know that clicking the buttons is just a part of the process. The more languages you know (HTML, CSS, PHP, etc.), the more customizations you can make to the client's site.

But is that all? We know HTML and CSS and they don't? We've built a dozen Joomla sites before and they are on their first one or two? What about those web firms based overseas who charge rates that are so low that we can't possibly compete here in the United States? They've built hundreds of Joomla sites — doesn't that negate the arguments just made?

As web developers, we have to get smarter about marketing ourselves and what skillsets we bring to the table to solve our client's problems. We need to understand what our client does in their organization and how they serve their clients in order to understand what technology can do to solve their problems.

Most technical books cover button-clicking really well. There are dozens of Joomla books that talk about how to create a poll, create a custom template, and install new extensions.

But not one of those books talk about *why* you should create a poll, what a custom template can do for you, or how to evaluate an extension before you install it.

Rather than writing another book on button-clicking in Joomla, I wanted to write a book about planning your Joomla site with maintenance in mind (rather than thinking about maintenance after the site is built), what kinds of problems a blog or a newsflash might solve, whether a custom template is right for every site, and how to upgrade your site.

These are the skills that you bring to your client. This is how you're different from the person who just installed Joomla for the first time yesterday and who has never before built a site. You know more than you think you do! Start marketing these squishy skills you have and take a genuine interest in your client's needs. Suggest ways that technology could solve some of their problems. Become a partner to your client, a true solutions provider, not just a button-clicker.

I touch on a lot of topics in this book, including user experience, user design, information architecture, business strategy, target audience identification, and much more. I don't go deep into any of them. If you're from any of these disciplines, you might even accuse me of barely touching on these topics. Truth is, each of the above topics is a genre of books by itself. I've just given you a start on these fields in this book. I encourage you to read up in these areas to expand your skills.

WHO THIS BOOK IS FOR

If you're trying to make money building Joomla web sites, this book is for you. If you're just trying to build better Joomla web sites, for profit or not for profit, this book is for you, too.

If you're trying to build a web site for the very first time ever, you might find this book a little advanced. I assume you know something about HTML and CSS, particularly in the templating chapters. I also assume you have good skills copying and pasting PHP and XML in those chapters. You don't need in-depth knowledge of PHP. Personally, I can write an `include` statement from scratch, but that's about the limit of my PHP skills.

If you're expecting chapters on module development, they're not in this book. I've really focused on front-end web developers. The book tends to be more intermediate level than some of the more beginner-level Joomla books out there.

WHAT THIS BOOK COVERS

This book covers Joomla 1.5 in depth. I do not touch on Joomla 1.0 or 1.6 (which, as of this writing, is still in the alpha stage). I also cover some softer skills of site organization, evaluating extensions for technology requirements, specification gathering, and more.

HOW THIS BOOK IS STRUCTURED

The book is structured in the order you'd normally work when building a web site.

Chapter 1, "I Want a Web Site and I Want It Blue — How Much Will That Cost," is all about business strategy and understanding your client and their needs.

Chapter 2, "Choosing the Right Technologies to Solve the Business Problem," is about assembling your team to build the web site and picking good Joomla extensions.

Chapter 3, "Downloading and Installing Joomla!," covers installing Joomla on a Linux web host running cPanel.

Chapter 4, "A Brief Tour of the Joomla! Administration Interface," discusses the Joomla interface, including Global Configuration, Media Manager, and some user-management tools.

Chapter 5, "In the Beginning There Was Content," is about content: sections, categories, and articles.

Chapter 6, "Creating and Configuring Menus," covers menus, blog configuration, and configuring menu modules.

Chapter 7, "Installing and Configuring Templates," talks you through the process of installing a commercially available or free template.

Chapter 8, "Modules That Come with Joomla!," covers the modules included with Joomla, including newsflash, breadcrumbs, and random images.

Chapter 9, "Components That Come with Joomla!," covers components like polls, banners, and contacts.

Chapter 10, "Plug-Ins That Come with Joomla!," covers plug-ins and installing your own editor.

Chapter 11, "Adding Extensions to Joomla!," explains installing third-party components, modules, and plug-ins.

Chapter 12, "Home Page Tips and Tricks," describes home page configuration and setup.

Chapter 13, "Custom Templates," walks you through creating your own custom templates from scratch.

Chapter 14, "Advanced Template and CSS Tricks," gets into more complicated template tweaks and configurations and CSS tricks, including some real-world examples.

Chapter 15, "Site Maintenance and Training," covers site maintenance and training issues for your client.

The Appendix, "Jen's Favorite Joomla! Extensions," lists some great Joomla extensions and developers I've used in developing web sites for my clients.

WHAT YOU NEED TO USE THIS BOOK

This book covers Joomla 1.5. If you are working with Joomla 1.0 or 1.6, you will find a very different environment, and much of this book will not match your environment. Most of the screenshots in this book were generated using Joomla 1.5.13 and 1.5.14. You should install the most recent version of Joomla 1.5 for security purposes. Although the screenshots might not exactly match your version of Joomla 1.5, they should be reasonably close.

In Chapter 3, I cover installing Joomla on an actual web host. If you want to follow along, your host should run Linux, PHP, plus the cPanel control panel software. If you already know how to install Joomla, you are more than welcome to use your existing Joomla environment, whatever that may be — on your local computer, on a Windows host, with different control panel software, etc.

CONVENTIONS

To help you get the most from the text and keep track of what's happening, we've used a number of conventions throughout the book.

> *Boxes like this one hold important, not-to-be forgotten information that is directly relevant to the surrounding text.*

> *Notes, tips, hints, tricks, and asides to the current discussion appear in boxes like this one.*

As for styles in the text:

➤ We *highlight* new terms and important words when we introduce them.

➤ We show keyboard strokes like this: Ctrl+A.

➤ We show file names, URLs, and code within the text like so: `persistence.properties`.

➤ We present code in two different ways:

```
We use a monofont type with no highlighting for most code examples.
```

We use bold to emphasize code that is of particular importance in the present context.

SOURCE CODE

As you work through the examples in this book, you may choose either to type in all the code manually or to use the source code files that accompany the book. All of the source code used in this book is available for download at `http://www.wrox.com`. Once at the site, simply locate the book's title (either by using the Search box or by using one of the title lists) and click the Download Code link on the book's detail page to obtain all the source code for the book.

> *Because many books have similar titles, you may find it easiest to search by ISBN. This book's ISBN is 978-0-470-57089-0.*

Once you download the code, just decompress it with your favorite compression tool. Alternately, you can go to the main Wrox code download page at http://www.wrox.com/dynamic/books/download.aspx to see the code available for this book and all other Wrox books.

ERRATA

We make every effort to ensure that there are no errors in the text or in the code. However, no one is perfect, and mistakes do occur. If you find an error in one of our books, like a spelling mistake or faulty piece of code, we would be very grateful for your feedback. By sending in errata you may save another reader hours of frustration and at the same time you will be helping us provide even higher quality information.

To find the errata page for this book, go to http://www.wrox.com and locate the title using the Search box or one of the title lists. Then, on the book details page, click the Book Errata link. On this page you can view all errata that has been submitted for this book and posted by Wrox editors. A complete book list including links to each book's errata is also available at www.wrox.com/misc-pages/booklist.shtml.

If you don't spot "your" error on the Book Errata page, go to www.wrox.com/contact/techsupport.shtml and complete the form there to send us the error you have found. We'll check the information and, if appropriate, post a message to the book's errata page and fix the problem in subsequent editions of the book.

P2P.WROX.COM

For author and peer discussion, join the P2P forums at p2p.wrox.com. The forums are a web-based system for you to post messages relating to Wrox books and related technologies and interact with other readers and technology users. The forums offer a subscription feature to e-mail you topics of interest of your choosing when new posts are made to the forums. Wrox authors, editors, other industry experts, and your fellow readers are present on these forums.

At http://p2p.wrox.com you will find a number of different forums that will help you not only as you read this book, but also as you develop your own applications. To join the forums, just follow these steps:

1. Go to p2p.wrox.com and click the Register link.
2. Read the terms of use and click Agree.
3. Complete the required information to join as well as any optional information you wish to provide and click Submit.
4. You will receive an e-mail with information describing how to verify your account and complete the joining process.

You can read messages in the forums without joining P2P but in order to post your own messages, you must join.

Once you join, you can post new messages and respond to messages other users post. You can read messages at any time on the Web. If you would like to have new messages from a particular forum e-mailed to you, click the Subscribe to this Forum icon by the forum name in the forum listing.

For more information about how to use the Wrox P2P, be sure to read the P2P FAQs for answers to questions about how the forum software works as well as many common questions specific to P2P and Wrox books. To read the FAQs, click the FAQ link on any P2P page.

Be sure to check out my blog at Wrox P2P, where I'll be writing about business strategy, user experience, and Joomla as well: `http://p2p.wrox.com/content/blogs/jen4web`

I Want a Web Site and I Want It Blue — How Much Will That Cost?

➤ Understanding business strategy, web site strategy, and user strategy, and how they compliment and contrast with each other

➤ Understanding a target audience and how it helps shape the message of your web site

➤ Assembling a team to build the web site

If you're like me, you've been asked something like the question in the chapter's title more than once when talking to a potential client. How do you answer it?

➤ Do you offer them a package of services for a fixed price?

➤ Do you ask them whether they want a calendar, blog, or some other piece of functionality with that?

➤ Do you ask them whether they want to update the web site themselves, or do they want you to do the maintenance?

All these questions are reasonable to ask at a certain point in the conversation with your potential client. But a far better place to start is at the beginning. For example, I might reply by saying, "Sure, we can make it blue. But before we start talking about how the site will look, please tell me a little about your business. What do you do for a living?"

Why would I want to do that? If the client is telling me to set up a few pages and a calendar, what could be simpler? Charge the client and move on to the next one!

Many freelancers run their businesses just like this, and they do reasonably well in a reasonable economy. But as the economy gets worse, clients hold on to their pocketbooks more tightly. They want to know they are getting the biggest bang for their buck, and they want to know that what you build is really going to work for them. And, of course, as the economy sours, moving on to the next client becomes progressively harder, because that next one is much harder to come by.

You bring more value to the table than just knowing which buttons to push to build a web site. You know all about technology trends and the latest cutting-edge Joomla extensions. You know about usability principles and how to make a clean interface. Maybe you had a client similar to this one before, and you know what worked for him. Perhaps it will work for this client, too.

You must market those strategic thinking skills and demonstrate how your good ideas add value to the service you deliver. Anyone can click buttons, but not everyone knows how to build a strategically sound web site. This chapter starts you on your way to doing that with your next client.

DEVISING STRATEGIES

When I was just getting started as a freelancer, I received a call from a housing developer who was selling his home in southern Vermont for $1.875 million. He needed to get some people in the door to look at the house and thought a web site might be a good way to do it. He wanted to know whether I had any suggestions.

We started by discussing his *business strategy* and *target audience*. Armed with that information, together we developed a *web site strategy* based on what he wanted to do and a *user strategy* based on what his site visitors would want to get out of the web site. Here's what we came up with during the discussion:

➤ **Business strategy.** His business strategy was to sell his home, hopefully close to the asking price.

➤ **Target audience.** His target audience had to be someone with enough money to afford a $1.875 million home. The average income for a southern Vermont family is about $44,000/yr, and most houses sell somewhere between $100,000 and $250,000, so the local people were clearly not the target. It was more likely that he was targeting someone from the big cities, like Boston, New York, or Montreal, which are in driving distance of the house. Big cities offer the possibility of jobs paying salaries that would support owning a home like this client's. Another target possibility was a corporate owner for the home, offering a retreat for senior executives.

➤ **Web site strategy.** Someone buying a house sight unseen, let alone a house with that price tag, is unlikely. Therefore, the web site strategy was to provide enough compelling information to get someone from a big city to come down for the weekend to walk through the house and hopefully buy it. The photos should be seasonal, to emphasize Vermont's four distinct seasons and the activities one can enjoy in each season. Therefore, the photos needed changed three to four times per year to show how the house looked at that particular season. The copy could also be adapted as the seasons changed, emphasizing skiing in the winter and hiking in the summer.

➤ **User strategy.** The visitors to this web site had their own agenda. The user strategy was to see lots and lots of beautiful pictures, get directions, read up on the house specifications, and see what there was to do in the area to make a weekend trip to see the house.

Based on this information, we built a web site of about 20 pages. We had a professional photographer take dozens of photos of the house and the grounds and even had a helicopter fly over the house with the photographer to take impressive seasonal photos of the house and the surrounding gardens. We had a content writer write all kinds of flowery content, generating warm, positive feelings about the beauty, serenity, and seclusion of the house, yet how convenient it was to grocery stores and shopping. We also included a page of information about regional events and attractions that might be of interest to someone visiting the area for the weekend. And most importantly, we included contact information to get in touch with the owner, via phone or e-mail.

We also had to think about a marketing plan for the web site, including how to get the site to show up in search engines, but we also did some cross-promotional advertising in the *New York Times* homes listing and other home listings in Boston and New York. (Remember that when you market a web site, you don't have to do all marketing on the Internet. Cross-promotional advertising means advertising in a different media — in this case, the newspaper.)

Eventually, the house did sell, close to his asking price. The site was successful, and we archived it.

Now, had this client simply said he wanted to sell his house and asked how much it would cost for a web site, I might have come up with some of this information without our having had the strategic discussion. Obviously, the site should contain photos of the house, along with some additional information about how many bedrooms, baths, and so on. However, would I have come up with the idea of including information about the local events and what to do in the area? Would I have thought to change the photos seasonally? It's likely I would not have caught all the nuances of the strategy without our discussion, and perhaps the house would have taken much longer to sell.

Understanding Your Client's Business Strategy

A *business strategy* is some type of plan that applies to an organization to help it achieve its goals. Although the term is "*business* strategy," it is not necessarily limited to businesses. A non-profit can have a business strategy, as can an educational institution.

In general, this plan covers the mission of the organization, its vision, how it conducts business, its plan for the future, the markets in which it competes, and the people it serves.

If I'm running a web development firm, I might tell you that my mission is to build web sites, that I sell my services building those web sites to make money, that I'm competing with the guy down the street, and that I serve the people in my community.

However, I could make that mission statement a bit more targeted. Do I build web sites for just anyone? What kinds of web sites do I build? Somehow, I need to differentiate the work that I do from the web site developer down the street. For example, I might use Joomla to build my sites, whereas he builds static web sites. I specialize in web sites for environmentally oriented non-profits, whereas he designs sites for small local businesses. My web sites start at 100 pages and go up from there, whereas he builds smaller sites, normally 10–20 pages.

The more targeted a business strategy becomes, the more targeted you can make your marketing plan, and the more of the target audience you can reach. A focused, well-crafted business strategy converts more people to customers, and you're more likely to make them happy with what you offer.

For example, if my web development business focuses on environmentally oriented non-profits, it's less likely the local church will call me about a web site.

Constructing a business strategy is hard work, takes a lot of thought, and, frankly, many people are too busy running their businesses to consider their strategy. If they did take the time to think about that strategy, however, they would find their business runs more smoothly and efficiently. The owners spend less time running the business, rather than the business running the owners.

To determine a business strategy, usually all you have to do is ask your clients what they do for a living, and listen very carefully to what they have to say. They should tell you exactly how they fulfill their mission goals — how they make money, how they recruit membership, how they solicit donations, and so on. They should talk about a typical customer or client, what this client needs from the business, and how the business fills that need.

For an established business, this conversation is fairly straightforward. In general, the business owner has little trouble answering any questions you ask.

For a new business or organization, however, you might ask some questions that are answered with, "Good question!" If your clients are unclear about their business strategy, encourage them to develop a strategy first, before putting up the web site. Plenty of local resources specialize in helping with this, such as SCORE, your local Small Business Administration office, and local and regional programs targeted at fostering small businesses.

 SCORE (Service Corps of Retired Executives) has more than 364 branches throughout the United States. SCORE volunteers help guide you through the process of setting up your business, as well as answering questions for existing businesses. It's staffed by volunteers, so there is no fee to use their services. You can learn more by visiting www.score.org.

Some business owners will tell you they need a web site because everyone says they do, but they're not sure why they need it or what they'll get from it. This is not really business strategy. What you want is something like the following:

➤ I want to offer a way for people to discover my store hours and location, plus an easy way to contact me by phone or e-mail. I want to reduce the number of phone calls my staff gets that deal with these very questions.

➤ I want to offer my products online, and offer a way for customers to find out what stores are near them that sell the product.

➤ I want to establish my expertise in a certain area, which will lead to consulting requests.

➤ I want to recruit new dealers for my products.

➤ I want people to subscribe to my publication and look up back issues.

Occasionally, while you try to find out the business strategy, the client will want to start talking about technologies. I've heard everything from the importance of a blog on a web site to how exactly certain database queries would be made. As soon as you go down the path of discussing technologies, you're discussing how exactly the site will function, not what problems the site will solve. Keep the conversation focused on strategy — what problems are you trying to solve? — and the technological solutions to those problems will be much easier to define.

Some Clients Should Not Have a Web Site

Consider how many sites you have visited that felt information-free and perhaps even half-finished. What was your impression of that organization? (Probably not positive, I'm guessing.)

This type of impression usually is a sign of an ambiguous business owner who got a site because someone (their spouse, a friend, a relative) urged her to get a site for the business. The owner wasn't necessarily convinced, and wasn't sure what to do with it, but now she has a web site so everyone will leave her alone.

Perhaps it's the type of small business where everything is done with paper and a non-computerized cash register. Although this seems impossible these days, these businesses are still around — and many are thriving.

A neglected-feeling web site might also be the sign of an overstretched owner who simply doesn't have time to think about updating the site.

If you are building a web site, and the owner doesn't seem particularly engaged in the process, make sure she understands the following about the commitment she is making by having a site:

➤ **The owner must commit to checking and answering e-mail every business day.** After all, web sites generate e-mails that must be answered. Visitors find not being able to contact the web site owner, preferably by e-mail, frustrating. (Famously, Southwest Airlines had no e-mail contact for years, but it had a web site. It finally offered e-mail contact in 2009 after customer insistence, but it states it has a five-business-day response window to e-mails.)

➤ **The site needs to be updated periodically.** How often? Of course, "It depends." Some sites can stand to be updated quarterly, whereas others should be updated every day. For example, an informational web site about your freelance Joomla business might be okay if it's updated quarterly. But if you're CNN, you should update your web site every day (perhaps even several times an hour).

➤ **The site is not a one-time investment.** A web site must be updated, redesigned, expanded, reworked, pared back, and have new functionality added. Nothing is worse than finding web sites that look like they were built around 1995 and have not been updated since. Rolling rainbow bars, starry backgrounds, spiders in webs, prominent hit counters, and little men in hardhats banging the ground with a hammer are generally considered "fashion no's" and hallmarks of a site that needs updating. Desperately.

➤ **Likewise, don't necessarily expect the site to "pay for itself."** This theme was common in the late 1990s and early 2000s. Site owners expected the web site to directly bring in revenue, or they would kill it. The web site is a piece of the overall marketing for the organization. Many people will read a web site and then call for more information, rather than purchasing a product on the site.

If your client doesn't seem to understand the preceding points, you might want to steer her away from a web site. Unfortunately, when sites are not updated regularly, they do go horribly out of date. Then the client is upset that the site isn't performing, and she was right all along, the web can't do a thing for her! Updating a site regularly, of course, is no guarantee of success — but not updating it regularly eventually leads to a business's goals not being met.

Aligning the Business Strategy with the Web Strategy

After you're clear on what a client wants to do with a site (the business strategy), it's time to think about how technology can help implement that strategy, meet goals, and solve any problems.

Some problems are easy. If the client wants to cut down on phone calls about the business location and operating hours, perhaps putting that information in the footer of the web page and again under "About Us" can solve the problem. (Of course, you don't know whether this method solves the problem until you test to see whether your users can find the location and hours easily.)

 Unfortunately, user testing is beyond the scope of this book, but I highly recommend Steve Krug's book, Don't Make Me Think, *which provides a great overview of the topic.*

Other problems are harder. For example, how does a business communicate its depth of experience in a certain area?

Suppose that you identify the problem you're trying to solve as showing that you are a Joomla expert on your web site for your freelance business. What are some possible solutions to that problem? Here are a few:

➤ **You put up a bunch of text explaining your depth of knowledge, degrees you have, and awards you've won.**

   ➤ *Advantage:* Cheap! Easy!

   ➤ *Disadvantage:* Who really reads that stuff? You're telling someone you are an expert, but you haven't demonstrated anything. Should you put up the text anyway? Sure, it can't hurt, but it shouldn't be the only solution to this problem.

   ➤ *Improvement*: Don't just say it yourself. Get testimonials from your clients and colleagues so you have third-party confirmation of how fabulous you are.

➤ **You list a bunch of sites that you've built in Joomla.**

   ➤ *Advantage:* Easy! Just a list of links, right? And Joomla has a Web Link Manager. Piece of cake!

   ➤ *Disadvantage:* A list of links shows off the sites, but it doesn't explain why the site is so great, what problems you solved for your client, or what the site is doing for your client now (increased traffic to the store by 10%, decreased phone calls for store hours by 5%, and so on). The Web Link Manager is beside the point, if it's not really solving your problem.

➤ *Improvement:* A list of links to the sites you've built, with some explanatory text about what problems the client wanted to solve and how you solved them. You want a screenshot of the site before and after you redesigned it as well so that visitors can see how much you improved the site. If you can incorporate the goals the site achieved, such as increased store traffic, even better.

➤ **You start a series of articles that talk about what problems you solve with Joomla, how you solve them, and why.**

➤ *Advantage:* It's in your own words, and it's your story. It's an authentic, believable voice.

➤ *Disadvantage:* You need to post articles regularly about what you do. Do you have time to do that? Who does it? How are the articles reviewed? Are they reviewed?

➤ *Improvement*: Again, including third-party verification of what you did is helpful. If you can get a statement from your client about how well your solution worked, it's a great thing to include in the articles.

Notice that I have not discussed implementation anywhere along the way in this list of possible solutions. Technologies might still spring to mind. It sure sounds like I'm describing a blog in the third bullet. The second bullet sounds like a series of case studies that talk about a client's problem and your solution, with a link to the final web site. The first bullet is a pretty standard About Us page.

Why do those technologies and solutions spring to mind so quickly and easily? Because I've essentially described them by describing the solution to the problem. Rather than stretching the technology to perform some ill-defined function on the site, technology is now serving the strategy in a clearly well-thought-out way.

I've also identified some potential problems and pitfalls with each of these solutions. If regular updates are problematic, I might want to think more about the first two solutions. If I'm looking for a solution that's a step beyond the usual, I will look at the third solution and less at the first. Now that I've thought through the upsides and downsides of each strategy, I can make a more informed and intelligent decision about which option is the right one for my web site.

If you're putting up any piece of functionality on your web site, it should go through the same vetting process. Be sure you can explain what problem it solves for the client.

Sometimes that problem seems very simplistic and/or trivial. For example, clients love slideshows, where there's a series of really big photos that fade in and out. They're particularly prominent on the home page of a web site. What function is this slideshow performing? It's "eye candy" for sure, particularly if the photos are good quality (or it's an eyesore if the photos are not). You might just be tempted to not ask too many questions about it, because the client asked for "interactivity" or "sizzle" for the home page.

Could a slideshow do more than that? Absolutely! It could set a mood for the site. A series of happy, smiling people doing various jobs conjures a different mood than a series of New England scenery photos. Slideshows can also be tied to branding. Think about the imagery that's used in commercials for companies. They're highly professional, job-focused people (airline commercials), or they're fun-loving, outdoorsy people (outdoor gear commercials), or they're people who are listening intently to your problems and trying to help you (bank commercials). Think about your client's slideshow the same way. Could you improve the message it sends and think about it serving as more than just "sizzle" for the site?

Before adding any functionality to the site, be sure to ask yourself why you're adding the functionality and what problem it's solving. If you're not sure, or you're putting it up because the client asked for it, ask your client a few discerning questions. Your client will love you if you suggest a different, "better" solution to the real problem he's trying to solve. You will have elevated yourself from a "button clicker" to a partner in providing solutions to the business.

Understanding Your Client's Target Audience

Web sites should be built with a certain type of visitor in mind. That person is part of the target audience. These are the people you want to buy or use your client's product or service.

Ask your client who the target audience is for the web site. Sometimes a client can provide a very specific answer for you. For example, the site is for men, ages 18–24, who have shoe sizes over size 12, who live in an urban environment.

Unfortunately, more often than not, your client may not have a clear answer about his customers. Sometimes the only guidance you get is "anyone who wants to buy our product." That's really not the answer, though.

Try to determine the following about your client's target audience:

➤ **Demographics.** Who are the site visitors? How old are they? How much money do they make? What are their hobbies, their jobs, marital status, or things they have in common?

➤ **Technographics.** Do they access the web site through a PC, a mobile phone, or some other device? Do they use Internet Explorer or Firefox? Which version(s)? Are they on dial-up or broadband Internet connections? Are they using newer or older computers?

➤ **Environmental factors.** Are they surfing at 11 p.m. in their bunny slippers? Or is it 9 a.m. and they're at work with a cup of coffee? Are they there for business or are they there to explore leisurely? Do they have nearby distractions demanding their attention?

➤ **Geographics.** Are they from only the United States or from other countries? Does the client need to serve multiple languages? Are visitors from rural locations or from urban areas? The vast majority of small businesses in this country serve a small geographic area. A car repair shop doesn't worry about serving customers 1,000 miles away, let alone 100 miles away.

➤ **User goals.** After you understand who the client's users are, you'll want to understand what they want to do on the web site. Are they there to be entertained? Find a product? Get specifications? Buy something? Research something? You'll also want to think about what the site owner's goals are for these users, as well.

After you understand these factors about the target market, you can create personas describing key users for your web site. *Personas*, originally described by Alan Cooper in his book, *The Inmates Are Running the Asylum,* are fictitious people with certain characteristics and goals that reflect the type of people a business wants to attract to its web site. These fictitious people are composites of certain classes of users you've identified as key audiences for the web site.

Suppose you're designing a site for a men's big and tall store. Historically, this store has served men who are 40 to 60 years old and are either taller or larger than normal. The clothing styles have been a bit on the older, more conservative side. You now want to communicate that the store is carrying clothes for a younger generation as well. The web site should provide a clear message that younger people are welcome and the clothes are appealing. However, you do not want to go so far as to alienate the older audience, for whom you'll still be carrying traditional clothing.

You might develop a handful of personas to help with this process.

➤ Mike, a 23-year-old recent college graduate, who is 6 feet 5 inches tall and wears a size 14 shoe. He needs some new clothes for his new job working at a bank. (This is a very typical persona for the site.)

➤ Sam, a 46-year-old doctor, who is 6 feet 4 inches tall and wears a size 15 shoe. He has shopped at this store for years and buys most of his clothes there. (In this case, Sam represents a target audience you do not want to alienate as you try to expand your market to the younger crowd.)

➤ John, 20, is 6 feet 7 inches tall and works as an assistant manager at a restaurant. He wants casual clothes to wear after work. (This might represent part of that new market you want to attract.)

➤ Sally, 23, is looking for clothes to give her boyfriend, Jack, 24. (Sally represents an atypical customer, but an important one, because women frequently spend money on clothes for the men in their lives.)

You might then develop the following story about each of these personas and what they want to accomplish on the web site:

Mike finishes up work at the bank at 5 p.m. He looks down at his old, scuffed loafers that he has been wearing since high school. He really needs some new shoes for this new job, but finding a size 14 anywhere in the usual stores was so hard. Mike opens Google and types, "men's shoes size 14 Nashua, NH" into the search box. It pulls up one result, a big-and-tall store a few miles away. Mike wonders whether this store is like all the other big-and-tall stores, featuring clothes for his dad. He works at a bank, but he really doesn't want to dress like he was 50.

How would you finish this story? The preceding describes exactly the kind of person you would like to visit your store. To get him in the store, you must make sure your store can be found in Google, and you must communicate that it's "not just your father's clothes" at this particular store.

How can we make this web site appeal to Mike, and therefore, convince him to drive over to the store after work for a look around?

➤ Show some pictures of some more modern-looking shoes that could be worn to work and would appeal to younger men. You might have younger models showing the clothes to enforce the message.

➤ Make it clear that large-size shoes are available.

➤ Feature store hours, address, and directions (note that Mike is going there after work one night).

Mike's goal is to make sure there's a shot that the shoes he needs are available at this store. If he sees clues on the site that the store can help him, he's likely to take a look.

On the flip side, think about how this imagery and message would impact Sam, the 46-year-old long-time customer of your store. If the shoe styles offered aren't classic, will this be a turnoff for Sam? Is Sam really an important audience for the web site, though? Sam has been going to this store for years already, and he probably has a good feel for what's offered. Sam probably won't make buying decisions based on what's on the web site, but maybe you need to keep him in mind for organizing the store.

MEASURING SUCCESS

Rarely do clients think about how they will measure whether a web site is successful. Many think that if the web site looks pretty (to them), and it's completed and launched, the visitors will just come. And if they don't come, the problem is search engine optimization! There's nothing flawed with the overall premise of the web site, or how it was built, or whether the technology is really addressing problems that need to be solved. And if visitors do come, well, the site's successful, isn't it?

Maybe. It depends, doesn't it?

Success can be measured in many different ways. Some ways are very tangible ("we reduced tech support phone calls by 10%," "online purchases increased by $500 per week"), whereas others are much less tangible ("I don't feel embarrassed to send people to my web site anymore"). Some goals might be based on the web site itself (increasing visitors' time spent on the site, the number of contact forms completed and sent in, or the number of newsletter subscriptions).

Measuring the success of a web site merits a whole book by itself, and I have only a few paragraphs. Suffice it to say that the success of the site should be defined upfront, as you define what problems the web site will solve:

➤ The problem I'm trying to solve is…

➤ I intend to solve it by…

➤ I'll know it's solved if the following happens…

Answering these questions now gives you a non-emotional, fact-based method of determining whether you've achieved your goals. Preferably, it's also measurable, as in the earlier examples. Sometimes it's not measurable — being able to send people to your web site without making apologies for how bad it looks is certainly a positive benefit, even if you can't measure it.

Perhaps a goal was to drive more traffic to the web site. Many people decide whether a problem like this is solved by measuring web traffic via Google Analytics. Clients should have clear goals as to what kind of traffic they're looking for, though! Getting traffic to a web site is easy. Just add some talk about the latest pop stars or a few dirty words, and traffic will miraculously arrive. Unfortunately, these visitors are not likely to buy something, call the business, or sign up for a newsletter. So be sure that when you talk about "driving traffic to the web site" with clients you're clear about what kind of traffic they want and what they want visitors to do when they get there — the goal is qualified traffic that is interested in what the business has to offer.

To learn more about measuring success and using Google Analytics to help measure that success, research the field of web metrics. A good place to start is the Web Analytics Association (`www.webanalyticsassociation.org`), founded by Jim Stearne, one of the leaders in the field of web metrics.

ASSEMBLING THE DEVELOPMENT TEAM

Back in the mid-1990s, as the commercial Web was emerging, there was the web master. The web master did everything where a web site was concerned, including setting up a server, applying security patches, installing software, writing HTML, and running the web site.

Now, more than 15 years later, sites no longer have a web master. The Internet has exploded, as have systems and processes pertaining to it. Knowing everything about server configuration, programming and scripting languages, HTML and CSS, and databases, not to mention graphic design, project management, search engine optimization, and content writing is impossible. Web masters have moved to areas of specialization.

Every day, newly minted freelancers enter the marketplace, ready to build web sites for a living. As a freelancer, you can make a reasonable living building small web sites. You probably have an area of specialization. Maybe you're a Flash whiz, or you do amazing graphic design, or you can make any CSS cross-browser–compatible.

Ultimately, though, you are not good at doing some things, and some things you do not enjoy doing. These instances are where the development team comes in. You can find freelancers to help in a wide variety of areas. I regularly hire help for:

- Graphic design
- Content writing
- Coding with Flex and Flash
- Coding with PHP and MySQL, particularly Joomla extension creation and modification
- Search engine optimization
- Video and audio creation and editing

If a client is looking for a completely custom template (not an off-the-shelf template), some help getting content written, and a custom contact form, I know that I need to hire a graphic designer and a content writer. I can probably take care of the custom contact form myself, using a Joomla extension, and I'll do the coding for the custom template, once the design is defined. To get that done, I call the graphic designer and the writer, and I get quotes from both of them for the work. I add a little bit to each price (called markup), because I'll need to do some project management along the way, making sure they've done their jobs correctly and completely. Then I add the cost of my own time to that quote and send the whole thing to the client. The client pays me for all work on the web site. My graphic designer and writer are subcontractors, and they bill me for the work they complete. I pay them with the money from the client.

Working with subcontractors means that you can expand the range of services you provide. For example, if a custom extension is required as part of the job, you don't have to turn the job down because you're unable to provide that part of the work. It also means you did not hire this expertise as an employee, meaning you'll have to continually find new work for that employee and give him or her a steady paycheck. Hopefully, you'll cultivate a relationship where your subcontractors will also hire you for their own projects.

Cultivating a network of subcontractors does mean you must spend some time networking and getting to know your fellow web developers and designers. A great way to do that is to attend a local Joomla user group meeting. Don't have a local user group? Start one up yourself (see Joomla's community web site, `community.joomla.org`, for more details). You can also network online via the Joomla forums or other developer groups around the Web. Your local Chamber of Commerce may sponsor some networking events, or you might have other user groups in your area (such as an Adobe user group, a PHP user group, or some other computer-related group).

After you hire a subcontractor, you'll want to get a signed agreement in place that defines, among other things, what he will produce for you, the timeline, and how much you're going to pay him. Getting a clear specification from the client about what's involved is important, so that your subcontractor can give you a fixed price for the job. I recommend staying away from open-ended hourly rates, because they can get out of control quickly. If you go with an hourly rate, be sure to specify an upper limit for the price charged for the work. Be sure to specify a schedule for production as well, so the subcontractor knows exactly what he needs to produce and by what date.

Subcontractor relationships can be risky. Despite their best efforts, people sometimes get sick. They also sometimes go on vacation or get swamped with other work to do. They have competing interests in their lives, like families and hobbies. Remember that you, as the contractor, are ultimately on the line for the work you have agreed to do for your client. Make sure your subcontractors are reliable and do high-quality work. Be sure to talk to their clients and get recommendations from other contractors. Also, you want to have at least two people to work with in each area where you need help. Sometimes your favorite subcontractor isn't available for one reason or another.

Choosing the Right Technologies to Solve the Business Problem

WHAT'S IN THIS CHAPTER?

➤ Is Joomla right for this client?

➤ Planning maintenance before building the web site

➤ Choosing the right extensions

Now that you've had a good conversation with your client about who they are, what they do, and what a web site can do for them, it's time to start thinking about the right technologies to build their web site.

Sometimes, Joomla isn't the right answer to their particular business problem. If Joomla is right for your client, maybe it's time to start thinking about extensions to make the site function the way you envision. You'll also want to consider maintaining the web site. Maintenance is the process of keeping a web site up-to-date with the latest content and the latest upgrades. Is your client going to help with content updates going forward? Are you going to take care of any security upgrades?

This chapter shows you how to move the business strategy to technological specifications. This includes making sure Joomla is right for your client, planning maintenance before you start building, and choosing the right extensions for this web site.

IS JOOMLA! THE RIGHT ANSWER FOR *THIS* CLIENT?

Your #1 consulting answer, which is almost always right in the world of web development is, "It depends."

Joomla is great software for building both small and large web sites. Editing for clients is easy. Plenty of functionalities are built into the core system, and you can download thousands of extensions to expand Joomla's functionality even further. (Refer to the Appendix for some examples.)

On occasion, you'll find a client that is *not* a good fit for Joomla, though. Here are some examples:

➤ If you need to have multiple people editing the site, but each person needs to have access to only certain parts of the site, this can be tricky to set up in Joomla. Extensions are available to solve this problem, called *access control lists* (ACLs). However, they can be very complicated to use and configure. Most developers agree that Drupal (`www.drupal.org`) has a better implementation of ACL as of this writing. ACL will be incorporated into Joomla 1.6.

➤ Having content that needs to be sliced and diced several different ways, such as viewing articles by relevant keyword, is also difficult to implement with Joomla without having the right extension to make it work.

➤ Sometimes a client just wants a simple five-page web site, and isn't planning on ever making changes. You might be better off with a simple HTML web site in this case (although you could also build this site in Joomla or WordPress, `www.wordpress.org`).

➤ Sometimes a client just wants a blog. Although Joomla can run blogs, WordPress is a better solution if a blog is the only requirement.

Before you take on Drupal, WordPress, and static HTML projects in addition to your Joomla work, you might want to rethink your own business strategy. I find that keeping up with the latest advances and upgrades for Joomla is challenging enough for me. I would not want to also keep up with the latest upgrades and updates for Drupal and WordPress. Therefore, I've decided that for my business, I'll stick to Joomla. This means if I am presented with a job that's not a good fit for Joomla, I will send that lead elsewhere.

"CAN JOOMLA! DO THAT?"

Sometimes, in the course of this conversation, the client will ask, "I need a blog, too. Can Joomla do that?"

Two red flags are in that sentence. You should address both of them very carefully.

The first flag is that your client has called for a very specific piece of technology with certain requirements. A blog is essentially a diary, displayed in reverse chronological order, with the most recent item at the top of the page. It's generally accepted that anyone with permission can add content to a blog. Generally speaking, one would expect to be able to add images, video, and links quickly and easily to a blog posting, without knowing technology in depth. Generally speaking, a blog is updated regularly. For some blogs, that's several times a day, whereas others update monthly. Most successful blogs, though, have a regular schedule, whatever that schedule is, so the readership is clear about when to expect new content.

Now, you probably already knew all of that. But does your client know that?

When a client asks me for a specific piece of technology, I ask two questions; first, "what do you mean by that?" Ask the client to define what a blog is. He could mean that he really wants an easy way to update the web site on his own, and his friend does that on her blog, so he's decided that *blog* means easy updates to all parts of the web site. That's not necessarily true, of course, but that's what a blog means to him.

The second question I ask is, "what problem would the technology solve for you?" You will get all kinds of interesting answers to the question, some of which have absolutely no relation to the technology the client has proposed. I've had many clients insist on a blog, because they've been told that blogs are good for improving search engine optimization. That's true, but they did not know that a blog that improves search engine optimization (SEO) is frequently updated, sometimes more than once a day, so the search engines get plenty of fresh content to read. When they find out they have to post every day (or at least several times a week), they drop the blog like a hot potato.

The real problem in the preceding example is that they want to improve their effectiveness in the search engines. A blog is one possible solution, but it's certainly not the whole strategy for improving SEO.

The second part of that client's question that raised the red flag for me was, "Can Joomla do that?" Well, certainly Joomla can produce a blog. Joomla does a lot of things — calendars, photo galleries, shopping carts, quote rotators, banner advertising, polls, and so much more. Joomla can do almost anything through custom programming if an off-the-shelf extension is not available.

However, the "Can Joomla do that?" question usually indicates that the client is worrying about the technology again, and perhaps they are failing to tell me about a problem they're trying to solve because they can't suggest a technological solution to the problem themselves. Frequently, I tell clients not to worry about what Joomla can or can't do. If I understand the problem they're trying to solve, I'll make Joomla solve the problem. How that technological solution works is of relatively little importance to the client. That is, after all, why they hired me.

THINKING ABOUT MAINTENANCE FROM THE CLIENT'S PERSPECTIVE

Before you evaluate which extensions you need and why, pick out a template, establish hosting, and so forth, you must think about maintaining the web site after launch.

Most web developers enjoy building web sites, but they aren't so thrilled about training clients, and they hate tech support questions after the fact. By thinking through what will happen maintenance-wise before you ever start building, you can make sure the maintenance process is streamlined for your client.

Is Your Client Tech-Savvy?

Sometimes your client knows HTML and/or CSS or has a background in web design. Some have been maintaining the site for years already, using a product like Dreamweaver, FrontPage, or Contribute. Other clients have a hard time using e-mail and Word. What is your client's technical ability level? What is the client going to be able to handle to maintain the site?

In general, your clients will be happy if they can make most or all of the routine, regular changes they make to their site. If they have some type of change that happens irregularly (quarterly, semiannually, annually), your handling those changes might be better. They won't remember how to make the changes, and just having you do them is probably more cost effective.

How Many People Are Involved with Maintenance?

In many small companies, non-profits, and educational institutions, an administrative assistant might make the day-to-day changes for the web site, whereas someone on the IT staff might do more complex tasks as required.

In larger companies and organizations, a dozen people might make updates to the web site.

Make sure you understand who these people are, what their technical backgrounds are, and what kind of changes each person needs to make. Is it okay for everyone to have access to the whole site? Or do you need to lock down the site so one person can only edit a few pages, while another person can edit a section of the site?

If you need to lock certain people out of certain parts of the web site, you will want to look at an ACL extension to accomplish this task. corePHP's Community ACL and Dioscouri's JUGA extension are both available (`www.corephp.com` and `www.dioscouri.com`, respectively). Keep in mind that configuring an ACL extension can be challenging, and having good tech support will make your job much easier. Both of these companies will help you configure ACL, which is why they charge a fee for their extensions.

How Frequently Will the Site Need To Be Updated?

Some clients update their web site daily, whereas others may only update their site every quarter. Sometimes just one page of the site changes, or just one application (like the calendar needs regular updating).

Be sure to understand which parts of the site need to be updated regularly and how often. You want to make sure that completing those regular updates is easy for your client.

Front-End Editing Versus Back-End Editing

You will also want to think about how your client will make changes and updates to the web site. Joomla offers two ways of editing the web site, editing from the "back end" and editing from the "front end."

The back end of the web site is the administrator screens, found at `www.yoursite.com/administrator`. This interface is very powerful, and this is where Joomla developers do much of their work in setting up a site.

The front-end editing capability of the web site is not always obvious to those new to Joomla. However, if you provide a way to log in from the public-facing side ("front") of the web site, and you provide users with enough permissions (see Chapter 4, "A Brief Tour of the Joomla! Administration Interface"), they can edit the site from the front end.

The front-end editing of the web site, however, is fairly limited in its offerings. As a super administrator, you can edit existing articles, and in some section and category layouts (see Chapter 5, "In the Beginning There Was Content"), you can occasionally add a new article, depending on the site configuration. You can upload new images and documents from the front end of the web site to use in an article.

However, you cannot add new articles to the site and give them their own menu link nor can you assign modules to a page.

Third-party components are spotty in their front-end support. Some provide everything the client needs, whereas others provide little front-end support at all. Be sure to look carefully at the front-end editing capabilities of third-party components, if it's important to your site when considering extensions for it.

Think carefully about what kind of access for updates your client will need. Is it all front-end access, or do they need to access the back end as well? Consider the following guidelines:

➤ If your client has few technical skills, consider offering front-end editing only, even if it means they can't do everything they want to do.

➤ If your client must access the back end of the web site for some reason (for example, they'll be using a shopping cart administrator interface there), you might want to offer only back-end editing access. This can be less confusing than going to the front end to edit articles and the back end to manage the store.

➤ If there is more than one person editing the web site, you might want to know the tasks that each person will need to perform, along with their technical level. It may make sense to give some people only front-end editing, while others have back-end editing.

Having trained dozens of clients to maintain web sites, I lean toward giving clients front-end editing access only; for non-technical people, it's just easier to understand front-end editing. Only when I have to provide back-end access do I train the client to edit articles from the back end of the site. Understanding how your client will edit content on the web site can impact which extensions you ultimately choose to include in the site, as well as decisions about overall site configuration.

THINKING ABOUT MAINTENANCE FROM THE ADMINISTRATOR'S PERSPECTIVE

When you take on Joomla clients, unless the clients have their own web hosting and IT staff, you're really taking on the client for the long-term. You'll build a site initially, but then you'll need to upgrade the site to the latest version of Joomla. Clients will frequently also want tweaks and upgrades as they work with their sites. Some clients will also expect search engine optimization work. Others might want you to do everything for them and will never touch the site themselves.

Before you start building the site — in fact, before you have a contract set up — you'll want to ask the client the following questions:

➤ What will the client be responsible for doing when the site is completed? (Typically this is editing text, posting new articles, adding photos to the photo gallery, events to the calendar, and so on.)

➤ If a problem occurs with web hosting, does the client call you or the web host directly?

➤ How does the domain name for the web site get renewed? Does the client handle it or do you bill the client and do the renewing?

➤ Does the client expect you to add new features, functionality, or content on a regular basis? How much direction is provided?

➤ Does the client expect you to implement a search engine optimization campaign?

➤ Does the client expect you to check for broken links on the site periodically?

There are many other questions to ask, but understanding your client's expectations about how you're involved going forward is very important. Some clients expect you to go away until you're called, whereas others expect a lot of ongoing help.

You also want to find out whether you'll need any subcontractors to help you with maintenance.

You also must discuss compensation for maintenance with your client. Generally, maintenance fees are handled in one of two ways. If you're expected to complete ongoing work for the client each month, having the client reserve a fixed number of hours for that work might make sense. Otherwise, you might want to charge your hourly rate. Be sure you disclose whether you bill partial hours or full hours. If you bill partial hours, billing in 15-minute increments is common. You also must spell out how any compensation for ongoing subcontractors will work.

Finally, you must consider what is *not* maintenance. This definition often depends on the size of a given job. For example, adding a new image or icon to a page on the site is maintenance. However, designing a new custom template from scratch might be a separate contract. A good general rule is if a job takes more than five hours to complete, it might be time to consider a separate contract for the work. You also want to make this clear to your client.

IDENTIFYING QUALITY EXTENSIONS

Once you've established that you'll use Joomla to build the client's web site, and once you've identified the types of features and functionalities that need to be included on the web site (blogs, calendars, shopping cart, etc.), it's time to go shopping for extensions.

As its name implies, an extension is an addition to Joomla that extends Joomla's core capabilities. For example, Joomla does not come with a shopping cart pre-installed. However, you can download a shopping cart extension that enables Joomla to behave as a content management system and a shopping cart. Extensions cover all kinds of areas:

➤ **The incredibly important.** JoomlaPack, a utility that backs up your Joomla site and allows you to restore it easily. (JoomlaPack is covered extensively in Chapter 15.)

➤ **Making your maintenance life easier.** Joomla Updater, which easily installs the next version of Joomla to your site (that is, Joomla 1.5.14 to 1.5.15).

➤ **Important functionality to some sites.** Blogs, photo galleries, calendars, forums, community building extensions, commenting software, search, site maps, and so much more.

➤ **Language functionality.** Install alternative languages for your site, or translations of the back end of your site.

➤ **The absolutely sublime.** Your horoscope, a Tic-Tac-Toe game, or a random quote from "The Simpsons" are all available to include on your site as well. (Just because you can, doesn't mean you should!)

As of this writing, nearly 4,000 extensions are in the Joomla Extensions Directory (known as the JED; see `extensions.joomla.org`). More are added every day. How on earth do you pick the "best" extension for your particular site? Is just downloading something and using it okay? Can you get into trouble that way?

Some extensions are widely regarded as "site essentials" in the Joomla community. Many experienced developers, regardless of the type of site they're building, always install these specific extensions.

For example, Joomla comes with TinyMCE as its default editor. The editor is the box where you enter the content and formatting for an article or for other information in Joomla. Other alternatives for editors are available; you do not have to stick with TinyMCE.

JCE, the Joomla Content Editor, has been around for almost as long as Joomla has, and it has a loyal following as being one of the best editors out there. You can view this extension in the JED at `http://extensions.joomla.org/extensions/edition/editors/88/details` (see Figure 2-1).

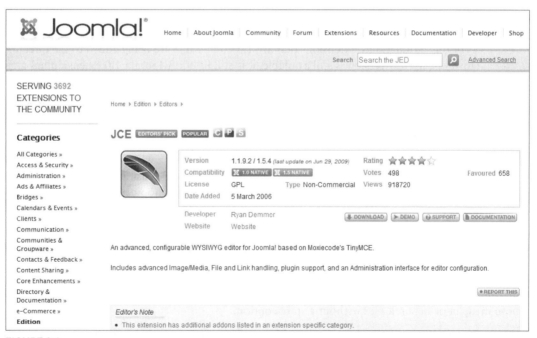

FIGURE 2-1

Note the following about this extension:

➤ The "Editor's Pick" icon appears after the name of the extension. Editor's Picks are featured extensions that are considered top-notch by the team of editors who review and run the JED. These editors are core team members of Joomla and other noted members of the Joomla community.

➤ The extension also features the "Popular" icon. This appears when more than 150 views of the extension occur per day. Popularity indicates either something unique in the JED or that many people think highly of the extension because they're looking at it and downloading it frequently.

➤ Note the version of the software, in this case, 1.1.9.2/1.5.4. Beware of extensions that are in alpha or beta development. They may change radically before they are ready for launch, or they may be buggy.

➤ Note the date added. This can give you some idea of the longevity of the extension. JCE was added in March 2006 (about six months after Joomla began). It's a very old extension, but clearly it's going strong.

➤ Note also the last update for the extension's listing, which appears after the version (June 29, 2009 in this case). This date gives you an idea of when the extension author visited the site. It can be a measure of how engaged and interested the author is in this extension. Some extensions are seldom updated, whereas others are updated regularly. More updates mean an engaged, active author for the extension, so you're more likely to get better tech support, more frequent updates, and so on.

➤ As of this writing, only extensions that are 1.5 compatible are being added to the directory. However, if a 1.0 version is still available, it is still listed. A Joomla 1.0 extension has a red icon, while a Joomla 1.5 extension has a green icon.

➤ Note how many votes and what rating the extension has. Getting five stars is easy if there's only a handful of votes but tough if there's a pile of votes. In this case, JCE has a four-star rating with 498 votes, which is a very good rating.

➤ Look at the most recent reviews, particularly with extensions with longevity, such as this one. Are most of the reviews good? If they're not good, has the extension owner responded to the review? Again, the review is a good measure of the current happiness (or unhappiness) of users, and it also gauges the responsiveness of the extension author.

➤ You might see some little icons for M, C, P, or S. They indicate whether the extension is a *m*odule, *c*omponent, *p*lug-in, or has an extension-specific add-on associated with it. You can see that the JCE extension has C, P, and S.

Be sure to watch for extensions that have not been recently updated, those with poor reviews, and those in alpha or beta releases without a stable option.

Also avoid extensions that are for Joomla 1.5 legacy wherever possible. *Legacy mode* is a backward compatibility mode that enables code that is more compatible with Joomla 1.0 to run within the Joomla 1.5 environment. This means you must enable a plug-in that comes with Joomla, called the Legacy Plugin, for these extensions to run. The Legacy Plugin adds significantly to the overhead for the web site. Furthermore, any Joomla 1.5 legacy component will definitely not run under Joomla 1.6. Be forward-compatible and work with Joomla 1.5 native extensions wherever possible.

Evaluating the Code

Many experienced PHP/MySQL developers will tell you to "evaluate the code" of an extension to make sure no security holes or other coding problems exist. They're frustrated that not everyone does this. Unfortunately, not everyone has the skills that these developers do.

Recently, I had a conversation with Victor Drover, owner of AnythingDigital (`dev.anything-digital.com`), and creator of extensions such as JCalPro and shSEF404. I told him that I don't have the PHP background to "evaluate the code" and asked what he would recommend someone like me do to determine what the other hallmarks of a well-written extension are.

These points apply to extensions available in the Joomla Extensions Directory (JED), or those not included there:

➤ **Is it encrypted?** "PHP is a scripting language," Victor said. "The code is there on the page, easy to read and understand. Encryption means you hide that code in such a way that the PHP cannot be read by a human, and you can't make any tweaks or changes to the code. As a policy, encrypted extensions are not allowed on the JED. If the code is encrypted, you don't know whether the extension author has done a good job or not, or whether security problems exist. I recommend you stay away from these extensions. If they require you to install IonCube or Zend Optimizer on your server to run these extensions, that's indicative that the code is encrypted."

➤ **Does it require you to change permissions on directories to install or use it?** "Joomla is set up in such a way that, if the extension author knows what he's doing, you should be able to get the extension to install without changing file permissions," said Victor. "Particularly dangerous is when you're required to give full read, write, and execute access (chmod 777) for a directory or a file. This is *usually* a security weakness, and it's an indication that you should uninstall the extension and not use it. In addition, you can search the source code with a good text editor such as TextWrangler (Mac OS X) or Editpad Lite (Windows) for '777'. These applications allow you to search all the files of the extension at once. If you find instances of '777' in the code, proceed with caution and be sure to inquire with the developers as to why this is needed — it might be legitimate."

➤ **Does the extension start with the correct first line?** "All Joomla extensions and templates start with the same first line of code," said Victor. "If that line of code isn't present, it indicates that the developer is not taking security seriously, and it leaves the extension and your entire site very vulnerable." Although looking at every PHP file for this entry can be tedious, it is essential. The line of code he refers to is

```
<?php defined( '_JEXEC' ) or die( 'Restricted access' ); ?>
```

This line of code is the same as the line of code you use to start a custom template. It's covered in Chapter 13.

➤ **Is there an index.html file in each folder?** "The index.html file is a blank page that simply prevents the filenames in the directory to be listed, if someone were to try to view the contents of an extension folder from the front end of the web site. It's a simple security measure so that no one knows exactly which files are contained in that folder," said Victor. "Most servers and web hosts prevent directory listing, but this file adds a little security in case your host doesn't offer this feature. (Unfortunately, this is more common than you might think.)"

➤ **Does it overwrite core files?** "Some extensions clearly state that changes or 'hacks' to the core Joomla files are required for operation," said Victor. "The problem arises when you update Joomla. These hacks get lost if the files are included in the update and are then copied to the server. While extensions that make changes to the core files are published on the JED, in general, beginners should avoid their use."

By following these guidelines, you can minimize your use of insecure extensions. Remember, hackers can also freely examine these extensions for vulnerabilities, so your doing the same is important. Over time, you will build a repertoire of safe extensions and trusted developers.

Using Commercial Versus Free Extensions

Most Joomla extensions are completely free to download and use. However, some extensions charge money for their work. Which is better? Right, it depends.

Obviously "free" is a very attractive price point. But consider that a free extension means there's not necessarily any obligation for quality support for that extension. It also means that there's less drive on the part of the author to keep updating the extension.

These points certainly are not true for all authors of free extensions. JCE, for example, is free and is extremely well maintained. However, having worked with hundreds of Joomla extensions, I have noticed that you are more likely to get poor support and/or few upgrades from free extensions than commercial extensions.

Commercial extensions clearly have a responsibility to provide high-quality support to their customers. The authors are also more likely to upgrade their products over time.

If you are the type of developer who needs to ask a lot of questions, who might not be good at figuring things out from documentation (or just by clicking around), or who might just prefer to be told how to do something, you should probably stick with commercial extensions for your site. You will need the support offered for the best experience.

Upgrading Extensions to Maintain Security

Not long ago, a very popular extension was pulled from the JED because a security hole had been discovered, but the extension's author had no intention of fixing the problem or upgrading it. Just because an extension is popular does not mean it is secure, maintained, or without problems.

Just as upgrading Joomla to the latest version when it's released is important, you must also stay current with new releases of your extensions. Not keeping up with these releases can lead to security issues on your Joomla web site, which might lead to being hacked.

Using Custom Extensions

One of Joomla's great strengths is its flexibility. It was built with extensions in mind. Extensive documentation is available on the Joomla web site describing the correct methodology for building Joomla extensions.

If one of the more than 3,000 extensions in the JED can't satisfy your client's requirements, one can certainly be written to do what he wants. My longtime engineer and good friend, Bill Tomczak, has done many wild and crazy things with Joomla extensions. One of the most unusual was making an old AS400 computer talk with Joomla.

Writing custom extensions, however, is not for the faint of heart. If you're going to write such an extension, you should have plenty of experience with PHP and MySQL, and you should understand what Joomla expects from its extensions.

You must completely and clearly understand what your client wants. Sometimes drawing pictures on paper (called *wireframe diagrams*) that outline exactly what the user sees, what the administrator sees, what kind of data goes into the system, and what kind of data comes out can help.

If you decide not to write the extension yourself, but to hire an engineer, inevitably he or she will have additional questions. The best service you can provide for that engineer is to fully understand the problem the extension is supposed to solve. Understand what the client wants to get out of it in the end. The wireframe diagrams can help communicate those requirements.

Generally speaking, engineers are not happy when you suggest ways for writing the code or making their magic happen. Let's talk car repair for a moment. If your car is making a funny noise, you might take it to a mechanic. My approach has always been to hand the keys to the mechanic and tell him to call me when he figures out what it is and how much it will cost to fix it. That's because I know nothing about car repair! I am delighted to let the mechanic figure out the solution to the funny sound that I want to go away.

Other people might drop their car off with instructions to replace the brakes. When they pick the car up later, the sound is still there. You can't go back to the mechanic and berate him for not fixing the funny sound. That was not what you asked him to do! You asked for him to change the brakes, and he did. Sometimes not suggesting solutions and just letting the engineer (and the mechanic) be creative and find their own best solution to your problem is better.

3

Downloading and Installing Joomla!

WHAT'S IN THIS CHAPTER?

➤ Comparing local vs. hosted installations

➤ Choosing the right web host with the right configuration

➤ Downloading and installing Joomla

➤ Remembering passwords (preferably, securely)

Joomla is a web application. A *web application* is a software program that runs on a web server and has a browser-based interface. Generally speaking, a web application requires a few pieces of technology:

➤ **Web server (hardware).** In a hardware sense, a web server is a computer that's hooked up to the Internet for the purpose of sharing information with the world. Web servers have their own operating systems. In the Joomla world, typically a server is running some variety of UNIX, or it is running Windows. Other operating systems are possible, but they are less frequently encountered.

➤ **Web server (software).** A software program called a web server deals with taking requests for web pages and sending them out to the requester (the *client*). This software is typically Apache, an open source web server, or Internet Information Server (IIS), the Microsoft web server that runs on a Windows-based computer. Other server software is possible, but you encounter it less frequently.

➤ **MySQL database.** The database is where all the Joomla information is stored. MySQL is the name of the open source database software that is almost exclusively used with Joomla.

➤ **PHP software.** PHP, which originally stood for Personal Home Page or Pre-Hypertext Processor (depending on whom you ask), is a scripting language that can talk to the database, extract its information, manipulate it if required, and create an HTML page that can be viewed by your web browser.

➤ **Joomla software.** Joomla is the program that runs on top of all the preceding pieces of software. It is written in PHP and its data is stored in MySQL.

Joomla requires that all the aforementioned pieces of technology be present in order to run. You have two options for running Joomla: You can configure your local computer to be a web server, running PHP and MySQL, or you can get a web host to provide those services for you.

In this chapter, I'll cover Joomla web hosting, downloading and installing Joomla, and a few words on security.

PLANNING THE INSTALLATION: LOCAL VERSUS HOSTED INSTALLATIONS

A local installation is an installation of Joomla that runs on your computer. The good news is that it is very quick to run. There is no lag time to get requests across the Internet to a distant computer. However, it also means that you cannot share the web site with anyone who cannot see your local computer. Depending on how you work and what you are trying to do, this can be a fairly large disadvantage.

For example, I regularly work with a graphic designer for the customized graphical look for the web site, an engineer who might provide custom code tweaks or custom extensions, and my client. Rarely are these people all located in my tiny hometown of Keene, New Hampshire, population of 20,000. Although my graphic designer lives just over the border in Vermont, only a 30-minute drive away, my engineers live in Colorado and Nebraska. My client is occasionally local, occasionally in Boston, or further away.

Having a local installation means that if I build my web site on my local computer, then my graphic designer, my engineer, and my client cannot see it until I push it up to a web host. A *web host* is the company that manages a series of web servers.

Some people ask what they should use for a web address (URL) when building a site on a web host. Typically, your host will have an obscure address (usually an IP address or an address containing a tilde [~] in it) that is used, temporarily, until you park your "real" address at that location. Unless someone types this obscure address into their computer, it's unlikely anyone will see your site while it is under construction. Unless someone links to your site, or you tell the search engines about it, your site should not be indexed until it's completed. You can also include a "do not index" instruction to search engines for your site until construction is complete, to ensure it doesn't get indexed.

My recommendation is that unless you have a very compelling reason *not* to develop your site on a web host, that is where you should build it.

If you do decide to build the web site locally, you will need to download software known as MAMP (Mac, Apache, MySQL, PHP), WAMP (Windows, Apache, MySQL, and PHP, sometimes also WAMPP, which includes Perl or Python as an additional language), or XAMPP, which runs on both Mac and Windows computers. This software is free to download and use. Any of the above installations are acceptable for running Joomla, so pick the best fit for your computer.

This chapter addresses building your web site on a web host, configured with Linux, Apache, the cPanel control panel, and the correct versions of PHP and MySQL for Joomla. These versions may change as Joomla evolves, so be sure to check the Joomla web site for the most recent version requirements for PHP and MySQL.

CHOOSING THE RIGHT WEB HOST

When evaluating web hosts, you'll find you have thousands of choices. Here are some important points to keep in mind when considering the right host for you.

Ensuring Your Host Is Running Windows or Linux/UNIX

My personal bias is that a Linux/UNIX system is the correct one for Joomla. If you must run on Windows (because it's a client demand), you can do that. If it's possible to have Windows run Apache instead of IIS, Joomla's search engine-friendly URLs will be formed correctly. If you're running a Windows server with IIS, Joomla will insert an extra index.php in the URL which is not present when Apache is the web server software.

Ensuring Your Host Is Running the Right Version of PHP, MySQL, and Apache/IIS

You can find the minimum requirements for running Joomla 1.5 on the Joomla web site at `www.joomla.org/about-joomla/technical-requirements.html`. Be sure to read these requirements carefully and compare them with your web host's versions of software. You should go for the recommended requirements. The minimum requirements are not optimal, since the technology is quite old.

Sometimes, you need other pieces of software to make certain extensions run (such as Zend Optimizer, IonCube, and so on). If you know you will need this software, make sure your host offers it. If you do not need it now, you might need it in the future, so find out whether your host can add the software to your account if you need it. I covered extension evaluation in Chapter 2.

Sometimes your web host will limit you to a fixed number of databases. If you are running Joomla, one database should be enough. You will also want to ask about file upload limits. Depending on how PHP is configured, the file upload limit may be as small as 2 MB. Find out if this can be over-ridden or altered in some way by the host if these limits are in place, in case you need to change them later.

Talking to Your Host about Its Backup Policies

I cannot stress the importance of knowing your host's backup policies. Your Joomla site will change every day. You must have a backup strategy for it.

Backups are critically important in several situations:

➤ **What if you are hacked?** It might seem unlikely, but a lot of bored people are out there who might like to hack your site just for some fun. You can do some things to prevent your site from being hacked, such as keeping your site and its extensions up to the latest version at all times (covered in Chapter 15). However, if a hacker is determined to get in, he will likely find a way. You must be prepared to remedy the situation by restoring from a recent backup.

➤ **What if you do something stupid?** Web developers are always trying out new extensions to Joomla. Sometimes those extensions do not work out as well as planned. Sometimes they work out really badly and cause the site to stop working altogether. Having a backup in a situation like this is a good idea.

➤ **What if the server catches fire?** Servers are kept in heavily air conditioned rooms for a reason — they run very hot. Occasionally, they catch fire, or the hard drive fails, or they get really hacked, or a piano falls on it, or any one of a number of improbable events happen. What is your host's plan to get that server back online ASAP if something *very bad* happens to your machine?

Some hosts make backups, but they are only for situations listed in the preceding bullet — that is, something catastrophic happens to the machine. They will not make these backups available to you. That is not a host you want to choose, no matter how cheap.

Other hosts make backups according to your schedule and your available disk space. A good plan is to have the host make a weekly backup as well as a daily backup for you. This means that the host makes a backup each day and overwrites it each night with the next backup. One backup is held for a whole week (generally Sunday to Sunday). If the daily backup is corrupted, the host can go to the weekly backup.

Your host's backups are important, but you should be making your own backups of your site on a regular basis as well. JoomlaPack (`www.joomlapack.net`) is an excellent extension for this job, and you can read more about it in Chapter 15 and the appendix.

Ensuring Your Host Can Respond to Your Questions and Problems

If you are like me, you do not know a lot about web hosting. You are very happy to have an expert on your team who can take care of those problems for you. And that is what your host should be for you in a successful business relationship — a partner on whom you can rely for anything you need, whenever you need it. If your host is flaky, has a lot of downtime, takes days to answer your problems, and is generally not responsive to your needs, it is not the right host for you. You need a professional host that responds quickly to any issues, who answers the phone, and whose servers are up and running regularly.

That might mean your host will cost a bit more than $10/month.

Does that mean those "cheap and cheerful" providers are not worth considering? No, not at all. If you are building a personal web site, or a site for a very poor client, a cheaper provider might be good enough for what you need. However, as you service larger clients, they expect their web sites to be up all the time, respond well to traffic, and not be down for weeks if the server catches fire. You do get what you pay for.

Ensuring Your Host Comes with a Good Control Panel

Unless you're a command line kind of person, you need some kind of interface for configuring your web server. Maybe you need to set up an email account or a forwarder, or you need to create a new database. Such tasks are easier with a graphical interface, at least for most of us.

The interface used in this book is cPanel, an open source interface for managing your web site, which came with my web hosting package. Other control panels are in use out there as well, but cPanel is rather popular. Your host might offer Plesk or other options for control panel software. Regardless of which control panel you choose, it should offer access to your files via a file manager (including uploads/downloads and zip/unzip functionality), the ability to create a database and a database user, and the ability to run a backup for you. Many additional nice-to-have features that you may also want, such as statistics and email access, are available.

cPanel can be configured in a number of ways that might not exactly match what follows here in the book. Many of the functions I'm covering here may not even be present in your configuration. In these rare cases, hopefully your web host will be willing to reconfigure cPanel with the needed features.

What the Web Host Gives You to Get Started

After you sign up for an account with your new web host, typically you receive an email a short time later. This email contains extremely important information about configuring and managing your account. Save it someplace where you can find it again.

The types of information in this email vary greatly, but there are usually some pieces of information that are always present. First, your web host will tell you what the FTP and cPanel username and password are for your account. FTP stands for *File Transfer Protocol*, and this is the methodology used for transferring files to the server. In my experience, the FTP and cPanel username and password are the same, but it's possible your host will give you different logins. You should also be given an address where you can find cPanel for your site, as well as an address to use in the FTP process. Make sure you take careful note of this information, as you'll need it to install Joomla.

Dealing with Clients Who Want to Host Their Own Web Sites

Occasionally, you'll encounter clients who want to host their own web sites on their own computers. These clients frequently include universities, K–12 schools, and larger companies. They should have IT staff dedicated to keeping this server running. (This staff might have other jobs as well, but maintaining the web server should be part of what they do.)

If your client does not have IT staff to keep the web server running, steer them towards a hosted solution. Web servers require frequent security updates, backups, tweaks, and so forth. Maintaining your own web server without the training that IT professionals have is not easy. Some clients think that they can just throw up any old computer on their (often inadequate) Internet connection and turn it into a good web server. Pay for a quality web host, or hire the IT people to maintain the web server.

Having said this, if my clients want to host their own sites, I set the expectation that they will install Joomla and prepare the server for me, so all I have to do is build the web site. For most clients, this expectation has not been a problem. I can then work with the IT staff to obtain any server access I might need in the course of setting up the site.

DOWNLOADING JOOMLA!

Joomla is freely available to download at www.joomla.org. On the home page is a button for down-loading the most recent version of Joomla (see Figure 3-1).

FIGURE 3-1

When you click this button, a second screen appears, containing a link to download the zipped ver-sion of the most recent full package version of Joomla — in this case Joomla 1.5.13 (see Figure 3-2).

FIGURE 3-2

Also note the link to download other Joomla packages. This link allows you to download other upgrade versions or other formats of the full Joomla installation package. You find out more about upgrades in Chapter 15, "Site Maintenance and Training."

Download the full package version of Joomla to your computer, but do not unzip it. I suggest you save it to your desktop, where you can easily find it later.

INSTALLING JOOMLA!

Installing Joomla is not difficult after you understand the outline of what you must do:

1. Create a database on your server.

2. Upload the installation package and decompress it.

3. Complete the installation wizard, which will make the Joomla files talk to the database.

4. Log in and change the username for the account.

5. Securely record the important usernames and passwords associated with this Joomla installation so that you can find them later.

Creating a Database

In the process of creating the database, you create the actual database (which holds the data) and a database user (which accesses the data). You then need to make them talk to each other. Be sure you record the database name, the database username, and the database user password, as you must type them as part of the Joomla installation process.

The database user is *not* the same as the FTP or cPanel information, and it's not the same as the username you'll have when you access Joomla itself. For security reasons, make sure all these passwords are unique.

To create the database and the database user:

1. Log in to cPanel and then click the MySQL Databases link, as shown in Figure 3-3.

2. Near the top of the MySQL Databases dialog page, as shown in Figure 3-4, you should see a box for creating a new database. Call your database "joomla," and click the Create Database button.

   Make sure that you write down the name of your database. Note that for this web host, the actual database name is not "joomla" — it is "start_joomla," "start" being the cPanel username for this hosting account.

   After you have created the database, click the Go Back button at the bottom of the page as shown in Figure 3-5.

FIGURE 3-3

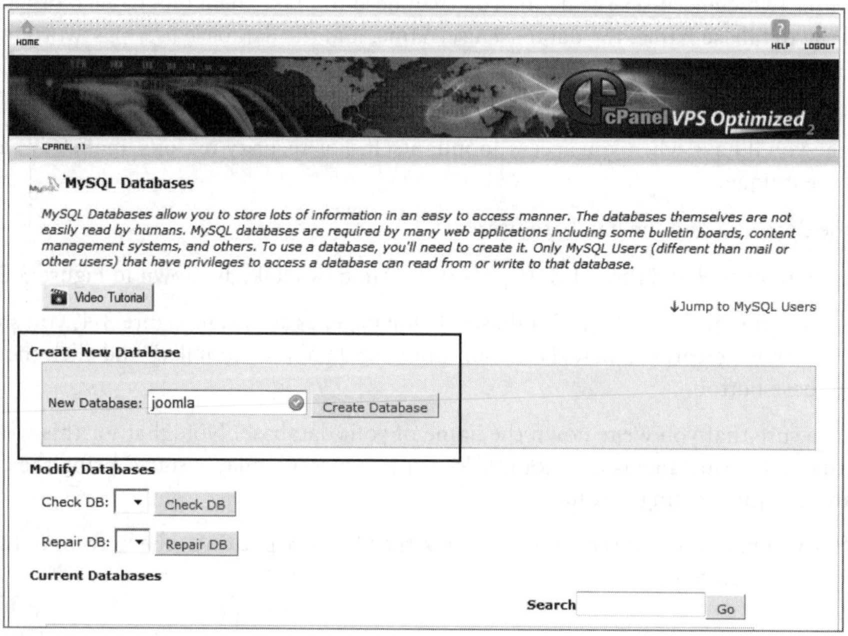

FIGURE 3-4

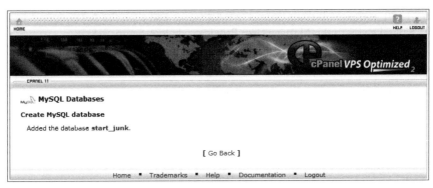

FIGURE 3-5

3. As shown in Figure 3-6, create a database user via the boxes further down the MySQL Databases dialog. Enter a username and password, and then click the Create User button.

Be very sure that you write down the username and password. Once again, note that the cPanel username is placed in front of your username, separated by an underscore. In this case, the database username becomes start_dbuser.

After you have created the database user, click the Go Back button at the bottom of the page.

New Database:		Create Database

Modify Databases

Check DB: start_joomla ▾ Check DB

Repair DB: start_joomla ▾ Repair DB

Current Databases

Search [   ] Go

DATABASE	SIZE	USERS	ACTIONS
start_joomla	0.01 MB		Delete Database

MySQL Users
Add New User

Username: dbuser ⊘ *Seven characters max

Password: ••••••••••⊘ Generate Password

Password
Strength:
▬▬▬▬
Very Strong
(100/100)

Password (Again): ••••••••••⊘

Create User

↑Jump to MySQL Databases

FIGURE 3-6

4. Next, you must associate the user with the database. Further down on the MySQL Databases dialog, in the Add User to Database section, select the username (start_dbuser) and database name (start_joomla) from the drop-down list boxes and click the Add button (see Figure 3-7). This will take you to the Manage User Privileges dialog (Figure 3-8).

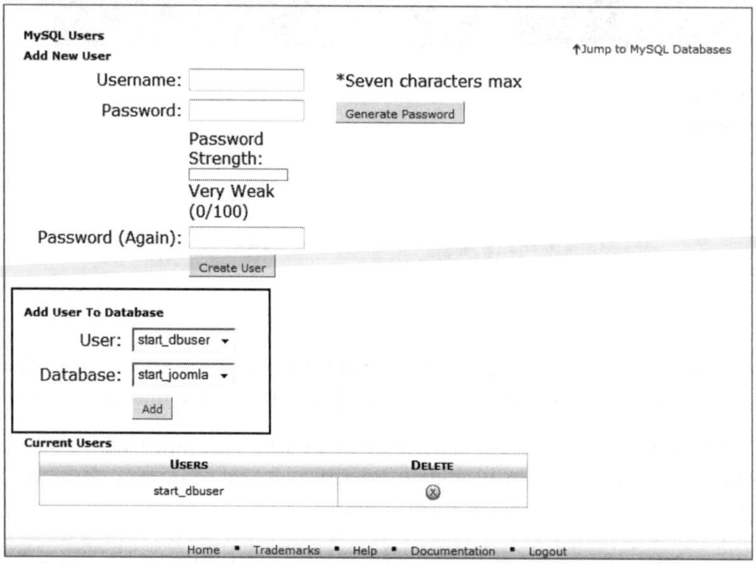

FIGURE 3-7

5. As shown in Figure 3-8, in the Manage User Privileges page, select All Privileges, and then click the Make Changes button. Once you have done this, click the Go Back button at the bottom of the page, which will return you to the MySQL Databases dialog.

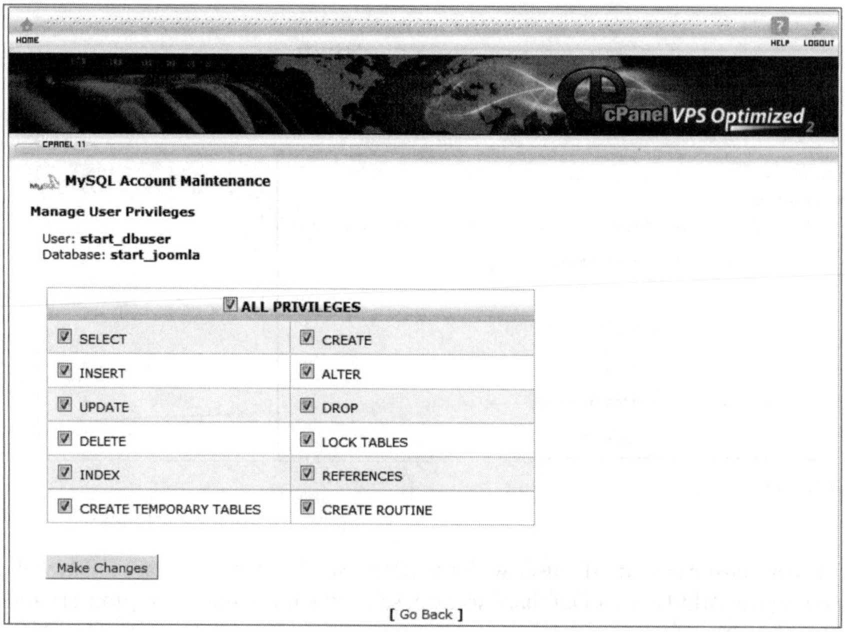

FIGURE 3-8

The MySQL databases dialog confirms that you've created the database and the user, and associated them, as shown in Figure 3-9.

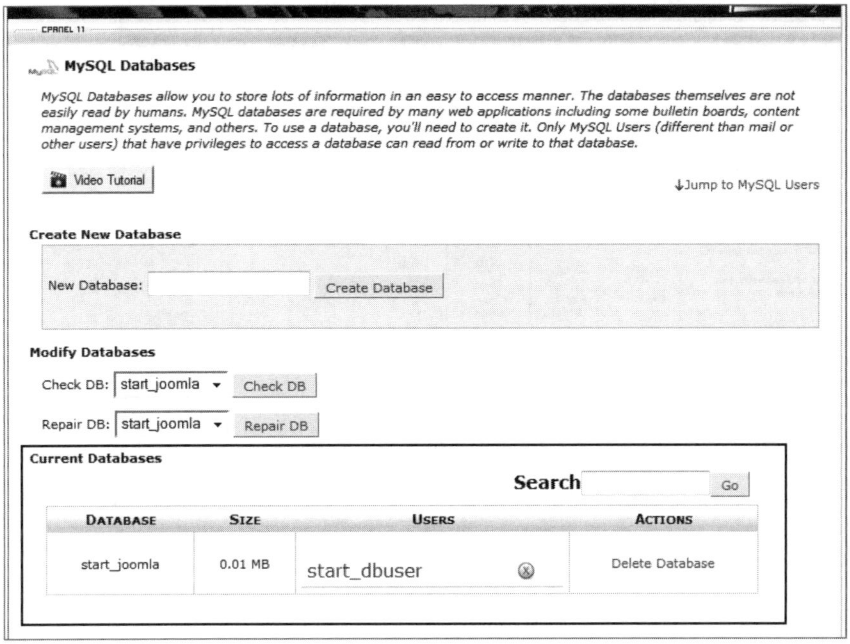

FIGURE 3-9

Uploading the Installation Package to Your Server

The next step for installing Joomla is to upload the zipped Joomla file to your server. You'll unzip it there, in the control panel.

Uploading each individual file by FTP is possible if you prefer (or if that's the only access you have). This method takes a very long time, even on a broadband Internet connection, but it works just as well.

You can upload the zipped Joomla file either through FTP according to your host's FTP instructions or through your host's control panel. I find that using the File Manager in cPanel is most convenient for completing these next steps:

1. From the home page of the control panel, click the File Manager link (see Figure 3-10).

    If you are prompted to do so after clicking the link, set it to show the root of your web site and to show hidden files. Remember that the web site root is not necessarily the root of your file structure. In the case of my server, the root of my hosting is a directory called *start* (which is inside of another directory called home). Inside of this, there is a directory called *public_htm* (or *www*). My web site lives inside of this directory, so I will want to upload Joomla to the public_html directory. (Also remember that directories and folders are interchangeable terms.)

FIGURE 3-10

2. In the File Manager screen that appears, click the Upload button, as shown in Figure 3-11. The Upload Files screen appears.

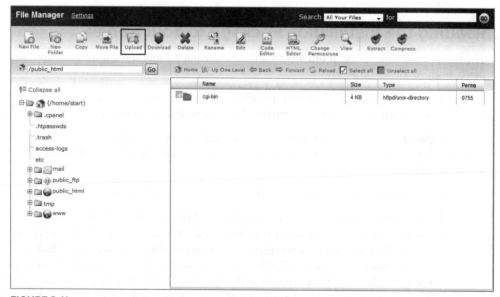

FIGURE 3-11

3. Click the Browse button to browse for your zipped file (see Figure 3-12). The upload will start automatically.

Leave this window open until the upload is 100% complete. If you close the window, you will quit the download in the middle of the process.

Upload files

Maximum File Size allowed for upload: 74.42 MB

Please select files to upload to **/home/start/public_html**

Joomla_1.5.13-Stable-Full_Package.zip: 97.38 KB: 1% Complete
ETA ~ 1m 18s @ 81.58 KB/s

Browse...
Browse...

Overwrite existing files: ☐

⊕ Add Another Upload Box

Back to /home/start/public_html

FIGURE 3-12

Decompressing the Installation Package

After the upload has completed, perform the following steps to decompress the installation package:

1. Go back to the File Manager screen and click the Reload button to reload the view.

You should see the zipped file listed in the listing of files and folders, as shown in Figure 3-13.

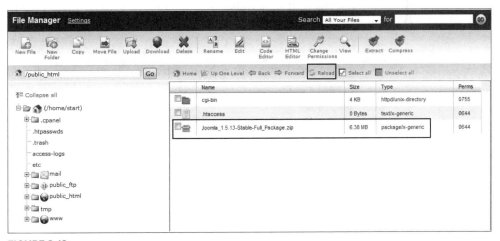

FIGURE 3-13

2. Select the check box next to the zipped file, and click the Extract button.

When prompted, extract to the web site's root directory (in this case, /public_html), as shown in Figure 3-14.

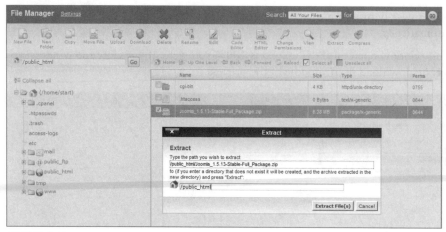

FIGURE 3-14

After the zipped file is decompressed, you will see a bunch of folders and files listed on the screen (click Reload if you do not). That's an indication that you're ready for the next step. Keep the File Manager window open because you're going to need it later.

Completing the Installation Wizard

To complete the installation wizard, perform the following steps:

1. In your web browser, open a new tab and go to the address for your web site's home page. You'll see an installation wizard there. As shown in Figure 3-15, the first step is selecting the language that should be used for installing the site. Choose your language from the list, and click the Next button. The Pre-installation Check screen appears.

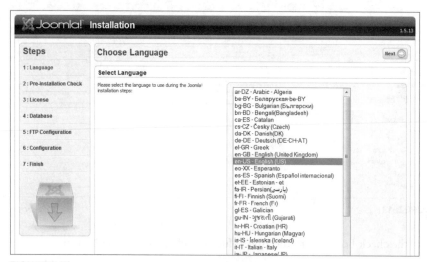

FIGURE 3-15

2. Joomla does a test to make sure you have a supported version of PHP on your server and that the server is configured correctly. If anything in the top section of the Pre-installation Check screen is set to No, be sure you talk to your web host about it to get it fixed. Underneath are recommended settings. Figure 3-16 shows the Display Errors turned on, which is not necessarily recommended by Joomla. However, Joomla will function just fine if Display Errors (or anything else in this list) are not at their recommended setting. Click the Next button. The License pane appears.

FIGURE 3-16

3. The License pane of the wizard contains the license under which Joomla is distributed (see Figure 3-17). You must accept the license to install Joomla. Click the Next button.

FIGURE 3-17

4. The Database Configuration window appears (see Figure 3-18). Remember when I told you to write down the database name, database username, and password? Now is when you'll need this information.

   a. Set your Database Type to mysql.

   b. Set your Host Name to localhost. (Your web host will tell you if it's something different.)

   c. Set your Username, Password, and Database Name to the settings you established earlier.

Click the Next button. If you entered everything correctly, the FTP Configuration screen appears. If you didn't, you'll get an error that Joomla can't connect to the database. You'll need to figure out what you entered incorrectly before moving to the next step.

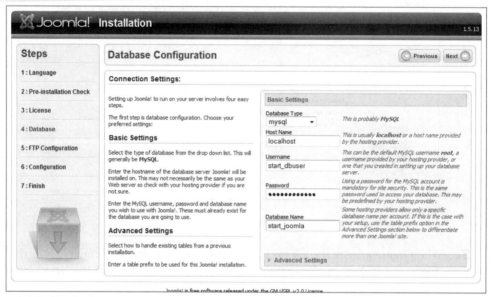

FIGURE 3-18

5. Figure 3-19 shows the FTP Configuration screen. Enable FTP by clicking the Yes button next to Enable FTP File System Layer, and then enter your FTP username and password. Click Autofind FTP Path, and the wizard will find the correct FTP path for you and put the path in the FTP Root Path box. Under Advanced Settings you might want to set Save FTP Password to Yes. This setting prevents your having to enter the password every time you upload extensions, images, and templates to Joomla. Click the Next button.

6. Finally, as shown in Figure 3-20, in the Main Configuration screen, you'll need to enter a site name, your email address, and an admin password.

You can change all these settings later, so don't worry if you don't pick the perfect site name the first time. Be sure you remember what your password is.

You can choose to install default sample data if you want. This data installs some informative articles about Joomla, along with some sample menus, modules, and components. You

Installing Joomla! | 41

can also look at how the sample site is constructed. Alternatively, if you're sure about what you're doing, don't install the sample data. This gives you a clean install, and you won't have to delete data after the fact. I did not install the sample data for this example, but many of the examples later in the book use the sample data.

When you're done, click the Next button. (If you choose not to install the sample data, you'll get a warning pop-up that you didn't install it. Just click OK and move on.)

FIGURE 3-19

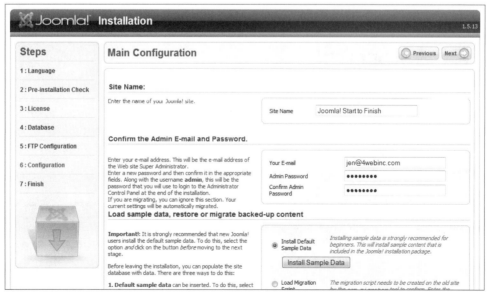

FIGURE 3-20

Congratulations! You've successfully installed Joomla. However, there's one final step you must do. Delete the "installation" directory from your server. You can do this by FTP or your File Manager. In the File Manager, simply select the check box next to the installation folder, and then click the Delete button. You will see a dialog box like the one in Figure 3-21. Click Delete File(s).

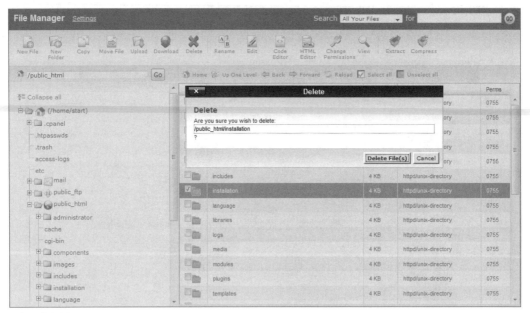

FIGURE 3-21

You're now ready to take a look at the front end of your site. If you did not install the sample data, Figure 3-22 shows how it should look. If you did install the sample data, you will see articles and menus on this page, in addition to the logo and template.

FIGURE 3-22

You're ready to log in to the admin side of Joomla. To get there, go to www.yourwebsiteaddress.com/administrator. (This assumes you did install Joomla into the web site root. If you installed Joomla in another directory, you'll need to modify this path accordingly.) You'll see the login dialog box as show in Figure 3-23. The username, by default, is admin, and you know your password.

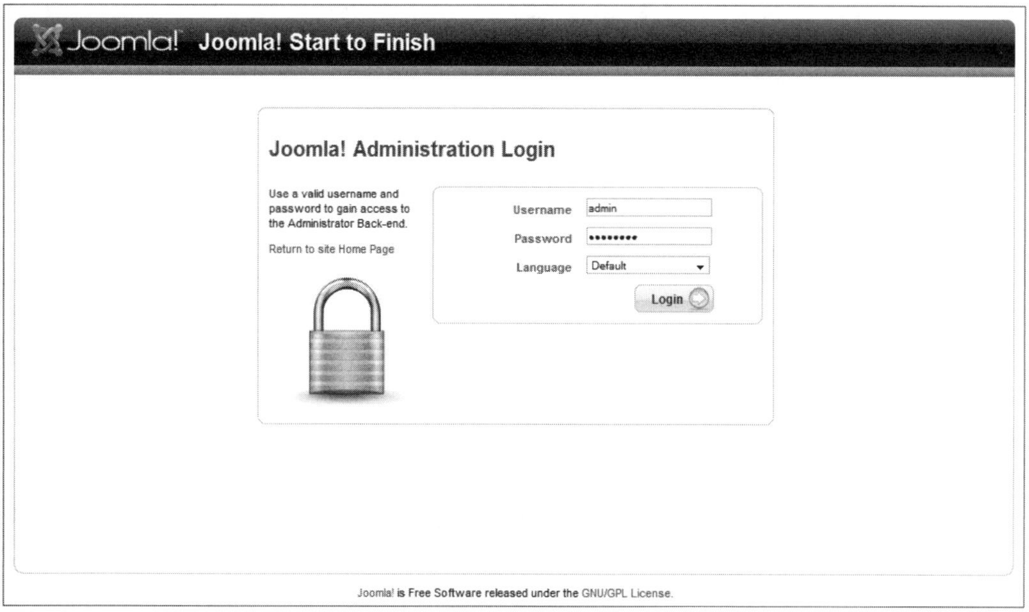

FIGURE 3-23

Changing the Username

Now that you've logged into Joomla, the very first thing you should do is to change the username for the default account. Rule #1 of any site's security is keeping the username and password secret. However, it's well known that Joomla always creates an account with a user ID of 62 and with a username of admin. This information can be used to hack into the web site — only the password must be guessed. By changing your username for admin, you can increase your site's security. Follow these steps:

1. When you log into Joomla, you'll see a control panel. Click on the User Manager option, as shown in Figure 3-24.

2. The only account created for your Joomla site belongs to Administrator (see Figure 3-25). Click the name to edit the information.

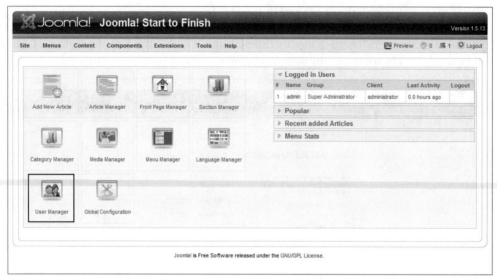

FIGURE 3-24

FIGURE 3-25

3. As shown in Figure 3-26, change the username to something other than Administrator. For example, you can change the name for the account from Administrator to your own. Click Save when you're done.

Storing and Remembering Passwords (Preferably, Securely)

You might not have a hard time remembering the FTP username and password, the cPanel login, the database name, username, and password, and the Joomla admin username and password for this first installation. But by your fifth site, assuming you've done the secure thing and created unique usernames and passwords for every Joomla installation, you'll definitely be having a few problems remembering them all. (And I haven't mentioned the username and password associated with your domain name, either, and other miscellaneous logins you might collect that are associated with your site.)

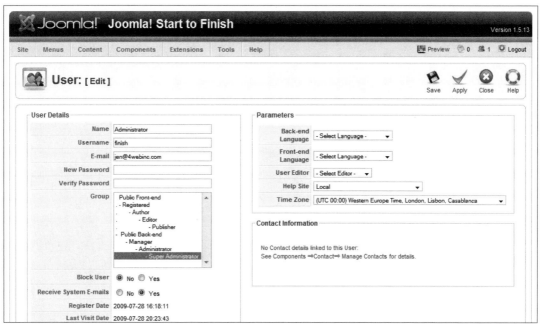

FIGURE 3-26

As a web professional, you need a safe, secure way to store all this information, so that you can access it as required.

Online services exist that will store your passwords for you, or you can get one to run on your local computer. These services should be password protected, of course.

Writing the information down in a Word document and password protecting the document is *not* good enough! Word password protection is notoriously insecure. Writing the information on a sticky and putting it under your keyboard isn't so secure, either. You're a web professional now, so act like one. Invest in a good program to keep your passwords organized and accessible. It will come in handy sooner than you think.

And finally, make sure you back up that password information. Should you ever lose it, you will be a very sorry web developer indeed.

A Brief Tour of the Joomla! Administration Interface

Now that Joomla is installed, it's time to take a peek in the back end of the web site. *Back end* is a term that refers to the administrative side of Joomla, where most changes are made. The term *front end*, in contrast, refers to the public-facing part of the web site.

The back end of your Joomla web site is typically accessible by the following address: http://www.yoursite.com/administrator. Unless you have done something to specifically change that address (such as install an extension that will change the URL), that's where the administrative interface is located.

This chapter will show you some features you'll use as your site's super administrator, including the global configuration, user management, mailing features, and clearing the site's cache.

GLOBAL CONFIGURATION

The Global Configuration is used for configuring the web site's functions. Here you can set the site name, change database and FTP information, set global metatags, and much more. Enter your username and password to access the back end of your web site, and click the Global Configuration icon (see Figure 4-1) or choose Site ➪ Global Configuration.

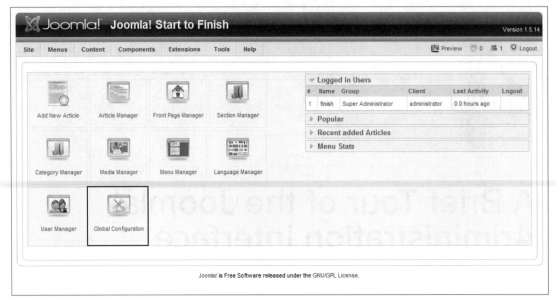

FIGURE 4-1

Global Configuration has three configuration tabs: Site, System, and Server.

 For most items in Global Configuration, you can roll your mouse over the title for a given item, and a tool tip will describe what that item does. In this chapter I cover Global Configuration items that you might want to change or that I use regularly.

The Site Tab

Take a look at the Site screen, shown in Figure 4-2.

You can see that it contains the following areas:

➤ **Site Settings**

    ➤ **Site Offline.** If you want to take your site completely offline, this setting is how you do it. Figure 4-3 shows the screen that appears if you take your site offline. Many developers take their site offline while developing a site on a web host. Those with a login can use it to see the site, while the general public cannot see it.

    ➤ **Offline Message.** In this box you can customize the message that appears when your site is offline.

    ➤ **Site Name.** Use this box to change the site name, which in this case is Joomla! Start to Finish.

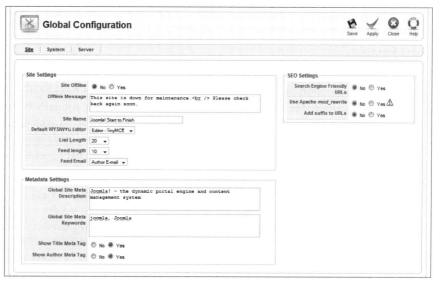

FIGURE 4-2

➤ **Default WYSIWYG Editor.** This is the default editor used throughout Joomla. *WYSIWYG* stands for What You See Is What You Get. By default, Joomla comes with TinyMCE. You could also set this box to no editor, meaning that everyone would need to code directly in HTML. However, these settings are global — they apply to everyone and everything by default. You can override the editor on a user-by-user basis in the User Manager, covered later in this chapter. There are also other editors you can install as extensions, covered in Chapter 11.

➤ **List Length.** This option refers to how many items you see on a screen, with 20 being the default. For example, the Article Manager provides a listing of all articles on the site (see Chapter 5). By default, you would see a list of 20 articles, broken up over a series of pages. By setting the list length to a larger number, you would see more items on fewer pages, whereas a smaller number produces fewer items on more pages.

➤ Metadata Settings

➤ **Global Site Meta Description** and **Global Site Meta Keywords.** You should change these for every site you build. The meta-description and meta-keywords, important for search engine optimization, will be included on every page of your Joomla site, except for those pages where you've overridden this setting on an article-by-article basis. I'll talk more about meta-tags and meta-descriptions in Chapter 5. Keep in mind that if you

FIGURE 4-3

don't change this setting, your meta-description and meta-keywords will be all about Joomla, and that's a sure sign of an amateur designer!

➤ **SEO Settings**

   ➤ **Search Engine Friendly URLs.** These are often called *SEF URLs*, and you want to turn this option on after your site is completed and in its final hosting location with the domain name pointing to the site. SEF URLs can occasionally be buggy when turned on while working in a staging site environment. SEF URLs are helpful for marketing. Rather than having to list a long URL with oddball question marks and inscrutable IDs, you can tell people to go to an address that's much more readable, memorable, and easier to type.

   ➤ **Apache** *mod-rewrite.* Your use of this option will depend on your web hosting setup. This setting is important if you're running Apache, but if you're running IIS, this setting should be left alone. To use this setting correctly, you must delete any existing .htaccess file on your web server, and then rename the htaccess.txt file that comes with the default Joomla installation to .htaccess. You can perform that action via FTP or in your site's control panel or file manager. This is an important step to get SEF URLs running if you're using Apache.

   ➤ **Add Suffix to URLs.** SEF URLs in Joomla, by default, look like directories; for example, www.yoursite.com/about/mission. If you prefer to have a suffix on your webpage, such as www.yoursite.com/about/mission.html, enable this option.

The System Tab

Figure 4-4 shows the System tab of the Global Configuration screen. This tab has fewer settings to cover, because the default settings are generally fine for most Joomla sites.

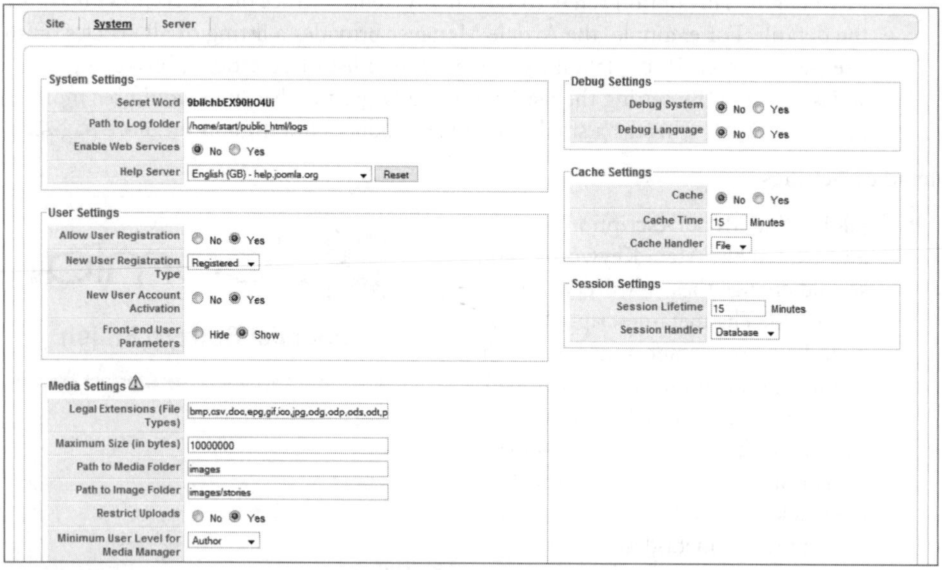

FIGURE 4-4

The System tab contains the following sections:

➤ **System Settings.** There's nothing to change here; leave everything in its default setting.

➤ **User Settings**

  ➤ **Allow User Registration** allows users to register for your web site. By default, this option is turned on. However, sometimes you don't want people registering for the site, even though a login box might be present. For example, you might have a fixed list of registered users and you want to approve all new users individually. If you turn off the Allow User Registration option by setting it to No, the Register link associated with a login box will not display.

  ➤ **New User Registration Type** sets the permissions level of the newly registered user. In general, this should be Registered. Higher levels of permissions (covered later, in the "User Manager" section) allow users — perhaps those registered automatically — to have additional content editing and creation abilities. (See Table 4-1 for a list of those abilities by user type.)

  ➤ **New User Account Activation** emails users a link that they must click before they can log in to the site. This tool helps to keep spam comments and postings to a minimum on your site.

  ➤ **Front End User Parameters** gives users access to certain settings from the front end of the web site, such as the language, their editor of choice, and where the Helplink goes.

➤ **Media Settings.** In this section, shown in Figure 4-5, you shouldn't have to change much. Although you can change the paths to where images are stored for your site, doing so is not recommended. Joomla was built with these image paths in place, and changing those paths might mean that not all extensions function correctly.

  ➤ **Legal Extensions** indicate what types of files may be uploaded to the Media Manager. Note the list includes non-image items. You can add to this list or remove items from it; just be sure to separate each extension with commas.

  ➤ **Maximum Size** is the largest size file you can upload to the Media Manager. However, beware that this setting is not the only place that file size is controlled on your web site! PHP has a file size limitation, by default, of a 2MB upload. Although Joomla's limitation is roughly 10MB by default, if PHP is set to its default of 2MB, then the 2MB limit wins. If you are having trouble uploading a file to the Media Manager, be sure to check your PHP settings, or talk to your web host, to allow larger uploads. To check your PHP settings, in the back end of Joomla, click Help and choose System Info. Under PHP Core Values, look for upload_max_filesize. This value is the maximum file size PHP will allow for upload. Make sure it is equal to or greater than the Joomla value.

  ➤ **Flash Uploader,** as of this writing, is not working correctly in Joomla 1.5 with a web browser running the Adobe Flash 10 plug-in. Therefore, this Flash uploader will not work. There are plans to fix the problem in later Joomla versions.

➤ **Debug Settings.** You should not need to touch the items on this screen.

➤ **Cache Settings.** You should not need to touch the items on this screen.

➤ **Session Settings**

➤ **Session Lifetime.** You might want to change this value to a higher number than 15 minutes. This value indicates how long you are logged in to the site, inactively, before you are logged out again. However, don't go too crazy with the value. If you make this number large, you're creating a security risk. I recommend keeping the session to an hour or less.

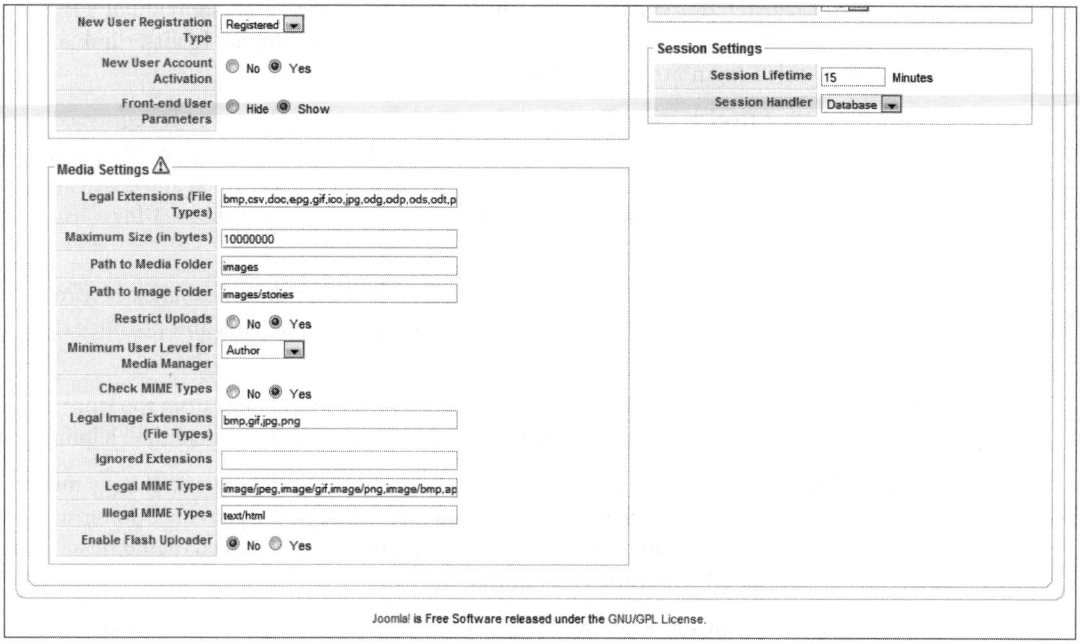

FIGURE 4-5

The Server Tab

After you've installed Joomla and it's working correctly, almost no reason exists for using the Server tab (see Figure 4-6).

Once in a great while, the temporary directory is not set up correctly. For the most part, your site will work just fine, but occasionally an extension will throw an error if it can't access the temporary directory. You change the path to that directory in the Server Settings section, with Path to Temp-folder.

In the Locale Settings section, you might want to change the Time Zone to your time zone. By default, this option is set to GMT.

Other than the aforementioned items, if the site is working well, then there is nothing else you should change on the Server tab. You already entered the FTP information and the database information when you initially set up the site. Mail is configured for you automatically. If the mail is not working, you might need to tweak these settings, but you generally do that task with the assistance of your web host.

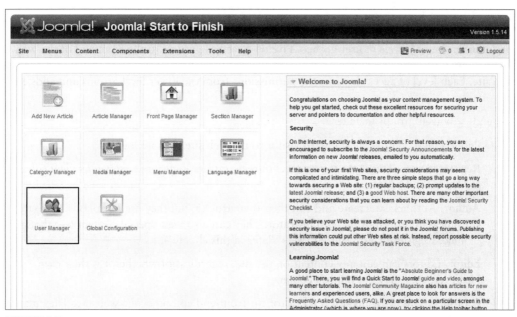

FIGURE 4-6

USER MANAGER

The User Manager is located in the Joomla control panel (see Figure 4-7), and under the Site menu.

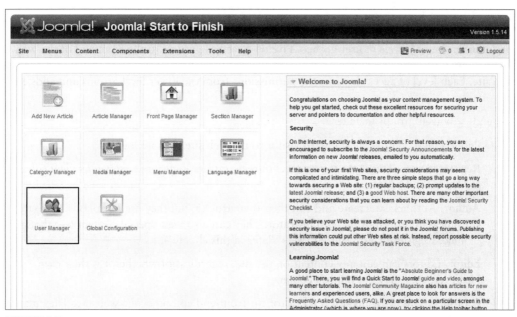

FIGURE 4-7

As the name suggests, the User Manager is where you manage any users associated with the web site. You created your first user when you set up the site. That user was originally called "admin" until you renamed it as part of the installation process.

Figure 4-8 shows the User Manager main screen.

FIGURE 4-8

Note that this site has only one user. That's because I recently installed this copy of Joomla, and I have not created other users. If I did have other users on this site, I could use the column headings — Name, Username, and so on — to sort my user list in any order, simply by clicking on the heading. Also note the drop-down menus in the upper right. These menus enable you to sort users by group level, or show only those users who are logged in.

User Groups

Joomla features eight levels of user groups. Five of these have access to the front end of the web site only (including, in some cases, editing privileges), while three have access to the front and back ends of the site. Each level of access inherits the permissions from the lower level groups and adds extra functionality.

Front end–only user groups include

➤ **Public/Guest.** This is the standard visitor to the web site with no login.

➤ **Registered user.** This is the lowest level of registration. Registered users may view content hidden behind a login.

➤ **Author.** Authors can create and edit their own articles, but they are not published to the site unless approved by an administrator. They can also view special content (see the section "Public, Registered, and Special Users" later in this chapter).

➤ **Editor.** Editors can edit any content on the site, regardless of whether it is their own. However, they may not publish content.

➤ **Publisher.** This is the highest level editor for front-end editing of the web site. They may edit any content on the site and publish new content.

Registered users, authors, editors, and publishers may not log into the back end of the web site.

Back end user groups include

➤ **Manager.** Managers have limited back-end functionality. They cannot change configuration, create menus, create users, or install or edit extensions and templates.

➤ **Administrator.** Administrators cannot create super administrators or administrators (though they can create lower-level users), edit templates, or mass mail users.

➤ **Super Administrator.** The Super Administrator is the highest level user and can do anything on the web site.

Table 4-1 compares the capabilities of the Manager, Administrator, and Super Administrator in the back end of Joomla.

TABLE 4-1: Back-end functionality of Super Administrators, Administrators, and Managers

MENU ITEM	SUPER ADMINISTRATOR	ADMINISTRATOR	MANAGER
Site			
Control Panel	X	X	X
User Manager	X	Can create users at Manager level or lower, edit own login; cannot change Super Admins or other Admins.	
Media Manager	X	X	X
Global Configuration	X		
Logout	X	X	X
Menus			
Menu Manager	X	X	
Menu Trash	X	X	
List of menus used on the site	X	X	X

continues

TABLE 4-3 *(continued)*

MENU ITEM	SUPER ADMINISTRATOR	ADMINISTRATOR	MANAGER
Content			
Article Manager	X	X	X
Article Trash	X	X	
Section Manager	X	X	X
Category Manager	X	X	X
Front Page Manager	X	X	X
Components	X	X	X
Extensions			Not a menu option.
Install/Uninstall	X	X	
Module Manager	X	X	
Plug-in Manager	X	X	
Template Manager	X		
Language Manager	X		
Tools			Not a menu option.
Read Messages	X	Although Read and Write Messages are not menu options, they can be accessed by clicking on the envelope icon in the upper-right corner of the screen.	Although Read and Write Messages are not menu options, they can be accessed by clicking on the envelope icon in the upper-right corner of the screen.
Write Messages	X		
Mass Mail	X		
Global Check-In	X	X	
Purge Expired Cache	X	X	

TABLE 4-3 *(continued)*

MENU ITEM	SUPER ADMINISTRATOR	ADMINISTRATOR	MANAGER
Help			
Joomla! Help	X	X	X
System Info	X	X	X

Creating and Editing Users

To create a new user, simply click on the New button in the upper-right corner of the User Manager. In the User Details section of the resulting User screen (see Figure 4-9), complete the requested information, including Name, Username, E-mail, New Password, and Verify Password, as well as the correct Group for this user. If you do not enter a password for the user, one will be automatically generated and included in a registration email sent to the user.

You would not enable the Block User option when creating a new user; however, if you ever want to prevent someone from logging in but you don't want to delete his or her account, this option is a good way to do it. Using the Block User option is the same thing as changing the green check mark to a red X in the User Manager main screen, in the Enabled column.

The Receive System E-mails option enables a given user to receive Joomla-generated emails, such as notifications of newly registered users.

The following options are available within the Parameters section of the User screen:

➤ **Back-end Language** and **Front-end Language.** You can set the user's back-end and front-end languages, assuming those language packs are installed.

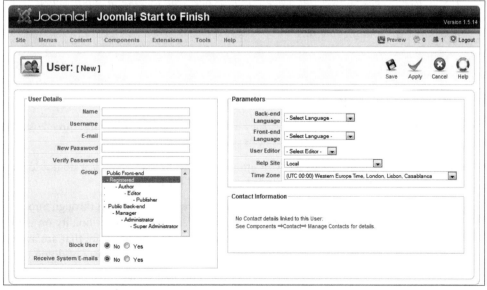

FIGURE 4-9

➤ **User Editor.** This option overrides the editor option specified in Global Configuration. This setting is helpful if you, as the web developer, want to have no WYSIWYG editor showing (so you can paste in HTML directly), while maintaining a different WYSIWYG editor for your client.

➤ **Help Site.** Change this option if you're interested in specifying a different language for Help; otherwise, the local version of Help will be used.

➤ **Time Zone.** This option, which enables you to set another time zone for the user, overrides the setting from the Global Configuration.

For most users you create, you need to specify only a name, username, password, and group. For most users, the standard settings developed in the Global Configuration will take care of the other options. You can use the individual settings here to override the Global Configuration, if you wish. For example, you might prefer to have No Editor rather than TinyMCE, if you like to work with raw HTML instead of a WYSIWYG editor. (However, your client is likely to prefer the WYSIWYG editor.)

When you're done with these User settings, click Save. Your users will receive a system-generated email to the address you specified, specifying their username and password.

Deleting Users

From the main User Manager screen, you can delete users by selecting the check box next to the user and clicking the Delete button.

You cannot delete Super Administrators from the User Manager. You must first demote them to a lower level, and then you can delete them. To demote a Super Administrator, click on the name, then change the group to a lower level than Super Administrator. (Anything at Administrator or lower will work.)

 If you want to keep a user but prevent him or her from logging in, simply click the green check mark next to the user. This turns it to a red X, and the user is now blocked from logging in.

Public, Registered, and Special Users

Although Joomla includes eight user groups, they are lumped into the following three larger groups for the purposes of managing content on the web site:

➤ **Public** includes any visitors to the web site who are not registered and/or do not log in to the site. By default, most items in Joomla are configured for public users.

➤ **Registered** includes all levels of registration, from Registered user up through Super Administrator. This level is useful for hiding some features and functionality on your public web site. For example, you might want to have some links on your site that are available only to users who are logged in. The Registered level offers a good way of doing this.

➤ **Special** excludes registered users, but includes authors and above.

MEDIA MANAGER

The Media Manager is accessible through Joomla's control panel or via the Site menu. The Media Manager is where all images are stored for your site, except for any images you might choose to associate with your template. The Media Manager is also the place you store other files you might use on your site, such as PDFs, word-processing documents, spreadsheets, presentations, and more. (Remember you can specify which file extensions should be included in the Media Manager in the Global Configuration.)

The Media Manager is comprised of two tabs: Thumbnail View and Detail View. Figure 4-10 shows Thumbnail View. Detail View generates a list of filenames with information about the image dimensions and file size, as well as the full filename.

The left side of the screen lists all the folders located inside of the Media Manager. The Media Manager's root folder is defined in the Global Configuration, by default, as the images folder, which is what this figure shows. Folders located within the images folder include M_images, banners, smilies, and stories.

Many longtime static HTML designers might find these folder names obscure, wonder why a folder called stories exists, and wonder why they would want to use this folder structure. I suggest that you work with the folder structure you have, not the folder structure you wish you had! Many extensions are coded with the assumption that these folders and files are in place in your Joomla installation. By changing anything, you potentially cause a lot of headaches later, trying to figure out why things aren't working.

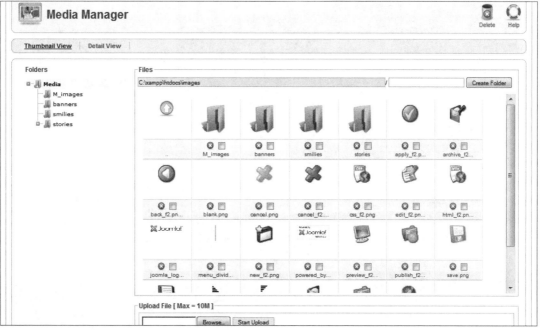

FIGURE 4-10

In any case, you should plan on putting any images associated with the content of your web site inside of the stories folder. You are welcome to make folders inside of the stories folder, or you might just upload your images there. Again, it seems awkward and redundant, but after you start working with this folder structure, you will grow accustomed to it.

The banners folder is designed for the banners component. Banner images associated with that component go in this folder.

The smilies folder, of course, is where you find smilies associated with the TinyMCE editor. You can add to these smilies if you want. If you want to turn off smilies, an option is available to do that from within the plug-in itself.

In the root images folder, as well as the M_images folder, are images associated with the functioning of Joomla itself. Some of these icons might already be familiar to you, such as the ones that appear as the Save and Cancel buttons.

Why Are There Cherries in My Web Site?

If you look inside of the stories folder, you'll see a number of images already in place, including an image of cherries, which is inside the fruit folder. All these images, including the food and fruit folders, are sample images that come with Joomla. You are more than welcome to delete all these images and folders from the stories folder. You will not affect the functioning of Joomla if you do this.

If you want a better look at any of these images, simply click on the image thumbnail. It appears full size in a shadow box, as shown in Figure 4-11.

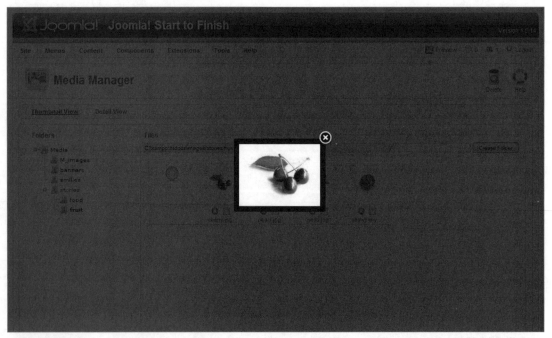

FIGURE 4-11

To delete an image, simply click the red X underneath the image thumbnail. If you want to delete more than one image, select the box under each image, then click the Delete button in the upper-right corner of the screen.

Creating New Folders

At the top of the main Media Manager screen, as shown in Figure 4-12, you can see a path to the current location. At the end of that location is a blank field, followed by a Create Folder button. You simply fill a name in that blank field and click the button to create a new folder.

Uploading Images and Files

At the bottom of the Media Manager screen, as shown in Figure 4-13, is a box to upload an image or another kind of document. Unfortunately, you can upload only one image or document at a time. Prior to the release of Flash 10, a Flash-based file manager would allow multiple documents and images for upload. However, due to a conflict between Flash and parts of Joomla, this upload manager is no longer working. (We disabled the Flash uploader in the Global Configuration earlier in this chapter.)

FIGURE 4-12

To upload a file, simply click the Browse button to find the file on your hard drive. Then click the Start Upload button to start uploading the file to the web site. The file will upload to the folder displayed in the Media Manager. So, for example, if you go into the fruit folder and start a file upload from there, it would upload to the fruit folder.

FIGURE 4-13

Note that right above the upload box, it tells you the maximum file size for uploading, which is 10MB by default. Remember my earlier warning — this is what Joomla thinks it can upload, as defined in the Global Configuration. However, PHP has its own file upload limit, which you might need to reset.

Unfortunately, no easy way exists for moving items from one folder to another within the Media Manager, such as a drag-and-drop capability. If you need to move files, you must download them to your hard drive, then re-upload them to the correct location.

Alternatively, you can create folders and do any image uploads via FTP or through your file manager in your web host's control panel. This method might be the easiest way to rearrange files or upload many files at once. Provided you upload these files to the stories folder or folders within the stories folder, Joomla will recognize the files.

SITE MANAGEMENT TOOLS

As a super administrator, you'll have some extra tasks for maintaining your site. These Joomla tools will help you do your job more easily.

Reading and Writing Messages

If you are logged in as a Super Administrator, you will see Read Messages and Write Messages as menu items under the Tools menu. They are not present for Administrators or lower, but you can still access Read and Write Messages by clicking on the envelope icon in the upper-right corner, as shown in Figure 4-14. If you choose Read Messages, you will get a screen called Private Messaging. If you choose Write Messages, you will get a screen called Write Private Message.

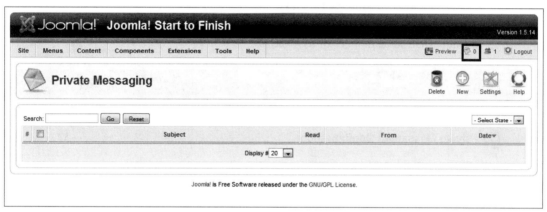

FIGURE 4-14

Choosing Tools ⇨ Read Messages opens the Private Messaging screen, shown in Figure 4-14, whereas the Write Messages option is the equivalent of clicking on the New button from that same screen.

As the Super Administrator of your site, you receive messages when authors or editors submit articles. You must approve the articles before publishing them, and you'll get a message alerting you to the fact that an article requires your review.

You can also send and receive messages to other users on the Joomla site. Simply click the New button (or choose Tools ⇨ Write Messages, select a user from the To drop-down menu, type a subject, type your message, and click Send, as shown in Figure 4-15.

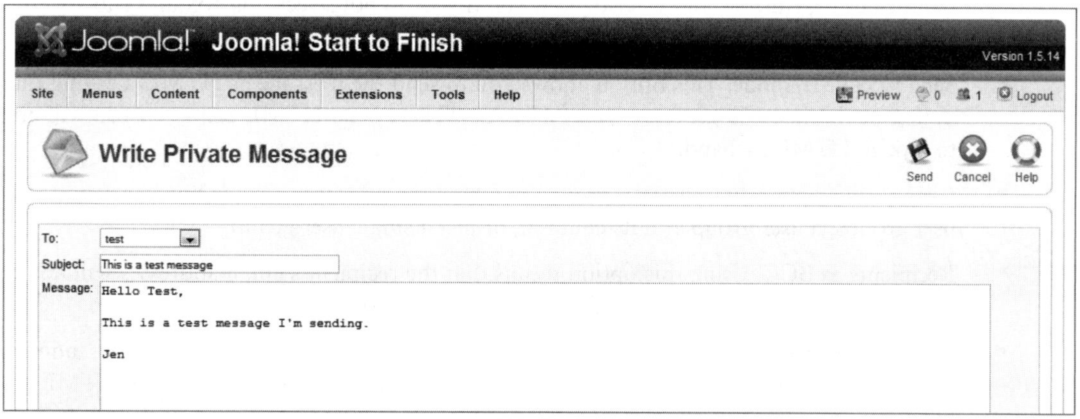

FIGURE 4-15

You might want to change the settings for the messages feature. Click the Settings button in the upper right of the Private Messaging (Read Messages) screen. Figure 4-16 shows the resulting Private Messaging Configuration screen.

> ➤ **Lock inbox.** Use this option to refuse all messages coming to you.

> ➤ **Mail Me on New Message.** This option generates an email alerting you that you have received a message on the web site. However, it does not send you the contents of the message — you must go to the site to read the message.

> ➤ **Auto Purge Messages.** Use this option to automatically delete any messages in your box that are more than some number of days old.

FIGURE 4-16

Mass Mail

Mass Mail is a way to send an email to all registered site users or to site users of specific user groups (see Figure 4-17). Mass Mail is located under Tools ➪ Mass Mail.

> ➤ **Mail to Child Groups.** Selecting this option means that if you choose Editor, the email will be sent to Editor, Author, and Registered users. If you do not select this box and choose Editor, the message is sent to Editors only.

> ➤ **Send in HTML mode.** This option allows you to send the message as HTML. Leaving this option unchecked will generate a text message. (There is no HTML editor, so you will have to type in HTML by hand.)

> ➤ **Group.** This option lists the user groups to whom the message will go. You can send to all user groups, a user group and its children, or just a single user group.

> ➤ **Recipients as BCC.** Using this option means that the recipient's email addresses will not be listed on the email. It's recommended you keep this option selected.

> ➤ **Subject** and **Message.** These boxes are fairly self-explanatory. Note that if you're sending an HTML email, then HTML should go in the message box. If you're not sending HTML email, just type normally, and this message will go out as text-based.

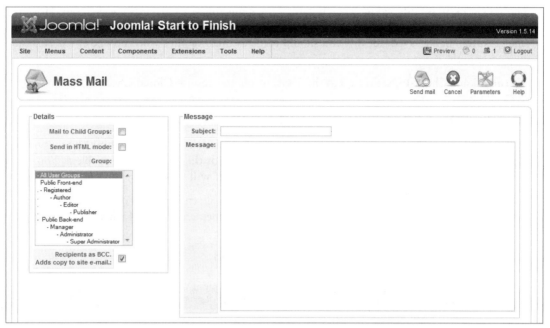

FIGURE 4-17

Note that Mass Mail is great for sending out administrative-type emails to a small list of users. Many web hosts have a limit for how many emails you can send per hour, as a spam reduction feature. If you are using this feature as an email blast to thousands of users, there's no guarantee that the message will even be delivered to most of those users. Furthermore, you may be flagged as a spammer on your server. Therefore, I recommend you use the Mass Mail feature judiciously and infrequently. If you want to send mass emails to all your users, and you want some guarantee that those messages will be delivered, then I strongly recommend an email service (such as MailChimp, www.mailchimp.com; Constant Contact, www.constantcontact.com; and iContact, www.icontact.com).

Global Check-In

Joomla is a powerful content management system for many reasons. One of them is because multiple people can work on the site at the same time. However, what happens if two people want to edit the same article at the same time? Whose changes win?

Joomla has a mechanism in place so that only one person can edit any given article at a time. When you edit an article, you check it out of the system. When you save it or cancel out of it, you check it back in.

For this reason, you should never click the Back button while editing in Joomla. By clicking the Back button, you may not check the item you're working with back into the file system. The item then stays checked out for the balance of that user's session. Once that person logs out (or is logged out), that checked out item becomes available again to other users. But when that user logs in again, that item which was checked out before is checked out again. This makes it hard for other users to edit that specific item.

Global Check-In is designed to check in any of the items that are currently checked out. However, if someone is currently working on the site and you run Global Check-In, you might prevent his or her changes from being saved. Ideally, you should run this functionality when no one else is currently logged onto the site.

To run Global Check-In, simply go to the Tools menu and choose Global Check-in.

Clean Cache and Purge Expired Cache

If you notice that when you make changes to a template, article, or module, those changes never show up on the site, Clean Cache is a good place to look for the source of the problem. You can find Clean Cache under the Tools menu. Selecting Clean Cache will take you to the Cache Manager.

Joomla occasionally caches items, that is, saves a copy of a given item, and doesn't update that copy with the new information for some time. Caching can happen regardless of whether you have enabled caching in the Global Configuration.

The screen for the Cache Manager is shown in Figure 4-18.

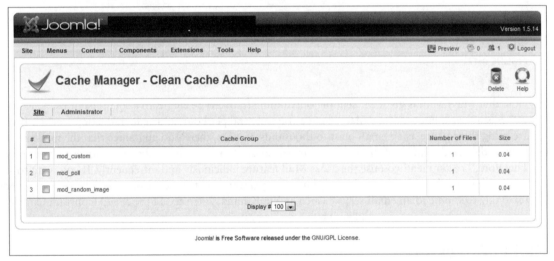

FIGURE 4-18

There are two tabs at the top of this window, one for Site and one for Administrator. The Site tab will show cached items for the front end of the site, whereas Administrator shows cached items for the back end of the site. You will almost never need to go to the Administrator tab. All the instructions below pertain to the Site tab.

To clear the cache, select the check boxes of the items you want to delete, then click the Delete button.

Finally, under Tools ⇨ Purge Expired Cache, you can delete any cached items that are hanging around past their expiration date. This option leaves any currently cached items alone, but it deletes the expired ones. This process can take some time if you have a lot of items cached on your site, so you might want to run this tool at a time when your site has less traffic.

5

In the Beginning There Was Content

Joomla, as I've pointed out before, is a content management system (CMS). Pay special attention to the big C in CMS — it's all about your content!

Content should always be the main focus of your web site. If your site is drop-dead gorgeous, perfectly functional, and coded like a dream, but it says nothing, it's completely useless. On the other hand, sites that have white backgrounds, Times New Roman black text, blue unvisited links and purple visited links, and straight HTML can still deliver great messages, despite being ugly as can be.

This chapter covers the heart of Joomla: visualizing, organizing, creating, and displaying your content.

CREATING A SITE MAP

After you have your strategic planning in place, you should put together a site map. A site map describes all the content on your web site, and it contains the navigation links that will form the menus on your site.

You might know the phrase "site map" as a link on a web site, which shows all site navigation on a single page. What we are planning is, in effect, this page of the web site.

Site maps can be created in many different formats. Sometimes you'll see a site map drawn in a program like Adobe Illustrator, Microsoft Visio, or in Inspiration. It can also be as simple as a bulleted list in Word.

Your client will have a lot of input into the site map. Even if you come up with a draft yourself, your client is likely to have things to add or remove from it. Therefore, if at all possible, I suggest you involve your client from the beginning when developing the site map.

A great way to involve clients is the "sticky note" exercise. You'll need a big table, a large piece of paper (a piece of brown wrapping paper works great), a bunch of sticky notes (size, color, and shape do not matter), and some pens. You'll also want to include representatives of the site's stakeholders.

Cover the table with a piece of paper, or hang the paper on a wall. The idea is to have a surface you can use to make notes and cover with sticky notes. You can roll it up and take it home with you, without losing any of the organization.

Take roughly 10 minutes and write down every idea that comes to mind about content that should be on the web site, one per sticky note. Encourage your client to focus on the content for the web site based on the target audience(s), goals for the site, and the message that needs to be sent. The client should not make notes about the photography for the site, the colors, the mood, and so on. This is a time to focus on the content only.

You might have some very broad ideas that merit an entire section of the site ("All of Our Products") as well as some very small ideas that don't even merit a page ("Copyright Statement"). Some of the items might be functionalities ("Search Box," "Calendar," and "Blog"). Throw all the sticky notes into a big, disorganized pile.

After 10–30 minutes, people usually start running out of ideas. At that point, have them start reading the sticky notes and grouping them into like-minded ideas. Some of those groups are easy. It's likely you'll have a few sticky notes that say "About Us." But you may also have a "Mission," a "Vision," a "Board of Directors," and "Staff Bios." These items might all be grouped together under the heading "About Us."

Some people might put one item under one heading, whereas others might put the same item under another heading. In such cases, discussing where the item should be located is worth it. If including the item in both locations makes sense, you can place the item in one location, with a link to that item from the other location.

 You do not want to create two copies of the same item. Make a note of which item is the link. When you're maintaining the site later and a change to a page is required, you should make it in one location only. This keeps you from having to remember to update the same information in more than one spot. Use the power of linking in Joomla to make maintenance easier on you, and to send a more consistent, user-friendly message to your site visitors!

As you're organizing the notes, you might find some notes that you want to discard on second thought, or you might find that some items are missing. Feel free to continue to add items (functionalities, ideas, new pages, new sections, etc.) or to throw them away as you organize.

As piles of notes accumulate, make sure you give each pile a title. This title will become the navigation name for that group of items.

Finally, you'll have a good-looking site map that you can take home with you. Roll it up and put a rubber band around it. When you get back to the office, type all the notes into your computer. A simple bulleted list works fine, with each layer of nested bullets indicating another level of navigation. For example:

- **Main Navigation**
  - Home
  - Web Sites
    - Technical Capabilities
    - Training
  - Portfolio
    - Site 1
    - Site 2
    - Site 3
    - Site 4
  - About
    - About Our Team
    - Our Partners
    - Contributions to the Community
    - Awards and Honors
  - Contact
  - Joomla4Web Blog
- **Footer Navigation**
  - Site Map
  - Privacy
  - Terms
  - Login

Note that you don't have to cram all the navigation items onto a single navigation bar. Having a "utility" navigation bar, which includes items like Home, About, Contact, Site Map, and Search, is common. Having a separate footer navigation bar, which might feature Site Map, Privacy Statement, Copyright, and any Legal Disclaimer, is also common. Plan out these navigation bars, then turn them over to your graphic designer. He or she can plan a design that accommodates your navigation bars and names.

When planning navigation bars, think about their general placement on the page and how the bars might expand or contract over time. The following are some common configurations:

➤ **Horizontal main navigation, left vertical sub-navigation.** If you have enough room to include your navigation in a horizontal layout across the top, you can list any secondary, tertiary, or deeper navigation on the left side. If you wind up adding lots of new primary navigation, however, you might run out of room for options.

➤ **All navigation on the left side.** If you have many navigation items, or a growing list of items, you could list them all in a vertical column. This option is good if you have lots of sub-navigation or particularly long navigation button names.

➤ **Horizontal main navigation with drop-down lists for sub-navigation.** This option has become quite popular in recent years. Keep in mind, though, that there's no way of knowing a drop-down list exists before one mouses over it. This can be surprising or confusing for some users. Occasionally, menus cover information of interest on the page, or they don't perform correctly if Flash-based elements are on the page (frequently the menus go behind a Flash movie). Issues can also occur with accessibility and search engines, depending on how these drop-down lists are coded. Use this option with caution.

➤ **Stay away from navigation on the right.** Highlighting certain pages or features in the right column is fine, but you should not put any critical navigation in that position. Users typically look on the left or the top for that main navigation, so they might miss navigation on the right. More importantly, however, display widths vary on monitors. If a user's monitor is small, the right column might be cut off, forcing side-scrolling to access the navigation, or the user might miss the navigation altogether. Having a right column in your design is fine, but be sure to group more critical page elements towards the top and left of the web page, where they're most likely to be seen by all visitors, regardless of computer configuration.

Keep in mind as well that you might continue to lump together and split navigation bars and navigation items as the site comes together. These changes are perfectly okay. The web site should be a dynamic document that changes as the site message needs to change.

DETERMINING WHERE THE CONTENT IS COMING FROM

Now that you've laid out your site map, it's time to figure out where all that great content is coming from.

Sometimes clients seem to expect that content will simply fall from the sky. Or perhaps they expect you to write it. Expectations should be made crystal clear about the source of every piece of content on the web site. Some content might come from an existing site, a brochure, or other existing materials. Others might be newly written. Some might be written by a professional content writer, whereas your client might write other pieces.

Don't forget about any images or diagrams, which also count as content. You must know which images go on which pages of the site, and whether your client has a specific preference as to where on the page the images should appear.

Here are some strategies to pull this all together to make the process go smoothly.

Tracking Content and Images

If you are not familiar with Google Documents (docs.google.com), you should become familiar with it. Google Docs is a great place for developing a shared spreadsheet. You can put this spreadsheet together, then share it with all members of your team. Anyone in your team may edit that spreadsheet, so both you and your client can continuously update it, without worrying about where the most recent version of the spreadsheet is located.

Start the spreadsheet at the same time you start your site map. Each item in the site map gets its own row.

In the columns, you can track items such as the source of the content (your client, the copy writer, you, brochure, old site URL, and so on), and what images are associated with that content. You should also track a due date for that content, or note that the content has been delivered. If the content is in process, make a note like, "Under review by Judy," "Waiting for photo shoot on 4/15," or some other similar note.

You can download and use the spreadsheet available on the book's web site at www.wrox.com.

Getting Content from Your Client

Getting content from your clients is sometimes the hardest task to do. They always have other things going on, and sometimes your web site is not their highest priority.

Because you've mapped out a list of milestones, the client should understand that if you don't receive all content by a certain date, you have every right in the world to move out the delivery date for the web site. Make this point clear to your client up-front, particularly if an important event is tied to the web site's timely launch (such as a tradeshow, advertising campaign, product rollout, and so on).

Sometimes clients will still deliver content late. One of the best pieces of advice I ever got was to figure out when you really need the content, and then set the deadline a week earlier than that. This is Scotty's first rule of engineering in *Star Trek:* Make sure the captain knows what he wants is impossible with the time you have, but pull it off anyway by overestimating the amount of time your piece will take to complete. You come out looking like a hero in the end, and you won't kill yourself trying to get it done.

Be understanding towards your client during this process. The hardest web site I ever worked on was my own. I'm too close to my own business to feel like I have a good, independent view of how it should be organized. I have a hard time writing good content for my site as well. Fortunately, I have a great friend who writes fabulous content, and she can give me the independent view I need to get work done.

If your client seems to be having a hard time writing his own content, suggest that he consider getting a content writer. Being critical of a piece of an existing piece of writing is often much easier than being creative and coming up with it from scratch.

UNDERSTANDING THE SCAM — SECTIONS, CATEGORIES, ARTICLES, AND MENUS

Now that you have your site map pulled together, and you know where all the content is coming from, the time has come to start putting some of that content into Joomla. You can put the content into Joomla even if you haven't determined the final look of the web site.

In Joomla 1.5, content is organized with sections, categories, articles, and menus (SCAM). This section goes through each of these items in detail.

Sections, categories, articles, and menus must be created in a specific order.

1. **Sections** are always created first.

2. **Categories** are created second, because a category cannot exist without being assigned to a section.

3. **Articles** are created next, because each article must be assigned a section and category.

4. **Menu items** are created last, because they can't exist without articles, categories, and sections. We'll cover menu creation and management in Chapter 6.

Creating and Editing Sections

A section is the top-level label for your content. You create sections via the Section Manager, located under the Content menu (see Figure 5-1).

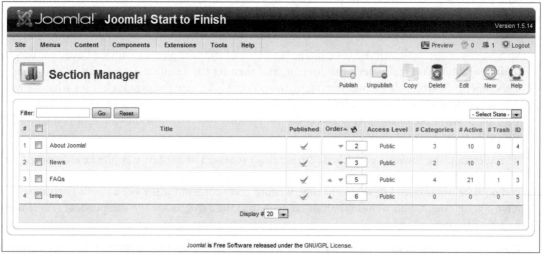

FIGURE 5-1

Click the New button; you'll see the Section: [New] screen appears, as shown in Figure 5-2.

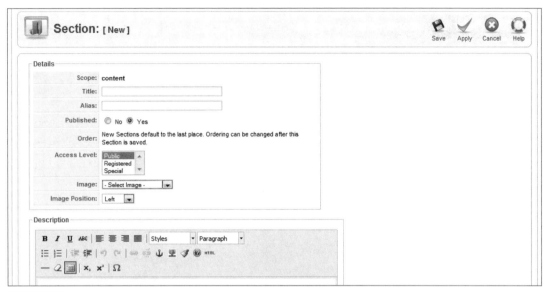

FIGURE 5-2

The only piece of information you must complete is the title of the section. Filling out the remaining options (described here) is optional:

➤ **Title.** This is the name of the section. It may include spaces, but you should probably avoid special characters or punctuation.

➤ **Alias.** This field is used, in some situations, for constructing a page URL. In other cases, it's not used at all. If you leave this field blank, an alias will be created for you.

➤ **Published.** Indicates whether the section is available to be used on the site and assigned to articles or not.

➤ **Access Level.** As described in Chapter 4, you may assign a permission level to your section.

➤ **Image** and **Image Position.** You may assign an image to the section if you want. Position, of course, sets whether that image will show up on the left, right, or center of the description. Depending on what options you use to display content, the image might or might not show on the web site.

➤ **Description.** You can write a description for the section. Depending on what options you use to display content, this description might or might not show on the web site.

Chapter 6 covers where the alias, image, and description appear.

Creating and Editing Categories

A category is assigned to a single section. Each section can have as many categories as you like, but each category can have only one section.

You create categories via the Category Manager, located under the Content menu (see Figure 5-3).

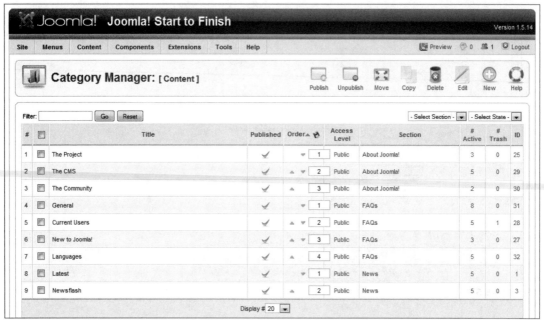

FIGURE 5-3

Click the New button and the Category: [New] screen appears, as shown in Figure 5-4.

FIGURE 5-4

You must supply the title of the category and the section with which it's associated. All other fields are optional:

➤ **Title.** This is the name of the category. It may include spaces, but you should probably avoid special characters or punctuation.

➤ **Alias.** This field is used, in some situations, for constructing a page URL. In other cases, it's not used at all. If you leave this field blank, an alias will be created for you.

➤ **Published.** Indicates whether the category is available to be used on the site and assigned to articles or not.

➤ **Section.** Choose section with which this category is associated. You should not create categories until the section with which it will be associated exists.

➤ **Access level.** As described in Chapter 4, you may assign a permission level to your section.

➤ **Image** and **Image Position.** You may assign an image to the category if you want. Position, of course, sets whether that image will show up on the left, right, or center of the description. Depending on what options you use to display content, the image might or might not show on the web site.

➤ **Description.** You can write a description for the category. Depending on what options you use to display content, this description might or might not show on the web site.

Chapter 6 covers where the alias, image, and description appear.

How Are Sections and Categories Related to Each Other and Your Content?

Joomla 1.5 offers a top-down approach to its content, requiring each article to be assigned one section and one category. As mentioned earlier, each section can have many categories, but each category can be associated with only one section.

How to associate content planned for a web site with the right sections and categories is a question that comes up constantly with those new to Joomla.

Section and Category Considerations

In Joomla 1.5, each article on your web site must be assigned a section and a category. However, you don't have to create any categories or sections for your web site. By default, Joomla offers a section called "uncategorized" and a category called "uncategorized." You could use "uncategorized" with each article on your site. This option works well if you have a small site, say 20 pages or less. The big advantage is you don't have to explain to your client which section and category to assign to each piece of content — there's only one — uncategorized.

However, as sites get larger, sections and categories are more useful. They can help you locate articles quickly and easily in the Article Manager. They also drive some pieces of functionality, such as a section blog, in which all articles of a certain section are displayed.

You can also use a mix of categorized and uncategorized articles on your site.

There are no right or wrong answers as to the "correct" sections and categories for a particular web site. You can create them as you want. They don't have to be tied to your site map, and as mentioned before, you don't have to create any beyond "uncategorized" if you don't want to.

However you decide to create sections and categories, you will eventually need to explain them to your client or someone else helping with the web site. Make sure that the organization and naming conventions of your created sections and categories is as intuitive as possible. You might also want to document how sections and categories should be chosen so that others can understand your thought process.

Site Map Considerations

You can easily apply sections and categories to your site map as a starting point. A section might be associated with each top-level navigation item: About Us, Products, Services. A category might be associated with subnavigation for the site map.

This way of assigning sections and categories to your content is the most intuitive. If you're looking for a specific article, and you know where it falls in your site navigation, you know exactly where to look for it and what category or section to assign it.

However, this assignment process contains some unintuitive pieces as well. Suppose you have a primary navigation item with only a handful of secondary navigation options. Do you create a category for each individual navigation item? Do you create a single category for all three secondary navigation items? And if so, what do you call it?

Again, there are not right or wrong answers to these questions. What I typically do is create a single category for the given section, often with the same name. That might mean that the Services section also has a Services category associated with it. The top-level page under Services might also be called Services, resulting in a section, a category, and an article, all with the same name.

You might think the obvious answer to the earlier situation is to use the "uncategorized" category for these items. In this case, the section is Services and the category is Uncategorized. Remember, though, each category can only be assigned to a single section. That means that the existing Uncategorized category already is assigned to the Uncategorized section.

Finally, think about your client's experience with maintaining the web site. What would your client find most intuitive to them? Should they have to create new categories when they want to create new articles? In my experience, clients have a difficult time deciding which category to assign to articles when many options exist. What I have decided to do, for most sites, is assign the same name to the section and category, regardless of the secondary navigation structure of the site. Only if I'm using a section or category to make a piece of functionality work (such as a blog, covered later in this chapter) do I deviate from this plan.

Functionalities Using Sections and Categories

A number of pieces of functionality in Joomla and its extensions rely on sections and categories to work correctly. For example, the blogging functionality in Joomla requires an appropriate section and/or category to be assigned for an article to appear in a blog. The newsflash module displays a specified number of articles from a given category.

If you're using a piece of functionality like the aforementioned ones, be sure to plan for such a section and/or category in your site structure. For example, suppose that in the News section of the site, you want selected items to display on the home page. You're going to pick which articles will display. In this case, you might create a category called Home Page associated with the News section. When you create your news article, you would then assign it a section of News and a category of Home Page, and it would show up on the home page automatically.

I discuss functionalities like blogs and modules like newsflash later in the book (Chapters 6 and 8, respectively), but for now, keep in mind that you might need to adjust your plan for sections and categories depending on what functionalities you pick for your web site.

What Are Articles?

Articles are the heart of your Joomla web site. They're the individual pieces of content, which are assigned a section and a category. Articles may contain a few words or pages of information, images, modules, plug-ins, and more.

You create and manage articles in the Article Manager, shown in Figure 5-5.

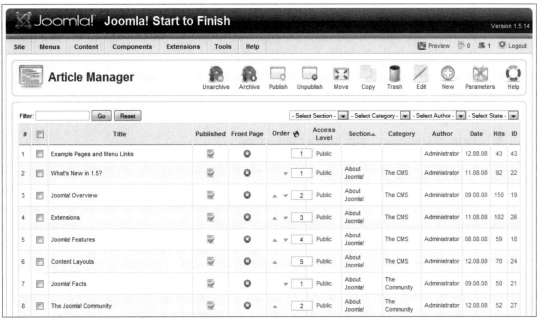

FIGURE 5-5

The Article Manager offers many options. Take a look at the buttons in the upper right. In all cases with these buttons, you first select the article(s) to which you want to apply these actions by clicking the check box by the article name, then you click the appropriate button. Here are the button descriptions:

➤ **Archive/Unarchive** are for archiving your old articles. This means they will not show up in standard article listings (like a blog), but will show up in archived listings. Archiving is useful if you have a very large, content-heavy site and you want to pull older articles from the main article listing, but still leave them accessible for users to your web site. If you want to keep an article in Joomla but not have it show on the web site, you can always unpublish the article.

➤ **Publish/Unpublish** are options you have seen throughout Joomla already. A published article is available to show on the web site, whereas an unpublished article is not. Published articles have a green check mark in the Published column, whereas unpublished articles have a red X. You can click this icon to toggle the published/unpublished state.

➤ **Move** moves an article from one section/category to another section/category. For one article, you can simply edit the article to change its section and category. However, if you have several articles that must have their section and category changed, you can select multiple articles (by selecting the boxes next to each article) and change their section/category all at once using the Move tool.

➤ **Copy** makes a copy of an existing article. Joomla asks you which section/category you want to assign the copied article.

➤ **Trash** sends an article to the Article Trash. Article Trash is only accessible to a Super Administrator. Functionally, the trash works the same as the trash on your hard drive. It holds articles until they are permanently deleted.

➤ **Edit** puts you into a screen for making edits to an article. You find out more about this screen in detail later in the "Editing an Article" section.

➤ **New** creates a new article (see the "Creating a New Article" section).

➤ **Parameters** indicate global article parameters. You find out more about these in the "Setting the Global Article Parameters" section.

➤ **Help,** of course, provides help for this screen.

Creating a New Article

To create a new article, click the New button. The new article screen is shown in Figure 5-6.

Items required to create a new article include:

➤ **Title.** This is the article title. It shows on the web page by default.

➤ **Section.** Select a section from the drop-down list. This list includes all sections, both published and unpublished.

➤ **Category.** After you have selected a section, the categories will populate this list.

➤ **The "big box."** This is where you enter the article itself. Note the buttons across the top that allow formatting of text, link creation, and more. I'll go through what you can do with the big box later in the chapter.

Underneath the big box are three to four buttons of information, depending on what version of Joomla you're running. If you're running a version of Joomla around 1.5.11 or prior (not recommended — upgrade!), you will see three buttons. Later versions of Joomla display four buttons if you are running the default TinyMCE 3.0 editor, which is the default editor that has been shipping with Joomla since

1.5.12. Installing a different editor for your site is possible, though. See Chapter 10, "Plug-ins That Come with Joomla!" The buttons are as follow:

➤ **Image** inserts an image into your article wherever the cursor is placed when you click the button. You can also upload images from this location, assign alt and title text, and align the image left or right.

➤ **Read more** inserts a line where the cursor is placed when this button is clicked. Anything above the line becomes introductory text, whereas the information underneath appears in a full article.

➤ **Pagebreak** breaks a very long page into smaller sections. An article index will be automatically generated.

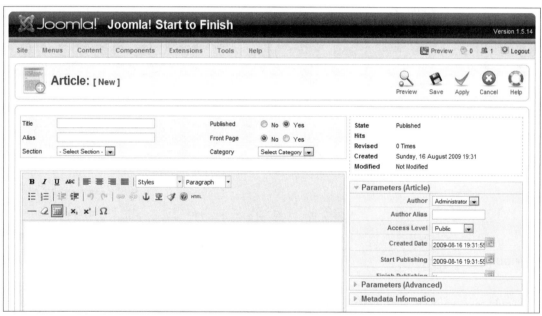

FIGURE 5-6

After you've created your article with this basic information, save it. Whether the article immediately shows up on the web site depends on how that article is linked to the menu. Chapter 6 covers these linking options.

Editing an Article

After you have created and saved your article, you might want to edit it.

You have two ways of editing an existing article. You can either edit it from the back end of the web site, or you can edit it from the front end. Which of these options are available to you will depend on the user permissions you have (see the User Manager discussion in Chapter 4). I assume that you're a Super Administrator, so you can edit any article from either the front end or the back end.

Front-end editing is somewhat more limited, in that many of the advanced article features are not available to you. However, for clients, front-end editing is ideal because it's so simple to do.

Editing from the Back End

To edit an article from the back end, first go to the Article Manager via Content ➪ Article Manager. Click on the title of the article you want to edit or click on the check box next to the article, and then click the Edit button, as shown in Figure 5-7.

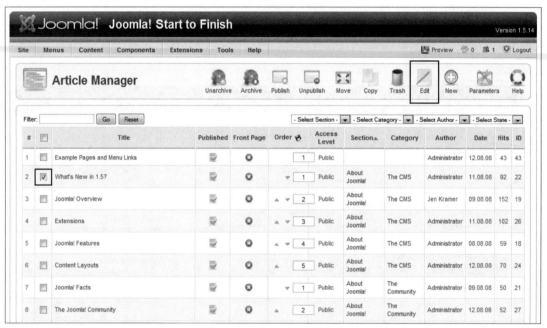

FIGURE 5-7

Apply saves your changes while leaving you in the editing screen. Save saves your changes and returns you to the Article Manager. Close closes the article without incorporating your changes.

Editing from the Front End

To edit from the front end, you must first log in. If you installed the sample data, there should be a login box displayed somewhere on the web site. If you did not install the sample data, you'll need to create and display a login box via the Module Manager (see Chapter 8). Go to the box and enter the same username and password that you use on the back end of the web site, as shown in Figure 5-8.

After you are logged in, you may see little change to the page, but the login box will disappear. Also note the appearance of a small pencil icon next to the titles of articles on the page, as shown in Figure 5-9.

Click on the pencil and an editing window appears for the article, as shown in Figure 5-10.

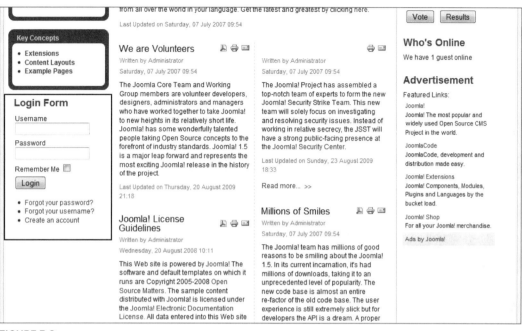

FIGURE 5-8

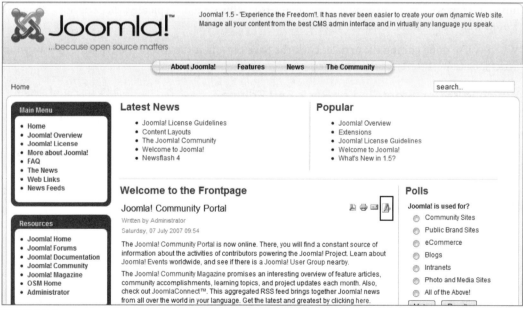

FIGURE 5-9

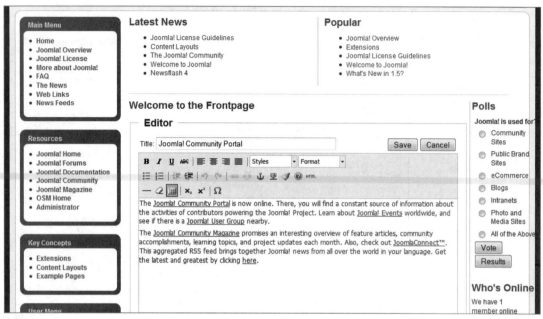

FIGURE 5-10

Note that fewer options are available for changing the article. All the advanced article features are missing. However, you can change some items from this screen. Typically, these options are all you would want your client to access anyway.

When you're done editing the article, click the Save button at the top of the window to save your article, or Cancel to reject any changes.

Which Is Better, Front-End or Back-End Editing?

As with many things web-based, determining which is better — front-end or back-end editing — just depends. Front-end editing tends to be very easy for clients. They log in, surf to the page to change, click the pencil, make the change, and save. However, fewer parameters are available to change from the front end, and the ability to make a new article from the front end is not always available.

Back-end editing makes most sense for web developers. You're likely logged in already, so going to the front end to edit an article is actually extra work.

However, both methods are completely legitimate, and both methods have their place in the site maintenance process.

Setting the Global Article Parameters

Back in the Article Manager, at the top of the page, is a link to the Parameters, as shown in Figure 5-11.

Click this icon for a long list of items to set, as shown in Figure 5-12. These items pertain to every article on the web site.

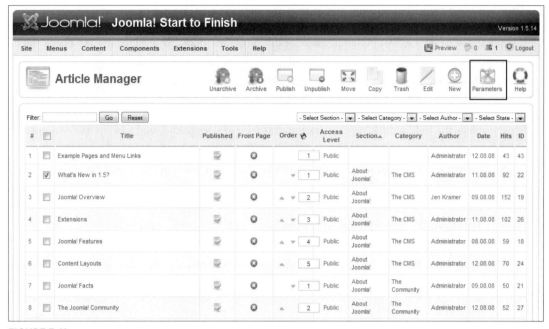

FIGURE 5-11

FIGURE 5-12

Although these are global settings, two places exist where these settings can be overridden: in the menu, and in the individual article. You find out more about that later in the chapter and in Chapter 6. If you happen to set a global preference here and it does not "take," you might need to check the individual article and its link to the menu structure, which might be overriding these settings.

➤ **Show Unauthorized Links** is for sites with some content for registered, logged-in users, and some content for the public. It determines whether links to that registered user content should display even if the visitor is not logged into the site. If the visitor is not logged in and clicks the link, a page appears stating that they are not authorized to view the content.

➤ **Show Article Title** determines whether the title should show for articles in general. With Joomla's default settings, the title does not show in a heading tag. Some developers like to turn off the article title, then include the article title contained in a heading tag in the article main body.

➤ **Title Linkable** determines whether the title will link to a full version of the article. (The choice is between a linked title plus a "read more" link or just a "read more" link.)

➤ **Show Intro Text** determines whether the introductory text should show. If you set this option to Hide, the intro text will show up on a blog page, which contains small introductory blurbs, but it will not show up when the visitor clicks through to the full article. This option is helpful if you want to have a teaser about the article, then show the actual article after clicking through.

➤ **Section Name** determines whether the name of the section the article is assigned displays on the page.

➤ **Section Title Linkable** means that if you click on the section name, you'll link to a section page.

➤ **Category Title** determines whether the name of the category the article is assigned displays on the page.

➤ **Category Title Linkable** means that if you click on the category name, you'll link to a category page.

➤ **Author Name** displays the author's name.

➤ **Created Date and Time** displays the date and time the article was created; that is, when the New button was clicked.

➤ **Modified Date and Time** displays when the article was last changed.

➤ **Show Navigation** shows some Back and Next buttons at the bottom of the article.

➤ **Read more… Link** is the link that displays when both intro and full article text exist, and when you are using something like a blog, where the intro text would display on one page with a "read more" link at the end of it.

➤ **Article Rating/Voting** allows users to vote on the article on a scale of 1 to 5.

➤ **Icons** indicates whether the icons for PDF, Print, and E-mail should display. If set to Hide, text will display instead. To get rid of the PDF, Print, and E-mail options, set each individual icon option to Hide.

➤ **PDF Icon, Print Icon,** and **E-mail Icon** are all individual controls for these three buttons, indicating which should display.

➤ **Hits** shows how many hits the article has gotten.

➤ **For each feed item show** is for showing either just the intro text or the full text in the RSS feed.

Figure 5-13 shows the bottom portion of the Article Parameters screen.

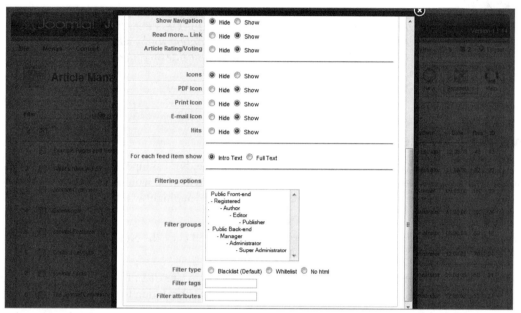

FIGURE 5-13

Filtering Options are quite a bit more complicated. I strongly recommend mousing over each title to read the tool tip help for each of these items. Essentially, filtering is in place to prevent your site visitors (for the most part) from trying to put in harmful HTML and other hacks into an article on a Joomla site.

Three options can help keep this type of attack from happening:

➤ **Blacklist.** Blacklisting means you can use any HTML except for the excluded tags. Those include applet, body, bgsound, base, basefont, embed, frame, frameset, head, html, id, iframe, ilayer, layer, link, meta, name, object, script, style, title, and xml. It also excludes the HTML attributes of action, background, codebase, dynsrc, and lowsrc. If you want to exclude other tags, you can enter these individually in the Filter Tags field, or exclude other attributes by entering them in the Filter Attributes field.

➤ **Whitelist.** You can whitelist tags and attributes, which means that you would list, in the Filter Tags and Filter Attributes fields, all tags and attributes that you would permit to be used on the site.

➤ **No html.** The final option is not to permit any HTML at all.

You assign blacklisting or whitelisting by group, via Filter Group. The chosen group level and lower will have the blacklist/whitelist restrictions in place. Groups above that level will not have these restrictions.

These filtering settings apply no matter which WYSIWYG editor you use, including no editor at all.

 If you are confused about which settings to use, try setting the group to Registered and the filter type to Blacklist. This setting is great if you do not have anyone contributing content to the web site except for known and trusted users. If you have people you do not know contributing content to the site, you may want to experiment with a higher group level, greater filtering (perhaps blacklisting with additional tags, or whitelisting), or both.

Advanced Article Features

Earlier in this chapter, I discussed how to create a new article, but I skipped over a bunch of additional items available to you to customize. I touched on the items you would use for every article you would ever create, but many other options are available that you might want to use every once in a while. Here are those additional settings.

To create a new article, go to Content ➪ Article Manager, and click the New button. Let's look back at the top of the article screen, as shown in Figure 5-14.

➤ **Alias.** This option may be used in the building of a web site URL. If you don't enter an alias, the title will be used to create the alias, with hyphens substituting for spaces.

➤ **Published.** If the article is published, it may appear on the site. If it's unpublished, it will not. (Remember an article may exist and be published, but it might not be linked anywhere on the site, and therefore it's not visible on the site.)

➤ **Front Page.** If you're using the Front Page Blog functionality, set this option to Yes to make this article appear on your home page.

On the right side of the page, next to the Published/Front Page/Category features, is some information that describes your article:

➤ **State** indicates whether the article is currently published. By default, articles are published.

➤ **Hits** indicates how many times the article has been seen on the web site.

➤ **Revised** indicates the number of times the article has been changed. Going to edit the article and clicking the Save button, even though you've not made a change, does count as a revision.

➤ **Created** is the date/time the article was originally created (when you click the "New" button).

➤ **Modified** is the most recent date/time that the article was last edited.

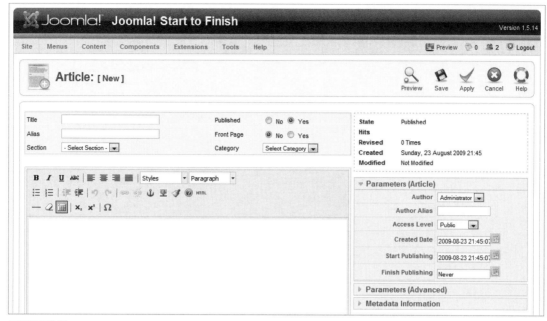

FIGURE 5-14

Underneath this box of information are more options in the accordion panes. First, click on
Parameters (Article):

➤ **Author.** The author of the article. By default, this will be your name from the User Manager.

➤ **Author Alias.** If you are posting an article for someone else, enter the person's name in the
Alias blank. If you are displaying the article's author on the web site, the Alias will show
instead of the Author.

➤ **Access Level.** Choose one of the three options, Public, Registered, or Special.

➤ **Created Date.** By default, this is the date/time you clicked the New button. You can change
this date if you want.

➤ **Start Publishing.** You can set up articles now to publish automatically in the future. Set
the Start Publishing date to sometime in the future, and the article will not immediately
show up on the web site or be available for use.

➤ **Finish Publishing.** If you have time-sensitive information you want to remove from the web
site, you can set the Finish Publishing date/time to automate that process.

Parameters (Advanced)

If you click on the Parameters (Advanced) title, the options shown in Figure 5-15 appear.

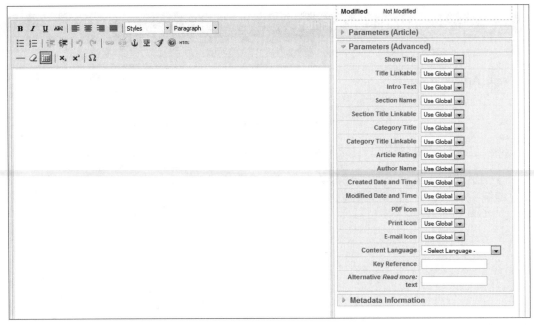

FIGURE 5-15

These parameters specify individual settings for an article, which might override the global article preferences and/or any settings for these parameters in the menu item for the article. Chapter 6 covers parameter hierarchy.

➤ **Show Title** determines whether the title should show for articles in general. With Joomla's default settings, the title does not show in a heading tag. Some developers like to turn off the article title, then include the article title contained in a heading tag in the article main body, which is why they might turn this setting off. (Alternatively, you could do this via Template Override, an advanced topic covered in Chapter 14.)

➤ **Title Linkable** determines whether the title will link to a full version of the article. (The choice is between a linked title plus a "read more" link or just the "read more" link.)

➤ **Intro Text** determines whether the introductory text should show. If you set this option to Hide, the intro text will show up on a blog page, which contains small introductory blurbs, but it will not show up when the visitor clicks through to the full article. This setting is helpful if you want to have a teaser about the article, then show the actual article after the user clicks through.

➤ **Section Name** determines whether the name of the section the article is assigned displays on the page.

➤ **Section Title Linkable** means that if you click on the section name, you'll link to a section page.

➤ **Category Title** determines whether the name of the category the article is assigned displays on the page.

➤ **Category Title Linkable** means that if you click on the category name, you'll link to a category page.

➤ **Article Rating** shows the current rating for this article.

➤ **Author Name** displays the author's name.

➤ **Created Date and Time** displays the date and time the article was created; that is, when the New button was clicked.

➤ **Modified Date and Time** displays when the article was last changed.

➤ **PDF Icon, Print Icon,** and **E-Mail Icon** options determine whether their respective icons are displayed.

➤ **Content Language** is for when you have more than one language pack installed on the site; you can choose which language should be associated with this article.

➤ **Key Reference** is an optional text key that can be used for referencing articles rather than the article ID.

➤ **Alternative *Read more* text** is for when you're using the functionality of having a "read more" break within your article; *Read more...* is what will display by default. You can specify other text in this field instead. This setting can be helpful for accessibility and for search engine optimization, because you can include more keywords that make it clear where the link goes.

Metadata Information

Click on the Metadata Information title and the options shown in Figure 5-16 appear.

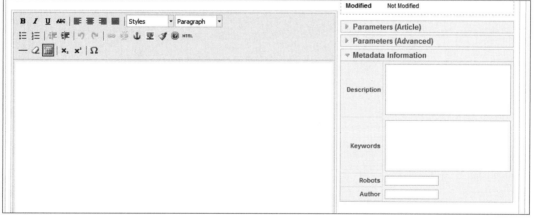

FIGURE 5-16

➤ **Description.** This area contains the meta-description for the article. This option overrides the global meta-description set in the Global Configuration. You do not need to put quotes around the description; Joomla will include quotes when this text displays on the site.

➤ **Keywords.** This area is for the meta-keywords for the article. They override the global meta-keywords set in the Global Configuration. List your keywords separated by commas. You do not need to put quotes around the list; Joomla will include them when this displays on the site.

➤ **Robots.** What you type in here will show in a robots meta-tag. Valid values for this meta-tag include index, follow, noindex, and nofollow, as separated by commas. The default value is "index, follow," so you do not need to put that in if that is what you want to do. Indexing indicates whether the page should be indexed for a search engine. Follow indicates whether the links in the article should be followed.

➤ **Author.** This meta-tag is used to indicate who is in charge of updates and changes to this page. By default, the author of the page is the name of the person who created it, from your user profile (set in the User Manager). This field is used to override that default setting with whatever you enter here.

The last part of the SCAM is Menus, which I'll cover next in Chapter 6.

Creating and Configuring Menus

WHAT'S IN THIS CHAPTER?

➤ Linking articles to the menu

➤ Creating blogs

➤ Creating split menus

➤ Hiding your site behind a login box

Now that you have content for your site, you're ready to create some menus to link it all together.

In the previous chapter you planned the menus as part of your site map, so you know exactly how many menus you need and the configuration in which you want them to appear.

Menus come in two pieces in Joomla. The first part is the list of links themselves, which are created in the Menu Manager and the Menu Item Manager. The second part of the menu is a module, which determines where on the page the menu will appear and which parts of the menu will display. I cover both halves of menu functioning in this chapter.

The chapter begins by describing how to use the Menu Manager to create menus, and then discusses how to use modules to make those menus appear on your web site. The chapter also gets into some fancier configurations for your menus, as well as how to integrate menus and articles to get you the results you want.

USING THE MENU MANAGER

The Menu Manager is a list of all the menus on your web site. You can have a single menu, or you can have dozens of menus. Fortunately, you already know how many menus you need, because you figured that out when you created your site map. A typical web site has from one to four menus. You must have at least one menu, which is why Joomla creates one for you (Main Menu) as part of the installation, even if you don't install the sample data.

Log into the back end of your web site, and in the control panel, find the link to the Menu Manager, as shown in Figure 6-1. Alternatively, go to the Menus navigation item at the top, and choose Menu Manager.

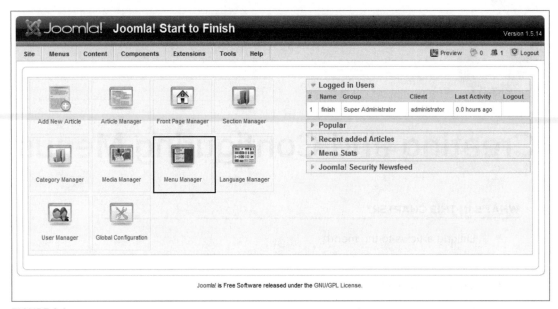

FIGURE 6-1

If you have installed the sample data for your Joomla installation, you'll see a screen like the one shown in Figure 6-2. If you did not install the sample data, you'll see one menu in the list: Main Menu.

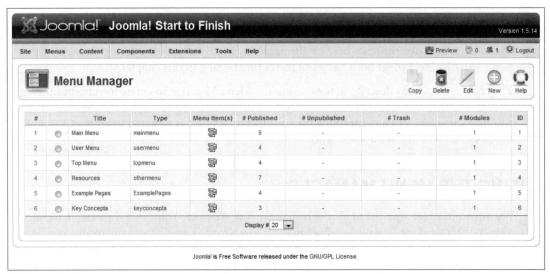

FIGURE 6-2

The Menu Manager provides key information about each menu, including:

➤ **Title.** The name of the menu.

➤ **Type.** Its unique name used in programming.

➤ **Menu Item.** A link to take you to the Menu Item Manager for the given menu, where you can add and edit individual menu items.

➤ **# Published** and **# Unpublished.** The number of items on each menu that are published or unpublished, respectively.

➤ **# Trash.** How many menu items are in the Menu Trash.

➤ **# Modules.** How many modules are associated with each menu

➤ **ID.** The database ID for the menu.

The upper-right corner of the Menu Manager also offers the following familiar buttons. Before clicking them (with the exception of New), be sure to select the radio button that corresponds with the menu you want to affect.

➤ The **Copy** button makes a copy of an existing menu.

➤ The **Delete** button deletes the menu and all menu items in it. Deleted menus and all of their menu items are gone forever when deleted. They do not go to the Menu Trash.

➤ The **Edit** button takes you to the Menu Item Manager for the selected menu. This is the same as clicking the pencil icon for the Menu Item(s) option.

➤ The **New** button creates a new menu.

➤ The **Help** button provides contextual help about this screen.

Take a look at one of these menus. If you look at the Main Menu item in the list, either by clicking on the title or by selecting the radio button and clicking the Edit button, you can change some basic properties about the menu, as shown in Figure 6-3.

FIGURE 6-3

➤ **Unique Name.** For Joomla to function properly, each menu must have its own unique name. Do not include spaces or funny characters (spaces, dollar sign, asterisk, etc) in this name.

➤ **Title.** This is the title of the menu that will show up in the Menu Manager, the module that drives the menu, and in the navigation in the back end of Joomla under Menus.

➤ **Description.** This describes the menu. It's not required if you don't want to have a description.

To create a new menu for your web site, click the New icon in the upper-right corner of the Menu Manager. You will get the screen shown in Figure 6-4.

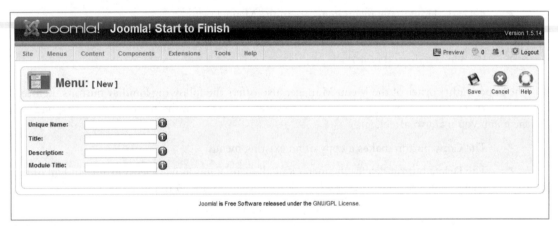

FIGURE 6-4

Fill in the unique name, title, and description, as described above. (Note the icon to the right of the blanks. You can hover over this icon to get helpful tool tips about what's required for each blank and how it is used.)

The last field is for the Module Title. When you create a new menu, a corresponding module is also created. The module is responsible for the display of the menu on your web site.

Click Save when all four fields are complete, and a new empty menu will be created, along with a new, unpublished module.

Now that you understand the basics about menus, it's time to get to the more interesting part: linking up your web site.

LINKING ARTICLES TO THE MENU

Chapter 5 covered Joomla's "SCAM" (Sections, Categories, Articles, and Menus). That's the order in which you create the content for your web site. If you don't have articles, you can't link them to a menu!

Take a look at the Main Menu in depth. To get there, choose Menus ⇨ Main Menu. (You can also click on the pencil icon in the Menu Item(s) column in the Menu Manager to get there.) The Main Menu appears in the Menu Item Manager, as shown in Figure 6-5.

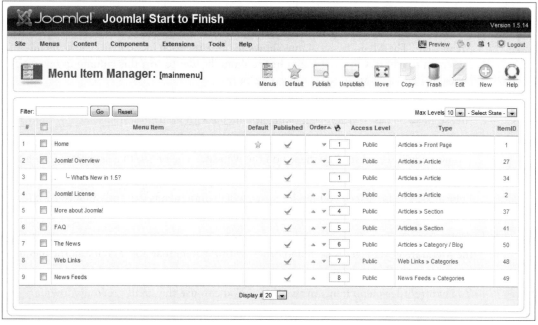

FIGURE 6-5

As with all Joomla screens, the Menu Item Manager is packed with information and possibilities. The following buttons appear in the upper-right corner:

➤ **Menus** takes you back to the Menu Manager.

➤ **Default** sets a single selected (checked) item as the default menu item for the whole site. That's typically the home page, although it does not have to be. The default page is the one that loads when you type www.mysite.com into a web browser. The default menu item cannot be deleted. When you create a new Joomla site without installing the sample data, there is always a home page set up as the default page.

➤ **Publish** and **Unpublish** publish or unpublish selected (checked) menu items, respectively.

➤ **Move** moves selected (checked) menu items from this menu to a different existing menu.

➤ **Copy** makes a copy of selected menu items to this menu or another existing menu.

➤ **Trash** sends selected menu items to the Menu Trash.

➤ **Edit** lets you make changes to a single selected menu item. You can also click on the menu item title to edit it.

➤ **New** makes a new menu item.

➤ **Help** provides contextual help for this screen.

The Menu Item Manager table provides the following list of valuable information about each menu item:

➤ **Menu Item.** The Menu Item column shows the title for each menu item. Click the title of each item to edit it. Click the Menu Item column header to sort this column in reverse alphabetical order. Click again to sort alphabetically.

➤ **Default.** The starred item is the default item for the site. There is only one default item for the site, so in some cases, you'll be looking at a menu with no default items.

Note that if you're looking at the drop-down Menu navigation item in the back end of Joomla, you'll see a list of all menus on the web site. The one with a star after the name is the menu that contains the default menu item.

➤ **Published.** The Published column indicates whether an item is currently published (green check mark) or not (red X).

➤ **Order.** The Order column enables you to reorder menu items on your web site. By default, the Menu Item Manager is sorted in order, with the item that appears first in the menu in the first spot in the Menu Item Manager.

You can reorder menu items in two ways. You can use the small green up/down arrows to nudge a menu item up or down a spot in the ordering, or you can enter numbers in the boxes and click the disk icon next to the Order column header. Many people refer to this as "Netflix ordering," after Netflix, the online video rental service that pioneered this type of interface.

➤ **Access Level.** The Access Level column indicates whether the menu item is public, registered, or special. See Chapter 4 for an explanation of these permissions.

➤ **Type.** The Type column indicates the type of menu item (article, blog, and so on). You learn more about these types in detail later in the chapter.

➤ **ItemID.** The ItemID column is the ID of this particular menu item. ItemIDs are critical to forming Joomla URLs for your web site.

Linking an Individual Article to the Menu

This section describes creating your first link from an existing article to the Main Menu. In the Menu Item Manager, click the New button in the upper-right corner. The screen shown in Figure 6-6 appears.

Under the type of Internal Link (the first item with the green arrow pointing down), Articles is the first item listed. Because you want to link to an article, choose Articles. However, many methodologies of linking to articles exist, as shown in Figure 6-7.

You can mouse over each available item for a tooltip that may help you choose which item you want. For this example, choose Article Layout, which is under the Article subheading. The Article Layout screen appears, as shown in Figure 6-8.

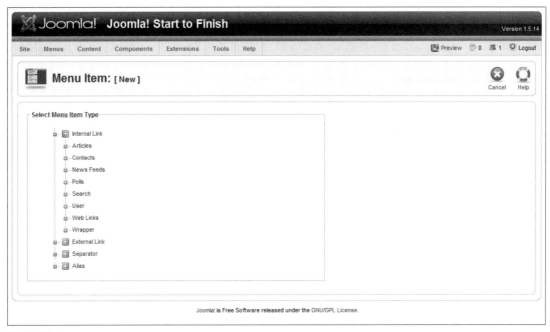

FIGURE 6-6

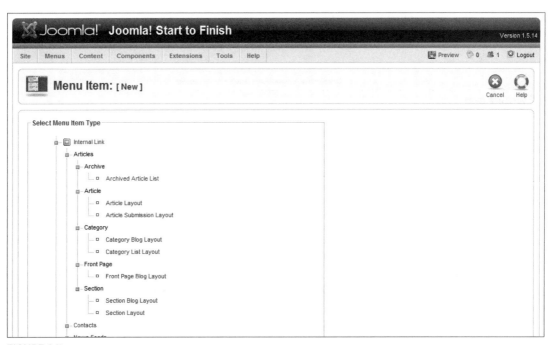

FIGURE 6-7

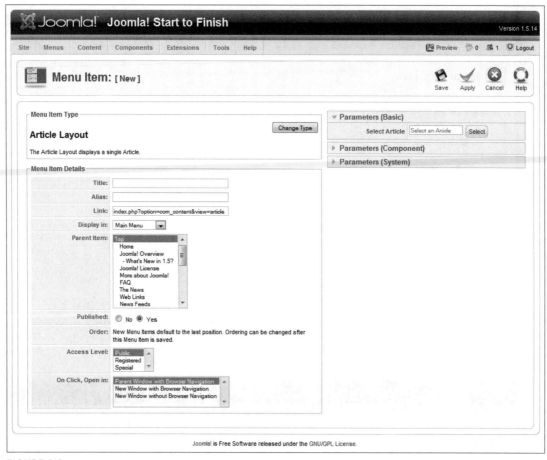

FIGURE 6-8

To make a link to your article, you must complete the following basic pieces of information:

➤ **Title.** This text will display as a navigation item (the clickable text in the link). Ideally, this will be the same text as your article title.

Users are most comfortable if they see a link that says "About Us" that, when clicked, takes them to a page with a title of "About Us." However, you might occasionally work with a verbose client who wants to title a page "Inside Our Fine Company and the Fabulous People Who Run It." That's a little long for a navigation item name, so you may be forced to shorten it to "Inside" or "Inside the Company." You should always make it clear what the relationship is between the menu title and the article title for the best experience for your users.

➤ **Alias.** If you have search engine–friendly addresses (SEF URLs) enabled for your site in the Global Configuration (see Chapter 4), the alias is what shows up in the URL. You should not use spaces or funny characters (ampersands, percents, asterisk, etc.) here; only use letters, numbers, hyphens, and underscores.

➤ **Link.** Leave this field alone. Joomla fills it in for you.

➤ **Display in.** Presumably, you want this link in the Main Menu, which is what displays. If you want the link to appear in a different menu, change this drop-down list to something else.

➤ **Parent Item.** If this is a top-level menu item (that is, it shows in the main navigation), the parent item is Top. If you want this item to appear underneath a navigation item as secondary or tertiary (or deeper) navigation, select that item from the list.

➤ **Published.** This determines whether the item is published.

➤ **Access Level.** This indicates whether this menu item is available to the general public (public), registered users only (registered), or authors and higher (special).

➤ **On Click, Open In.** In general, if you're linking to an article on your own web site, you'll want it to open in the same window users are already in, and you'll want them to have access to the back button and other browser navigation. Generally, you'll leave this option set to Parent Window with Browser Navigation.

Under Parameters (Basic) on the right, notice the Select Article box. Click the Select button to select your article from a list by clicking on the article name, as shown in Figure 6-9. You can filter this list by section and/or category using the Select Section and Select Category drop-downs menus, respectively, to reduce your choices. The filter box will filter the list based on whatever you enter into the box. You can use the filter box in combination with the Select Section and Select Category drop-downs, or you can use it on its own.

FIGURE 6-9

These are all the items you must complete to create a new article link. To save your changes, click the Save button in the upper-right corner. To apply your work while keeping the screen open to continue editing, click Apply. The Cancel button deletes all changes, and the Help button provides contextual help.

After you click Save, Joomla creates your new page, and it appears in the Menu Item Manager list. It usually winds up being the last item, as shown in Figure 6-10.

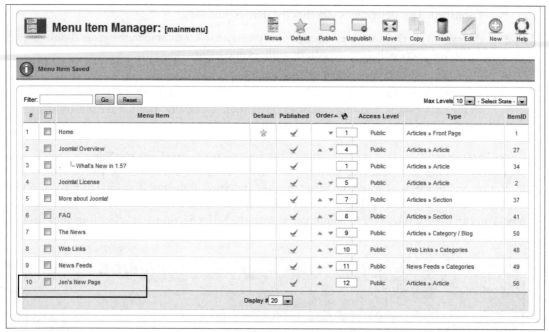

FIGURE 6-10

The last position might be right where you want this article, or you might want it further up the list. Use the up and down arrows in the Ordering column to nudge the article to where you want it. In Figure 6-11, I used the arrows to move the article to appear in-between FAQ and The News.

You can also see how this new menu item looks on the front end of the web site. Click the Preview link in the upper-right corner of the Menu Item Manager, and the home page for the web site will open in a new tab or new window in your web browser, as shown in Figure 6-12.

Note that the link shows up under Main Menu, on the left side of this web page, exactly as specified to appear.

Parameters (Component) Settings

The Parameters (Component) section of the Article Layout screen (see Figure 6-13) includes some items that should look familiar to you, such as Show Article Title, Title Linkable, and so on. You saw these settings back in the individual articles, where you could also set them (refer to Chapter 5, "In the Beginning There Was Content").

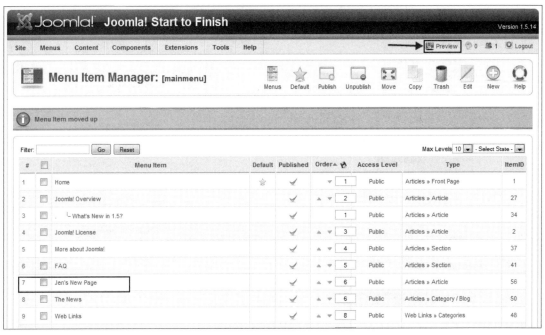

FIGURE 6-11

FIGURE 6-12

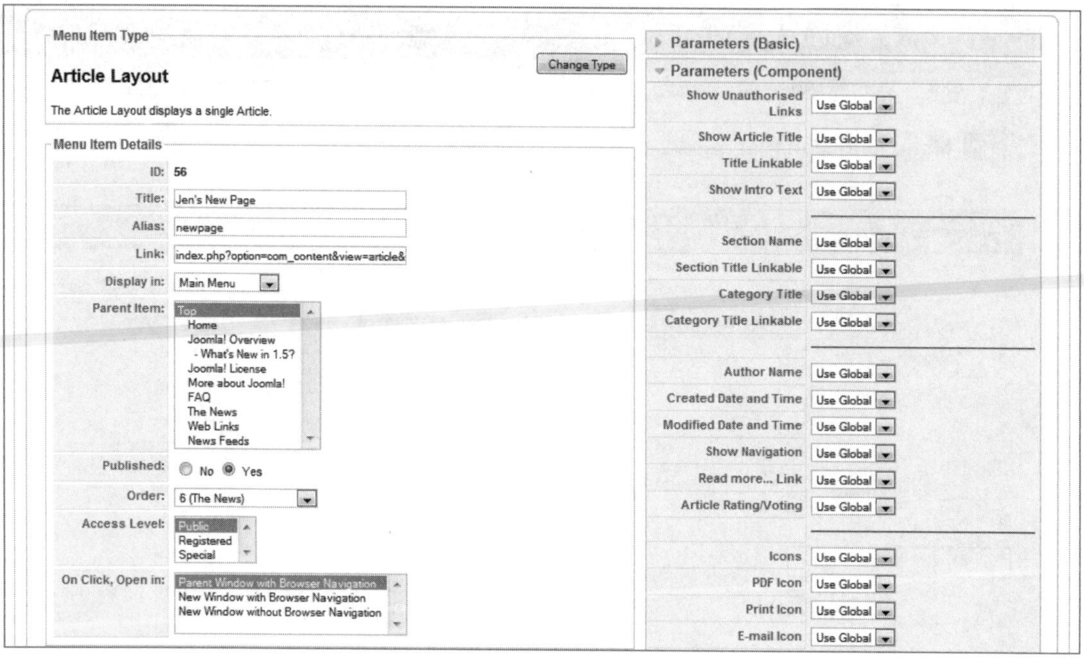

FIGURE 6-13

So, which is better — setting these variables here, under the menu, or setting them under the individual article? What about those Article Parameters? And which setting wins?

For an individual article like this, the settings with the highest priority are those on the article, followed by those on the menu, followed by the Article Parameters. For example, if Show Title is set to Yes in Article Parameters, No in the article, and Yes in the menu, the title will not show.

There is little point in changing these settings in the menu for an individual article. As you'll see later in the chapter, the menu settings are useful for blogs, in particular.

However, for individual articles, I recommend you not touch the Parameters (Component) settings within the menu item. You could easily wind up confusing yourself later. Set your Article Parameters to what the majority of the articles on the site require, and then use individual article settings to override those settings, as required. For now, however, ignore these menu settings.

Parameters (System) Settings

Figure 6-14 shows the Parameters (System) settings.

Enter a title in the Page Title field to include an additional title at the top of the page, and then use the appropriate Show Page Title option to specify whether the page title should appear on the page.

The page title is completely separate from the article title, which may or not display depending on how you've configured the Article Parameters and the individual article settings. The page title appears above the article title, if present. Note that the page title also becomes the HTML title for the page — that is, the text associated with the <title> tag.

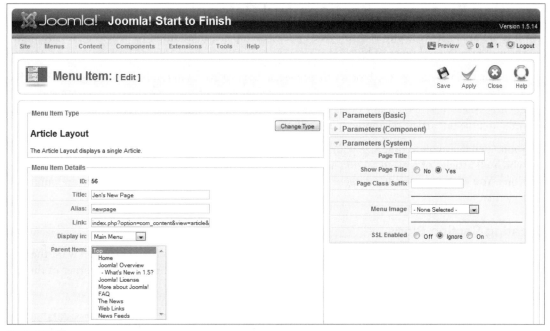

FIGURE 6-14

A key feature of Parameters (System) is that when you enter a title in the Page Title blank but set Show Page Title to No, the Page Title is still the `<title>` for the page, even if it does not show in the main body of the page. This feature can be crucial for search engine optimization (SEO) rankings. To boost SEO rankings, include extra keywords or concepts in the `<title>` tag, even if you don't want those words to appear on the page itself.

If you don't enter any text in the Page Title field and set Show Page Title No, the `<title>` for the page is the same as the article title, even if the article title does not show on the page.

The Page Class Suffix field enables you to add a suffix to the end of the CSS classes in use — on this page only. For example, if you enter *jen* as the suffix for this page, you would have a class of "contentheadingjen," instead of having a class of "contentheading." Again, note that the suffix applies to classes on this page only, within the article content, and not to classes on other pages. I'll talk more about suffixes and their uses in conjunction with modules and templates in Chapter 14.

The Menu Image drop-down list enables you to pick an image from the Media Manager to appear with the link in the navigation options. The menu image will not show unless the module that displays the menu is set to show menu images. By default, modules are set to not show menu images, so if you turn this setting on, chances are you will not see any image in your menu. I cover this topic in more detail later, in the section, "Presenting Image-Based Menu Navigation."

You can use the final option in System section, SSL Enabled, to specify whether the page will display starting with `https://` instead of `http://`. Although an in-depth discussion about Secure Sockets Layer (SSL) is beyond the scope of this book, suffice it to say that enabling SSL is critical for sites with shopping carts and other pages with sensitive information.

Creating Blogs from Sections and Categories

In Joomla, blogs are a way of displaying articles on a page, in addition to providing functionality in the more traditional sense of blog.

Blog functionality can be used for writing blogs, a diary of events in reverse chronological order. Blogs are also a great tool for showing press releases, upcoming events, new product announcements, frequently asked questions, or any other reason you would like a page with short bits of text, a Read More link, and the full article on another page following that Read More link.

Joomla enables you to organize your blogs in one of two types. You can publish a *section blog*, in which all articles of a given section are published (optionally grouped by category within that section). You can also publish a *category blog*, in which all articles of a given category are published together.

Creating Section Blogs

To create a section blog, start in the Menu Item Manager for the menu in which you want the section blog to appear, such as the Main Menu. Click the New button in the upper-right corner of the page. Choose Articles, and then Section Blog Layout, as shown in Figure 6-15.

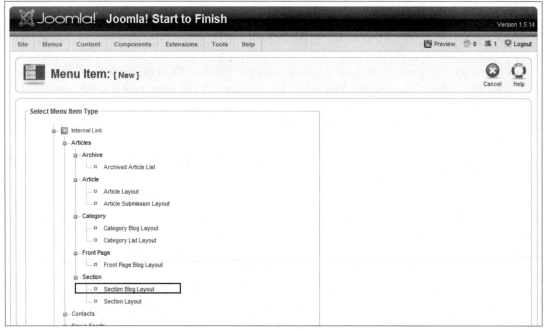

FIGURE 6-15

The Section Blog Layout screen appears, as shown in Figure 6-16.

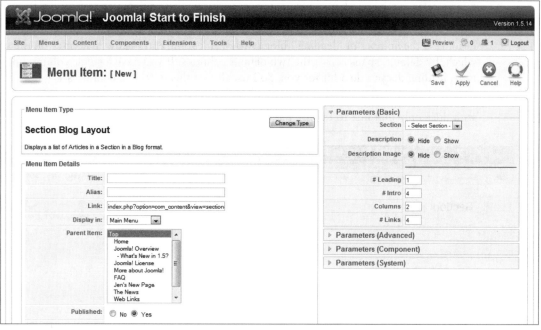

FIGURE 6-16

On the Menu Item Details side of the screen, the fields to complete are the same as the Article Layout: Title, Alias, Link, Display In, Parent Item, Published, Access Level, and where the item should open on click.

The Parameters side of the screen has its own unique attributes, which require a deeper look.

Parameters (Basic) Settings

The Parameters (Basic) section of the Section Blog Layout screen includes the following options:

➤ **Section.** Select the section for the blog from the drop-down menu.

➤ **Description.** This is the section description. You can create or edit these descriptions by going to the Section Manager (under Content ⮕ Section Manager), selecting the section, and scrolling to the bottom of the screen, where there is an editor for a description (see Figure 6-17). The description is extremely handy if you need to have some fixed text at the top of a blog page.

➤ **Description Image.** This is the image associated with the section (also shown in Figure 6-17), which you can configure in the Section Manager.

The final four options under Parameters (Basic) are best described out of order:

➤ **Columns** are straightforward. Do you want your blog entries to appear in 2 columns (the default) or some other layout? I almost always set this to 1 column.

➤ **# Intro** refers to the number of blog entries that display with title, intro text, and a Read More link in their default setting. The default setting is 4.

➤ **Leading** is the number of "leading" blog entries. A leading entry is the first entry on the pile, which, by default, spans across the two default columns. If you have a single column on the page, leading doesn't do a lot for you. So I usually set this to 0. The default is 1.

➤ **# Links** refers to the number of blog entries at the bottom of the page, in bulleted list format, with titles only that link to the full blog entry. The default setting is 4.

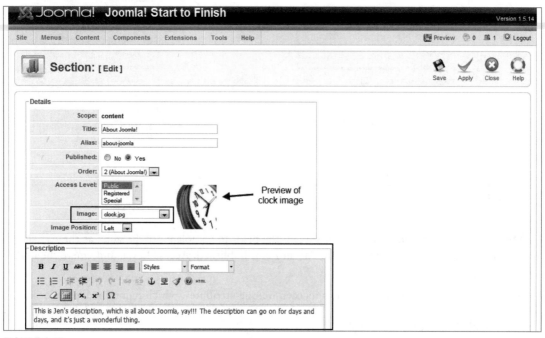

FIGURE 6-17

Figure 6-18 shows the section blog I set up for my site. I've turned off the Description and Description Image, and the Columns are set to 1, # Intro to 2, # Leading to 0, and # Links to 4.

Parameters (Advanced) Settings

Now that you've established which section's articles make up your blog and how many articles you'll display at a time, it's time to look at the order in which those articles should be displayed. The settings are shown in Figure 6-19.

➤ **Category Order** refers to the categories within the section and the order in which those categories should appear. The four choices for ordering are:

➤ **Order by Primary Order Only** means for Joomla to ignore the category separation and simply list all articles in their primary order, as they appear in the Article Manager.

➤ Title (**alphabetical**) and Title (**reverse-alphabetical**) are straightforward: They display the categories in A–Z or Z–A order.

➤ **Order** means to display the categories in the order in which they appear in the Category Manager, with their articles underneath each category. Reorder the categories in the Category Manager, using the ordering up and down arrows, if you want them to appear in a different order.

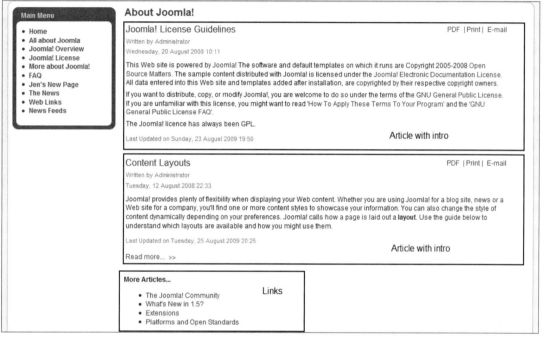

FIGURE 6-18

➤ **Primary Order** refers to the order of the blog entries themselves. Again, you have several ordering options:

  ➤ **Title** (alphabetical or reverse alphabetical)

  ➤ **Author** (alphabetical or reverse alphabetical)

  ➤ **Number of Hits** (from most to least hits or the reverse)

  ➤ **Time Published** (oldest or most recent first)

  ➤ **Ordering** (the order in which the articles appear in the Article Manager)

➤ **Multi Column Order** determines whether the display of blog entries goes down the column or across the column, if you have a multicolumn layout (see Parameters [Basic]).

➤ **Pagination** refers to the number links on the bottom of the page (see Figure 6-20). Auto means the pagination will be generated automatically as needed.

➤ **Pagination Results** refers to the showing of "Page 1 of 4." (See Figure 6-20.)

➤ **Show a Feed Link** determines whether an RSS feed should display (see Figure 6-20).

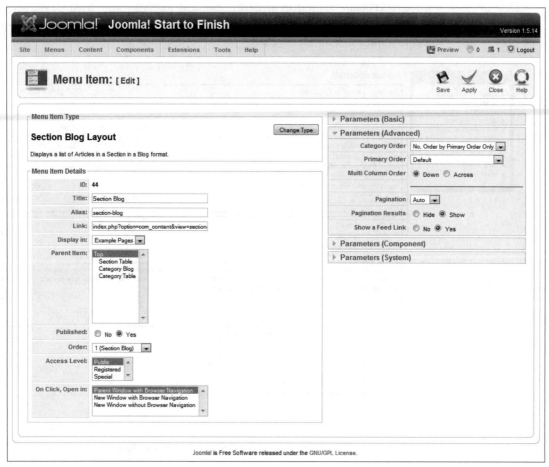

FIGURE 6-19

Figure 6-20 shows the bottom of my section blog, featuring Pagination, Pagination Results, and Show a Feed Link.

Parameters (Component) Settings

As shown in Figure 6-21, the settings under Parameters (Component) are the same as those in the Article Manager.

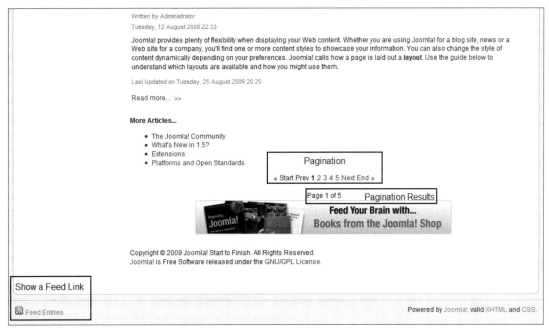

FIGURE 6-20

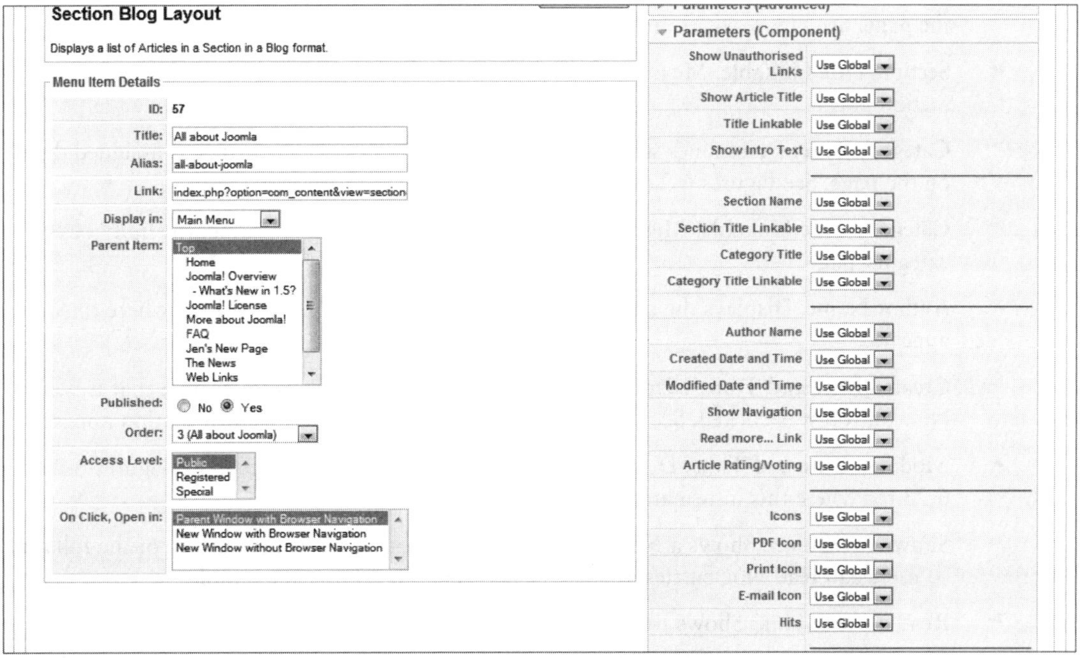

FIGURE 6-21

The following reviews what each item is and what it does (then I'll talk about how to configure these in light of the different places to set them).

➤ **Show Unauthorized Links.** If this option is set to Yes, regardless of a visitor's login status, the section blog will show the intro text for all articles. When visitors click on the Read More link, they will get a login box, requiring them to log in to read the full article. If you want everything hidden from visitors unless they're logged in, set this option to No. In that case, only the articles that can be read without a login will be displayed. This feature is nice if you have a membership site, and you want to give visitors a taste of what they could get if they become members.

➤ **Show Article Title.** Determines whether the title should show for each individual article.

➤ **Title Linkable.** Determines whether the individual article titles will link to a full version of the article. (The choice is between a linked title plus a Read More link, or just the Read More link itself.) If this option is turned on, the titles on the section blog page will link to their full articles. After visitors go to a full article, the article titles on those pages also link to the full article — in other words, it links to itself.

➤ **Intro Text.** Determines whether the introductory text should show. If you set this option to Hide, the intro text will show up on the section blog page, which contains small introductory blurbs, but it will not show up when users click through to the full article. This feature is helpful if you want to have a teaser about the article as the introductory text, then show the actual article after users click through.

➤ **Section Name.** Determines whether the name of the section the article is assigned displays on the page. See Figures 6-22 and 6-23 for where this name appears.

➤ **Section Title Linkable.** Means that if users click on the section name, the link goes to a section page.

➤ **Category Title.** Determines whether the name of the category the article is assigned displays on the page. See Figures 6-22 and 6-23 for where this title appears.

➤ **Category Title Linkable.** Means that if you click on the category name, the link goes to a category page.

➤ **Author Name.** Displays the author's name. See Figures 6-22 and 6-23 for where this name appears.

➤ **Created Date and Time.** Displays the date and time the article was created; that is, when the New button was clicked. See Figures 6-22 and 6-23 for where this information appears.

➤ **Modified Date and Time.** Displays when the article was last changed. See Figures 6-22 and 6-23 for where this information appears.

➤ **Show Navigation.** Shows a Next and/or Prev (Previous) link at the bottom of the full article so users can read blog entries as a series. See Figure 6-23 for an example.

➤ **Read more... Link.** Shows the Read More link (or what you've specified as the Read More text in the individual article) if there is introductory text and full text associated with a given article. If this option is turned off, only the introductory text will show. Users will not be able to get to the full article unless you've made the article title linkable.

➤ **Article Rating/Voting.** Shows the current rating for this article and offers users the ability to vote when the full article is displayed. See Figure 6-23 for an example.

➤ **Icons.** Specifies whether the icons or text should display for PDF, Print, and E-mail options.

➤ **PDF Icon, Print Icon,** and **E-mail Icon.** Determine whether the option to create a PDF for the page, put the page into printer-friendly format, or the option to email a friend is available. The previous setting determines whether these options display as icons or text. See Figures 6-22 and 6-23 for where these icons appear.

➤ **Hit.** You would expect this option to show how many hits per article, wouldn't you? It does, but not in the section blog or category blog. Hits only shows in some of the other layouts. Why it's included as an option in the section blog is anyone's guess. It doesn't matter how you set this option — it will not show up in your section blog. (Thanks to Brian Teeman for straightening this one out!)

➤ **For Each Feed Item Show.** This option sets whether you're exporting the intro text or the full text for each article.

Parameters (System) Settings

The Parameters (System) panel contains the same settings as those for an individual article (refer to Figure 6-14).

Examples

Figure 6-22 shows a section blog's top-level page, with many of the previously mentioned options labeled. All settings were configured in the Menu item for this blog.

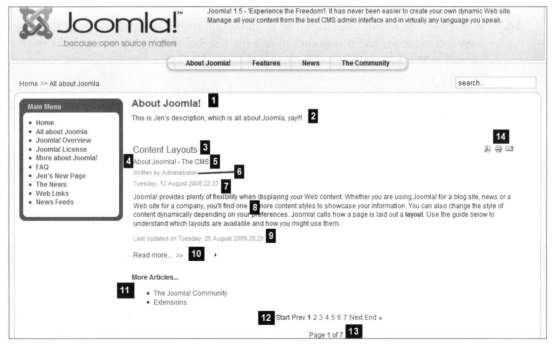

FIGURE 6-22

Here are the label descriptions for Figure 6-22:

1. **Section Title** is acting as the page title, because Show Page Title, under Parameters (Advanced), is set to Yes, but Joomla displays the section title because no text was in the Page Title field.

2. **Show Section Description** is set to Yes under Parameters (Basic).

3. **Show Article Title** set to Yes under Parameters (Component). The article title is also linked. Clicking it takes users to the full article.

4. **Show Section Name** is set to Yes, as is Section Title Linkable. Clicking the section name essentially reloads this page (that is, it generates a section blog).

5. **Show Category Title** is set to Yes, as is Category Title Linkable. Clicking the category name creates a category blog.

6. **Author Name** is set to Show.

7. **Created Date and Time** is set to Show.

8. **Show Intro Text** is set to Show under Parameters (Component).

9. **Modified Date and Time** is set to Show.

10. **Read more... Link** is set to Show.

11. **More Articles.** These are links to more articles. Under Parameters (Basic), # Leading is set to 0, # Intro is set to 1, Columns is set to 1, and # Links is set to 2.

12. **Pagination** is set to Show (under Parameters [Advanced]).

13. **Pagination Results** is set to Show (under Parameters [Advanced])

14. **PDF, Print, and E-mail Icons** are all set to Show, and Icons is set to Show. Note that if users logged in to the site had permissions to edit articles, they would also see a pencil icon (for editing) in the right corner, next to these icons.

Clicking on the Platforms and Open Standards article link opens a full article, as shown in Figure 6-23. (You may need to go through some of the pages in this blog to find the link, via the Pagination links at the bottom of the page.)

The following are the label descriptions for Figure 6-23:

1. **Show Article Title** is set to Yes. Article title is also linked. Clicking it will reload this page.

2. **Article Rating/Voting** is set to Show.

3. **Show Section Name** is set to Yes, as is Section Title Linkable. Clicking the section name generates a section blog.

4. **Show Category Title** is set to Yes, as is Category Title Linkable. Clicking the category name creates a category blog.

5. **Author Name** is set to Show.

6. Created Date and Time is set to Show.

7. Full text for the article.

8. Modified Date and Time is set to Show.

9. Show Navigation, under Parameters (Component) is set to Show.

10. PDF, Print, and E-mail Icons are all set to Show, and Icons is set to Show. Note that users who were logged in to the site and had permissions to edit articles would also see a pencil icon (for editing) in the right corner next to these icons.

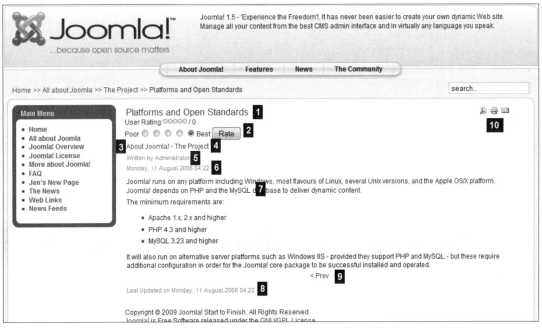

FIGURE 6-23

Creating Category Blogs

To create a category blog, open the Menu Item Manager for the menu in which you want the category blog to appear, such as the Main Menu. Click the New button in the upper-right corner of the page. Choose Articles, and then Category Blog Layout, as shown in Figure 6-24. The Category Blog Layout screen appears, as shown in Figure 6-25.

On the Menu Item Details side of the screen, the fields to complete are the same as in the Article Layout screen: Title, Alias, Link, Display In, Parent Item, Published, Access Level, and where the item should open on click.

The Parameters side of the screen has its own unique attributes, which require a deeper look.

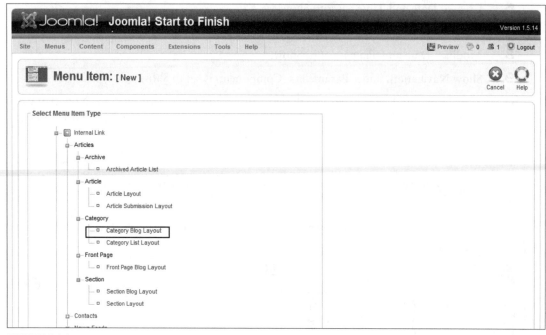

FIGURE 6-24

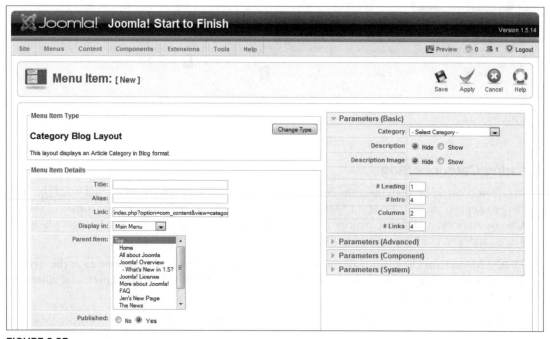

FIGURE 6-25

Parameters (Basic) Settings

The Parameters (Basic) section of the Category Blog Layout screen includes the following settings:

➤ **Category.** Select the category for the blog from the drop-down menu.

➤ **Description.** This is the category description. You can create or edit these descriptions by going to the Category Manager, selecting the category, and scrolling to the bottom of the screen, where there is an editor for a description (see Figure 6-26). The description is extremely handy if you need to have some fixed text at the top of your blog page.

➤ **Description Image.** This is the image associated with the category (also shown in Figure 6-26), which you can configure in the Category Manager.

FIGURE 6-26

The final four options under Parameters (Basic) are best described out of order:

➤ **Columns** are straightforward. Do you want your blog entries to appear in 2 columns (the default) or some other layout? I almost always set this to 1 column.

➤ **# Intro** refers to the number of blog entries that display with title, intro text, and a Read More link, in their default setting. The default setting is 4.

➤ **# Leading** is the number of "leading" blog entries. A leading entry is the first entry on the pile, which, by default, spans across the two default columns. If you have a single column on the page, leading doesn't do a lot for you. I usually set this to 0. The default setting is 1.

➤ **# Links** refers to the number of blog entries at the bottom of the page in bulleted list format, with titles only, that link to the full blog entry. The default setting is 4.

Figure 6-27 shows the category blog I set up for my site. The Description and Description Image options are turned off, and the Columns are set to 1, # Intro is set to 2, # Leading is set to 0, and # Links is set to 4. However, only three articles are in this category, so visitors will see two articles with intro text, and one link item.

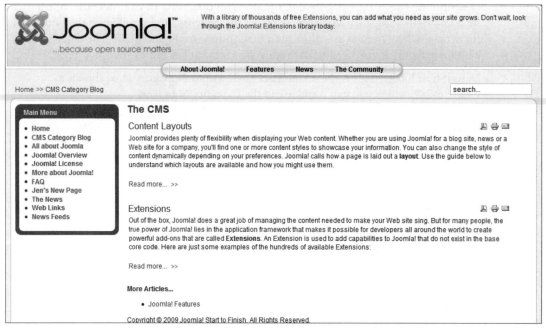

FIGURE 6-27

Parameters (Advanced) and Parameters (Component) Settings

The settings in the Parameters (Advanced) and Parameters (Component) screens are the same, and they work the same, as those in the Section Blog Layout screen described previously in this chapter.

Parameters (System) Settings

The Parameters (System) panel contains the same settings as those for an individual article, described previously in this chapter.

Creating Article Lists from Sections and Categories

Sometimes, you just want a list of available articles, rather than having them display in blog format. For example, you want a list of questions for a FAQ, with each question as a separate article. The Section Layout and Category List Layout are what you need for this type of list.

I present these two layouts together, because they fit together very well. Figure 6-28 shows a Section Layout.

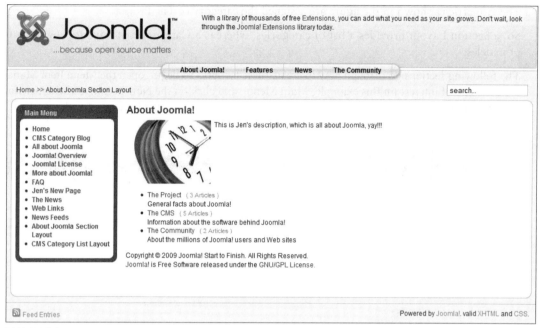

FIGURE 6-28

In this figure, you can see the three categories associated with the About Joomla section: The Project, The CMS, and The Community.

When visitors click on The Project link, a Category List Layout appears, as shown in Figure 6-29.

FIGURE 6-29

The two articles shown in the figure are assigned the category of The Project.

So, a Section Layout provides a list of categories, whereas a Category List Layout provides a list of articles.

The following sections go through how to create these layouts. To begin, open the Menu Item Manager for the menu of interest (in this example, Main Menu), and click on the New button in the upper-right corner. On the next screen, choose Articles, then either Section Layout or Category List Layout, as shown in Figure 6-30.

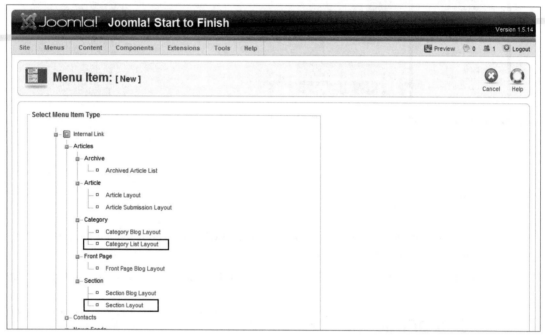

FIGURE 6-30

Take a look at the Section Layout options first, and then the Category List Layout options.

Section Layout Options

The settings in the Menu Item Details section of the Section Layout screen should be familiar to you by now, so take a look at the Parameters side of the screen, as shown in Figure 6-31.

The Parameters (Basic) section offers the following options, and Figure 6-32 shows you where each of the parameters appears on the web page:

1. **Section.** Choose the section from the drop-down menu.

2. **Description.** This is the Section Description, which you set for this section within the Section Manager. See the "Creating Section Blogs" section earlier in this chapter for more information.

FIGURE 6-31

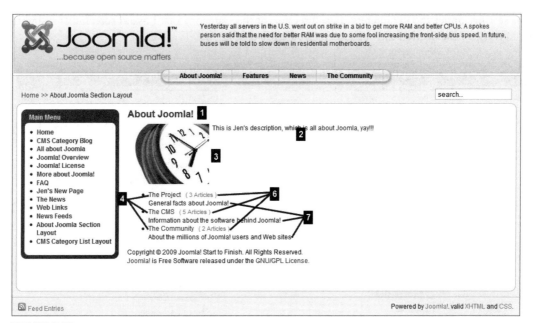

FIGURE 6-32

3. **Description Image.** Again, you set this option in the Section Manager.

4. **Category List - Section.** This option controls whether the list of categories shows up on the Section Layout page. If you set this option to Hide, a list of categories does not appear, so there's no way to navigate to another page! I recommend you always set this option to Show.

5. **Empty Categories in Section.** This option sets whether categories that exist within the section, but don't have any articles, should show or be hidden. In this case, we don't have any empty categories, so there is nothing to show in this figure.

6. **# Category Items.** After each category name, you'll see something like "(5 items)." This option is where you can set whether these show or not.

7. **Category Description.** Use this option to show the category description after the name of the category, or hide it.

The settings under Parameters (Advanced) work just like the Parameters (Advanced) settings covered in the "Creating Section Blogs" section of this chapter. The Order drop-down menu refers to the order in which the categories should appear (alphabetic, reverse alphabetic, or the order in which they appear in the Category Manager). The Article Order is the order the articles should be sorted after a category is chosen.

Finally, the settings under Parameters (Component) and Parameters (System) work just like the settings you've already seen, as described in "Creating Section Blogs" earlier in the chapter.

Category List Layout Options

The settings under the Parameters (Basic) section of the Category List Layout screen differ slightly from those of the Section Layout screen (see Figure 6-33).

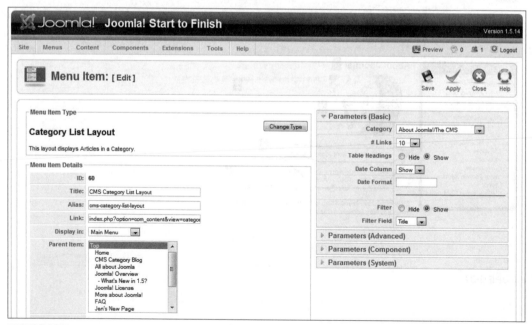

FIGURE 6-33

1. **Category.** Choose your category from the drop-down menu.

2. **# Links.** Choose how many links you want to display on the page.

3. **Table Headings.** Determines whether each column in the table should have headings.

4. **Date Column.** Shows the Created date in the column or not.

5. **Date Format.** Determines how the date will be formatted. If you know PHP, you can change this formatting.

6. **Filter.** Shows or hides the filtering box.

7. **Filter Field.** Applies the filter to the field you choose (Title, Author, Hits). It's applied to Title in Figure 6-34.

The Parameters (Advanced) section includes the following options:

8. **Primary Order.** This is the order in which the articles are displayed. In this case, this is displaying in default order (not shown in the diagram).

9. **Pagination.** Shows or hides the pagination at the bottom of the page. In this case, there are only five articles to display, though the display # is set to 10. This means that even though the pagination is set to Show, there is nothing to show since the number of articles for this category does not exceed the display # field (not shown in diagram).

10. **Display Select.** From the drop-down menu, choose the number of articles to show on this screen.

You've seen all the options in Parameters (Component) and Parameters (System) earlier in this chapter. The following are a few quick tips to keep in mind:

➤ To get rid of the Hits column, set Hits to Hide under Parameters (Components).

➤ Likewise, to get rid of the Author column, set Author Name to Hide under Parameters (Components).

Figure 6-34 shows the Parameters (Basic) and Parameters (Advanced) options.

Note that two articles in the Article Title list say "Register to read more." These articles are for registered users only. They show up in this list because Show Unauthorized Links is set to Yes. If this option were set to No, these links would not even appear.

 As you can see in Figure 6-35, I've turned off as many parameters as I can for my Category List Layout. I just want a list of articles! This is as close as I can get.

Those numbers won't go away! Argh!

Unfortunately, no easy way exists to turn off those numbers. There is, however, something called a *template override*, which enables you to format this page exactly how you wish. However, you do need a solid background in HTML and maybe a little PHP background to complete the task. For more on template overrides, see Chapter 14, "Advanced Template and CSS Tricks," which uses these numbers in an example.

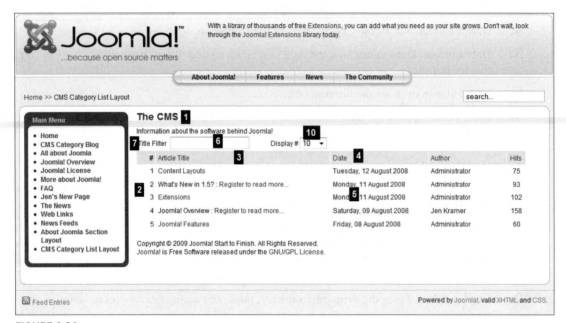

FIGURE 6-34

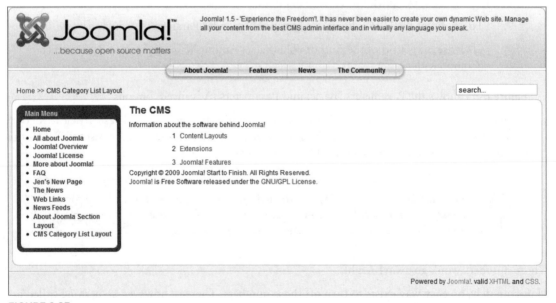

FIGURE 6-35

Menu Overrides from Articles and Which Setting Wins

For many of the parameters covered in this chapter, there are three places to set their inclusion or exclusion on the page. There's a setting in the Article Parameters, the same setting in the individual article, and a third setting in the menu item. So which one wins?

➤ The **lowest priority** goes to the Article Parameters. Think of this priority as the global setting for your articles. The individual article setting and the menu setting override anything set in Article Parameters.

➤ The **second priority** is the menu settings. This priority overrides the Article Parameters, but not the individual article settings. These settings are extremely useful when configuring blogs. This priority overrides any Article Parameter setting, but it still sets a pile of posts to appear in a certain way, without setting each article individually.

➤ The **highest priority** is the individual article setting. Use this only if a specific article needs the override. For example, perhaps one article would not have the article title display, but every other article does display the article title.

Some developers like to set all three locations to display or not display something. They say, for example, not to display the author name in the Article Parameters, in the individual article, and in the menu item. This is just creating extra work, and later, if you change your mind, you may have a hard time unraveling what you did in the first place.

Learn to take advantage of this series of overrides, and you'll save yourself a bundle of time and prevent headaches. For example:

➤ If you never, ever want to have an article's author display on your site, set it in the Article Parameters. Set all the article settings and menu settings to just Use Global (which is set by default).

➤ If you want to display the author name in one section blog, set the menu settings for the section blog to show the author name. All articles should stay set to Use Global (the default). That way, you have one place to change your mind later. You *can* change it on a per-article basis, but if you ever change your mind, you would need to edit dozens, hundreds, or even thousands of articles.

➤ If you don't want to display the author name for one post in that same blog — for example, an announcement in the blog, where an author name isn't relevant — then setting the author name on a per-article basis makes perfect sense. However, if 80 percent of the posts include author names and 20 percent of the posts do not, I would set the blog to show the author name in the menu setting, and then set individual articles to not show the author name. It's less work that way.

MAKING MENUS SHOW UP ON THE PAGE

At the beginning of the chapter, I mentioned that menus are comprised of two parts: what happens in the Menu Manager, and the module that drives where the menu displays.

When you create a new menu in the Menu Manager, a corresponding module is created, provided you entered a module title (see "Using the Menu Manager" earlier in this chapter). Modules are found in the Module Manager, under the Extensions menu, as shown in Figure 6-36.

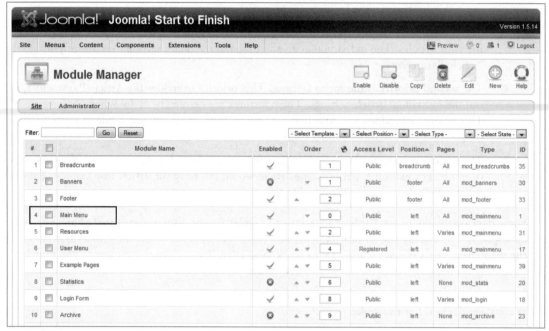

FIGURE 6-36

Chapter 8, "Modules That Come with Joomla!," covers all the parts of the Module Manager. For now, find the Main Menu module, and click on the title to edit it. You should get something like Figure 6-37.

Take a look at each item in the module configuration, starting with the Details section on the left side of the screen:

➤ **Title** is what you click on to get into the module to edit it.

➤ **Show Title** indicates whether the title should show on the web page. Sometimes you'll want the title to be there, but more frequently, you may not want to include it.

➤ **Enabled** indicates whether the module is published.

➤ **Position** is where, within the template, this module will appear. Templates are coded with specific module positions. If done correctly, those positions will appear in this drop-down menu. See Chapter 13, "Custom Templates," for more on this topic.

➤ **Order** determines for a given module position, what appears first, what appears second, and so on.

➤ **Access Level** determines, as you've seen before, whether access to this module is Public, Registered, or Special.

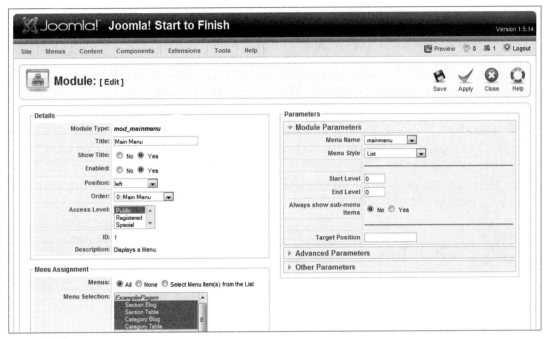

FIGURE 6-37

In the Menu Assignment area, you can choose to have this module display on all menus for the site, none of the menus for the site, or selected menu items only. You can choose those items in the Menu Selection box. Remember to Shift+click to select a bunch of sequential menu items; Control+click to select non-contiguous items.

The right side of the screen contains the Module Parameters area:

➤ **Menu Name** is a drop-down menu containing all menu names on the site. You can associate this module with any menu and change it at any time.

➤ **Menu Style** offers four choices, with only one you should use. Use the List option, which is chosen by default. This option formats your list into a nested bulleted list. This HTML markup can then be formatted to just about anything via CSS. The three items marked Legacy are left over from the Joomla 1.0 days. These write out table-based markup, with one menu item per cell. It leads to bloated, slow-loading, non-search engine–friendly markup, so stay away from options other than List.

➤ **Start Level** and **End Level** indicate the points at which the menu should start and stop displaying. I cover these settings in detail later in the chapter.

➤ **Always Show Sub-Menu Items.** Normally, when Joomla builds navigation for a given page, it shows the sub-navigation specific to that page only. For example, if you're on the Mission page in the About Us section of the site, you would see Mission, Vision, and Values spelled out under About Us. However, under the Products menu item, you would not see a list of products to explore, unless you went to the Products page. Always Show Sub-Menu Items means that all sub-menus show all the time.

➤ **Target Position.** Used only for JavaScript values for positioning a pop-up window. JavaScript is beyond the scope of this book, but this blank allows you to specify top, left, width, and height values for the pop-up. Mouse over the words "Target Position" for more information.

Modules have many more settings, which are covered in later chapters. But these settings are what you need to get your module configured and showing on the web page.

While you're editing the Main Menu module, I suggest making a quick change. It always bugs me that the Main Menu, by default, has its title showing. If you've been surfing the Web for five minutes or more, you understand the concept of a navigation bar, so why does it need a label? Yet many Joomla sites have this "Main Menu" item, because developers never turn off the title.

On the Details side of the screen for managing the Main Menu module, set Show Title to Hide (No). Save the module, and look at the home page of your web site (see Figure 6-38).

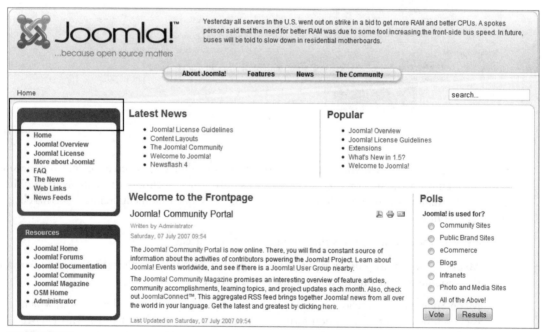

FIGURE 6-38

The title is gone! But the box looks a little off. This template is designed to have headings on top of these modules on the left side.

Because this is the main menu for the site, what if it appeared toward the top of the page, where the About Joomla!/Features/News/The Community navigation bar is located? As for that top menu, what if you just got rid of it? It's a lot of duplicate content, so turn it off.

This is Joomla, and these kinds of changes are easy. You simply do the following:

1. Figure out what the module position is for that top menu bar. You already know that your main menu is in the Left position.

2. Edit the module for the Main Menu, and set it to appear in the position for the top bar.

3. Unpublish the top bar.

To figure out what the module positions are, you can use a little-known feature of Joomla. If you add ?tp=1 after the URL for your web page (for example, www.joomlastarttofinish.com/?tp=1), you can get an outline of where all the module positions for the template appear on the page and what their names are. See Figure 6-39 for an example.

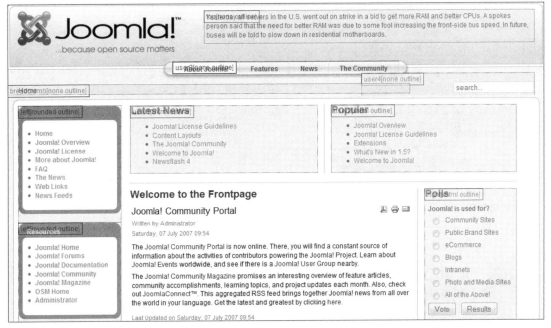

FIGURE 6-39

It's a little hard to read there (and easier in color), but user3 is where that top menu bar is currently living.

Next, return to the Module Manager and the settings for the Main Menu module. Set the position to user3, as shown in Figure 6-40.

Refresh the front end of the web site to see what you have now. Remember to take out ?tp=1 at the end of the URL to get a clear picture, as shown in Figure 6-41.

Note that you now have two navigation bars on top. That's because you haven't completed the third step: unpublishing the old top navigation bar.

In the Module Manager, find the navigation bar among all the modules. The best way to do it is to use the Select Position drop-down menu at the top right, as shown in Figure 6-42, and tell it to show just those modules with a position of user3.

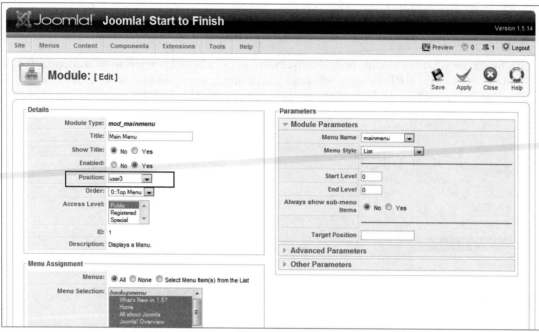

FIGURE 6-40

FIGURE 6-41

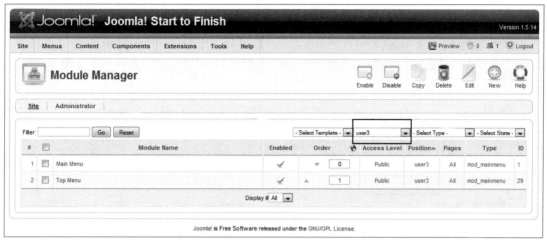

FIGURE 6-42

Only two items are in the user3 position: the Main Menu (which you want to stay there) and the Top Menu. Click the green check mark in the Enabled column to disable (unpublish) it. The green check will turn to a red X. Now check the front end of your web site, as shown in Figure 6-43.

FIGURE 6-43

Great! You've simplified your site's navigation options, gotten rid of redundant navigation, and your main navigation now goes horizontally across the page. Are you done? Almost. Do a quick test to see what happens on pages with subnavigation. For example, if visitors were to click on the Joomla! Overview link, they would see a secondary navigation item called What's New in 1.5?, as shown in Figure 6-44.

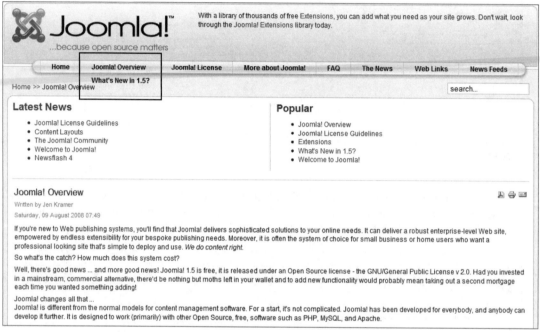

FIGURE 6-44

Most web sites would put that navigation on the left side. But all of this navigation is built into the same menu, the Main Menu, as you did in the Menu Manager. Is it really possible to split the menu into pieces, to just show the secondary navigation for this item on the left side?

Absolutely it is! The next section takes a look at how an all-in-one navigation bar looks, where the primary, secondary, and deeper navigation is all in one place. Then I describe how to split up the navigation into pieces.

Displaying the Menu All in One Place

Just for a moment, I've moved the Main Menu navigation bar back from user3 to the left position on the web page, as shown in Figure 6-45. (This is still the Joomla! Overview page.)

Notice that a bulleted list makes up this menu. Top-level bullets have a solid black bullet next to them, whereas subnavigation bullets (in this case, What's New in 1.5?) have a circle bullet.

You could use CSS to change the appearance of this menu to make it look however you want. You see some of those possibilities in Chapter 14. So although this might not be the most attractive menu in the world, it's very functional. What the top-level menu items are is clear, and clearly the What's New in 1.5? item lives underneath the Joomla! Overview.

Nothing is wrong with keeping your navigation all on the left side like this. It's clear, it's functional, and it works just fine.

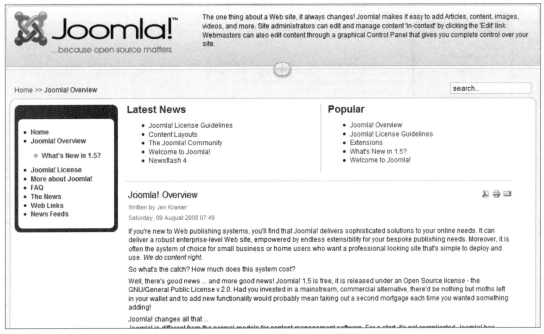

FIGURE 6-45

Configuring the Module for Split Menu Presentation

However, many people really want to have main navigation horizontally, across the top, and they want any subnavigation to appear on the left. How do you make this happen?

A typical approach by Joomla newbies is to make a second menu. So you'll have Main Menu, with your top-level navigation items, and then in your Menu Manager, you'll create a second menu called Joomla! Overview, for example. In that menu, you'll place a single link, What's New in 1.5?. You'll tell that menu to live on certain pages only. What could possibly go wrong?

Unfortunately, the breadcrumb can go wrong. The breadcrumb indicates the hierarchy of pages, starting at the home page, and progressing deeper into the site. Figure 6-46 shows the What's New in 1.5? page. Take a look at the breadcrumb. It has a correct hierarchy.

If you move Main Menu to the top and create a second, separate menu for What's New in 1.5?, the look is correct, but the breadcrumb is all wrong, as shown in Figure 6-47.

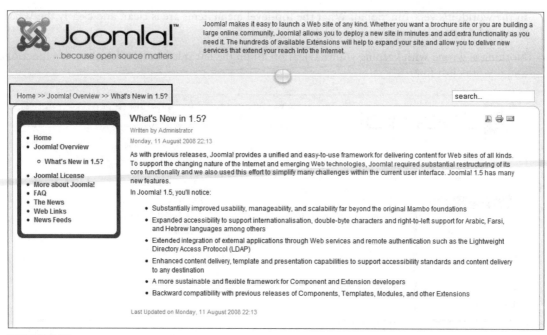

FIGURE 6-46

FIGURE 6-47

Remember that the menu contains all the links, but the module drives where those links appear and which links appear.

To get the menu to appear as it does in Figure 6-48, and have the breadcrumb to work correctly, perform the following steps:

1.   Start in the Module Manager (Extensions ⇨ Module Manager). Find the Main Menu module and click on the title to open it.

2.   Change the following settings, as shown in Figure 6-48:

➤   Set the Position from left to user3.

➤   In the Module Parameters section, take a look at the Start Level and End Level items. These are currently set to 0 in both cases. This means that all levels of navigation will show. Change the End Level to 1. This means that only the first level of navigation will show, and secondary navigation will not show.

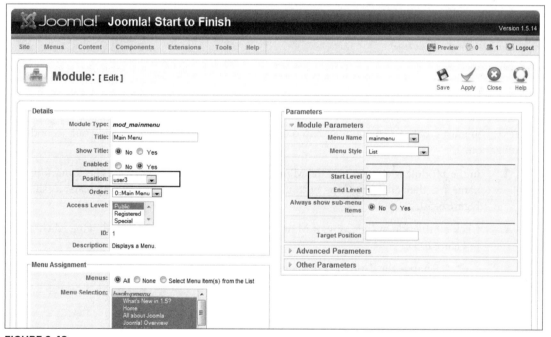

FIGURE 6-48

Now take a peek at the front end of the web site. If you go to the Joomla! Overview page, you should see something like Figure 6-49.

You might be surprised to see no left column at all. This template is programmed to move all the content to the left side of the page and not even write in a left column if no modules are assigned to that position. See Chapter 14 for how to do that.

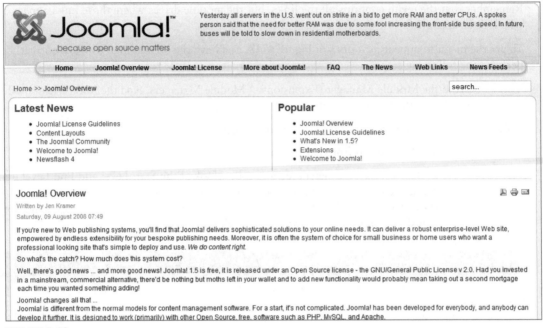

FIGURE 6-49

Next, you must create a new module, based on the Main Menu module, to hold your secondary navigation.

1. In the Module Manager, find the Main Menu module. Click to place a check mark next to its name and then click the Copy button. A Copy of Main Menu module appears, as shown in Figure 6-50.

2. Click on the title of the Copy of Main Menu module, and make the following edits, as shown in Figure 6-51:

   ➤ Change the Title to Left Menu - Joomla Overview so you know what this is. You do not need the title to display, so you can turn that off.

   ➤ Set Enabled to Yes.

   ➤ Set Position to Left.

   ➤ Assign the module to appear on the Joomla Overview and What's New in 1.5? pages.

   ➤ Set Start Level to 1 and End Level to 0. This means to start after the primary navigation, and to show all navigation after that.

3. Under Advanced Parameters, set Module Class Suffix to _menu. (I explain what this is in Chapter 14.)

4. Save the module settings.

Now look at the Joomla Overview page from the front end of the site. You should see something like Figure 6-52.

FIGURE 6-50

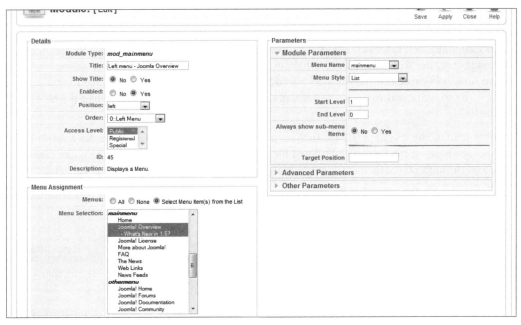

FIGURE 6-51

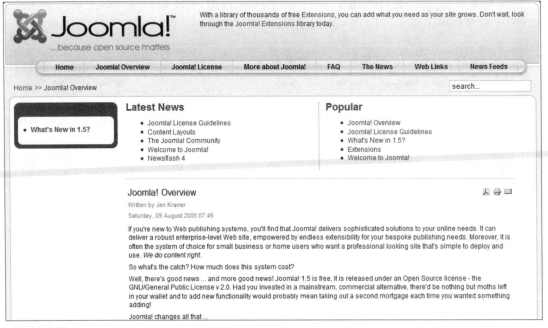

FIGURE 6-52

PRESENTING IMAGE-BASED MENU NAVIGATION

Back in the old days of FrontPage and Dreamweaver, when the world was still figuring out the Web, occasionally developers created navigation bars by using a series of images. Sometimes we used images because we wanted some off-the-wall, non-web-safe font for the navigation. Sometimes we used images because the :hover CSS pseudoclass was not widely supported, so the only way to get a rollover to work was to create two images and swap them by JavaScript when the mouse rolled over the link.

A content management system (CMS) such as Joomla is terrific because it generates a menu for you from the database, in the form of a bulleted list. This means that you or your client can create new pages, and through no particularly superhuman efforts, link those pages to your web site.

The moment that talk turns to image-based menu navigation, we get into a different realm. Some distinct positives and negatives exist to image-based menu navigation:

➤ Positives

➤ Rather than "being stuck" with the fonts that everyone typically has on their computer (like Arial, Verdana, Trebuchet, Times, and Georgia), you could use any font you wanted to display the text, because the text is stored in an image.

➤ You have exact control over how large the font size is and how it will display on the page.

➤ **Negatives**

> ➤ Every time you create a new menu item, you must create at least one image to display. This means you need some kind of image-editing program, expertise to run it, expertise to align the letters and get them laid out exactly correct, and so forth — in other words, skills your client is unlikely to have, so you'll need to create the image(s) every time.

> ➤ You've negated the advantage of easy menu creation in the CMS. Now it's a real pain in the neck.

> ➤ You potentially create some accessibility issues for visitors who are not able to read your image-based navigation. And if there's an accessibility issue, Google and other search engine spiders may also have difficulty reading and navigating your web site.

I strongly, *strongly* encourage you to stay away from image-based navigation. Many PR and branding companies argue that having the exact correct font in the navigation is critical to their marketing efforts. Branding definitely has a place on a web site, but it's not in the navigation bar. Use branding elements in the colors on the site, the logo, or some supporting graphics, by all means! But please keep your branding away from the navigation bar and the content. Keep these spaces easy to read and simple to maintain, and you're more likely to have an up-to-date web site, which will outweigh any tiny loss from a branding opportunity.

Having said all this, the three steps to creating an image-based navigation bar are as follow:

1. Create the image(s) and upload them to the Media Manager in the images/stories folder. Do not place the images anywhere else in the directory structure.

2. In the Menu Manager, for the menu item you want to assign an image to, in the individual menu item under Parameters (System), choose the image from the drop-down menu (see Figure 6-53).

3. Go to the corresponding module for that menu. Under Other Parameters, as shown in Figure 6-54, set Show Menu Images to Yes, set any menu alignment you want, and if you want the menu image to be clickable (in addition to the text), select that option as well.

Now take a look at the front end of the web site. As shown in Figure 6-55, for the Joomla! Overview item, I've assigned it the clock image from the Media Manager. Note that the bullet for this menu item still displays, but the text for Joomla! Overview does not display. Visitors would just have to know to click on the clock to get the Joomla! Overview. (If I had created a "real" navigation image, it would include the text, so this would not be an issue.)

The other menu items in this list do not have images, only because I have not assigned images to these menu items. I could continue to assign images, one at a time, and they would display in the menu.

The bullets do not have to be there, either. You could use CSS to get rid of the bullets, as mentioned before, and you could style this menu nicely, with or without images.

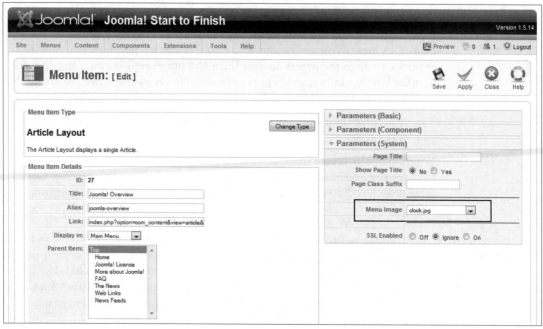

FIGURE 6-53

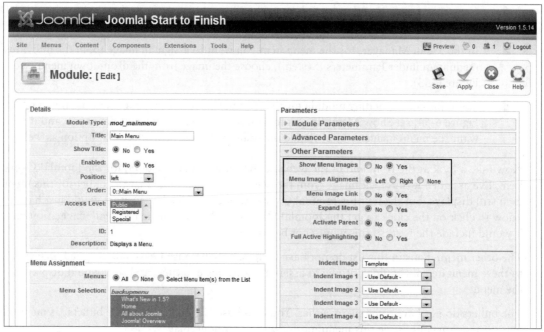

FIGURE 6-54

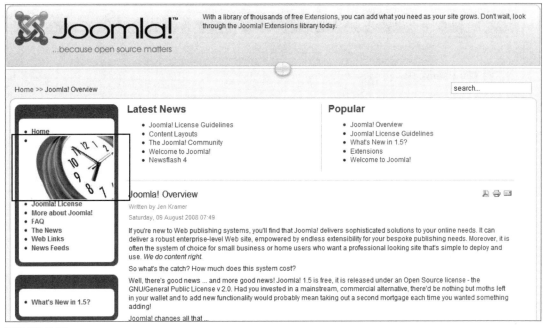

FIGURE 6-55

CREATING SPECIAL MENU ITEMS

So far, this chapter has discussed linking articles to menus in one way or another. Joomla also includes many other options for creating other types of menu items.

Creating a Wrapper Menu Item

Those of you who are familiar with HTML probably know that a wrapper is Joomla's word for an *iframe*. This is a web page within a web page. The Joomla template wraps around the content area for the web page. In the content area, another web page displays.

To create a wrapper menu item, from the Main Menu Item Manager, follow these steps:

1. Click New, and then select Wrapper (twice), as shown in Figure 6-56.

2. In the next screen, as shown in Figure 6-57, enter a title for this menu item, its parent, and then set the Wrapper URL (on the right) to Google's home page.

3. Flip to the front end of the web site and refresh to update the menu. Click on the Sample Wrapper Page (which you just created), and you should see a page similar to the one in Figure 6-58.

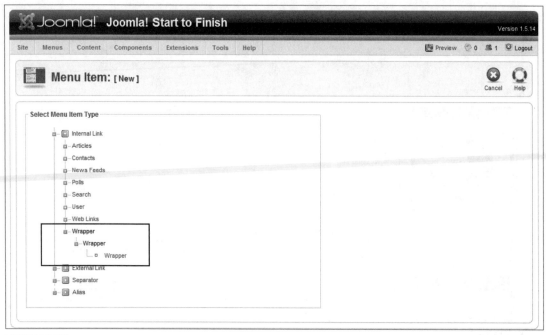

FIGURE 6-56

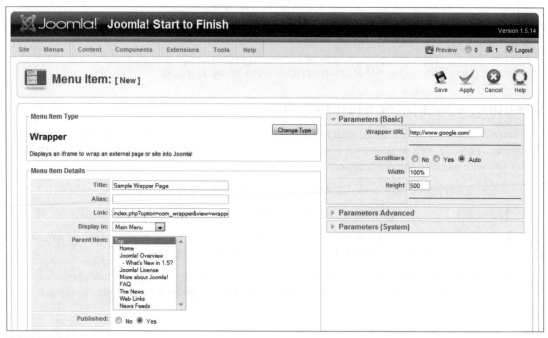

FIGURE 6-57

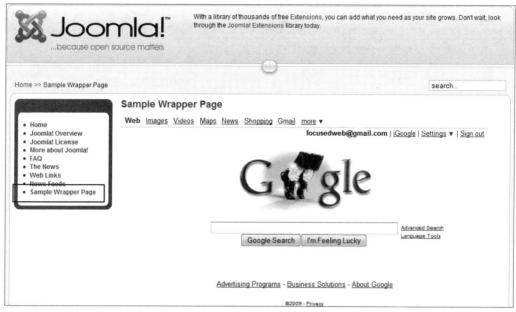

FIGURE 6-58

Although your wanting to run Google in your web site is unlikely, the wrapper functionality is very handy if you have an off-site functionality you want to incorporate quickly and easily. Functionalities like donations, job listings, press releases, and more may do well running in a wrapper like this.

Creating an Alias Menu Item

One of the big advantages of a CMS is the ability to have a given piece of content appear in the site only once, but you can link to it as often as you want. To have a menu item appear in more than one location, you use something known as an *alias*.

What's wrong with making more than one link to a given piece of content? As you'll find out in Chapter 8, you must assign modules to each link individually. You would have extra configuration to do if you created a link in more than one location.

Suppose that you want the What's New in 1.5? menu item to show up on the main navigation, as well as under the Joomla Overview navigation item. To do so, return to the Menu Item Manager and click New, and then Alias, as shown in Figure 6-59.

The alias screen is shown in Figure 6-60. Unfortunately, although you click Alias to get here, the screen is called Menu Link. They are the same thing.

Type in the title for the menu item under the Details section, and assign a parent item. Under Parameters (Basic), select the location where this item is already linked from the drop-down menu.

Now, when you look at the front end of the web site, the link for Alias for What's New will take you the same place as clicking on Joomla! Overview, then What's New in 1.5?. All module assignments are also maintained.

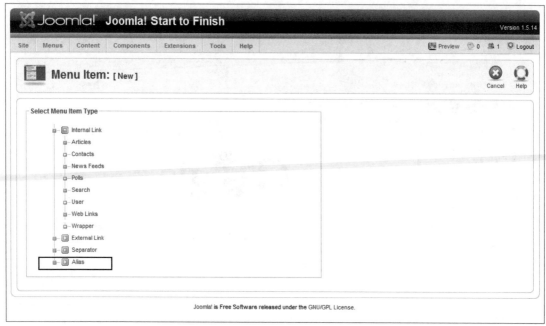

FIGURE 6-59

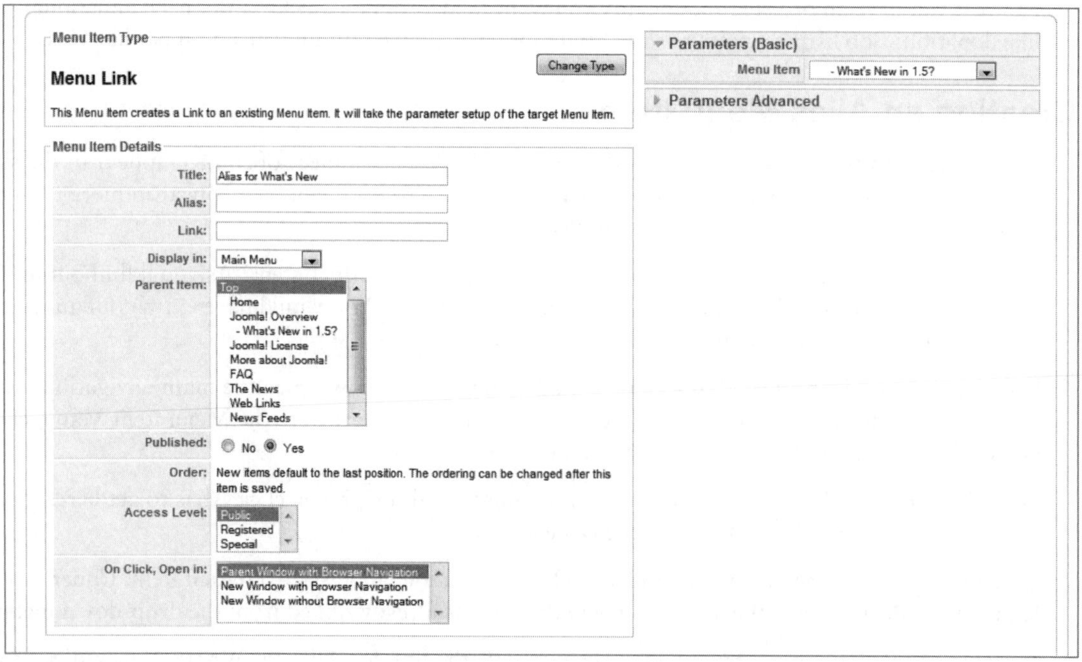

FIGURE 6-60

Creating an External Link Menu Item

Sometimes you just want to link to another page that's not on your web site, but you want to include that link in your menu. The External Link option is the way to do that.

If you've installed the sample data in Joomla, the Resources menu consists of a series of external links.

To create an external link menu item:

1. From the Menu Item Manager, select the New button and then the External Link item.

2. In the External Link screen, shown in Figure 6-61, enter a Title for the link and the URL, including http://, in the Link box. At the bottom of the Details section, set the On Click, Open in: drop-down menu to New Window with Browser Navigation. That way, when people are done with the offsite link, your web site is still open in the browser window.

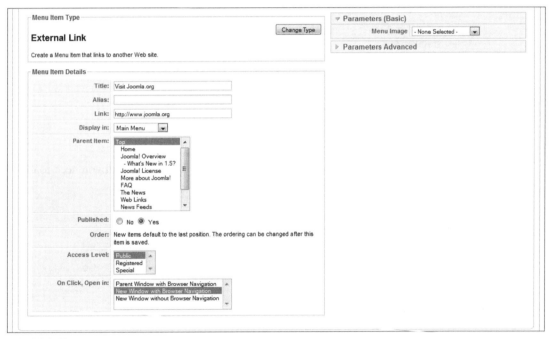

FIGURE 6-61

Creating a Separator Menu Item

A *separator* is a non-linked item that might appear in your menu. It helps to break up long lists of items.

To create a separator menu item, follow these steps:

1. In the Menu Item Manager (under the Menus menu, choose the menu to which you wish to add the separator, like Main Menu), click New, then Separator. A Separator screen similar to Figure 6-62 appears.

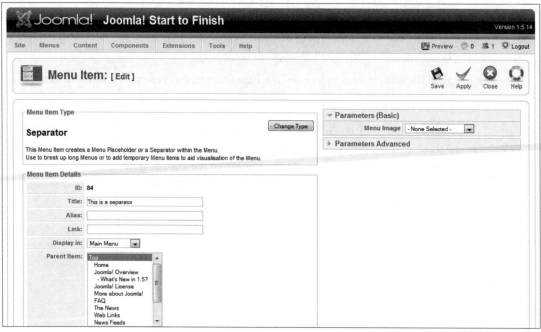

FIGURE 6-62

2. Type in the title and choose the parent item — and that is essentially all you need to do. The item will appear in your menu, as shown in Figure 6-63.

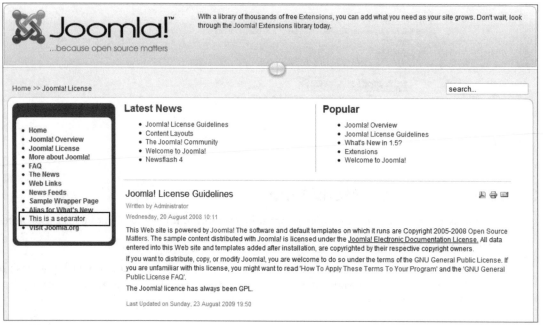

FIGURE 6-63

Obviously, this is not the best name for a separator! If you do use text as a separator, make it clear that it's not clickable and that it's breaking up your menu. You'll probably need to do some styling to make it more effective. A separator is a great place to use an image as well, if you want to throw in a fancy line that would divide up the menu. You can choose the image on the Parameters (Basic) section of the Separator menu item configuration screen.

CREATING MENUS FOR SPECIFIC USER CLASSES

Occasionally, you might want to have an entire menu appear when a user is logged in. Logged-in users have special needs, relative to the general public, because they might want to change a password or modify their profile.

Creating Registered User Menu Items

Making a menu item appear only to a registered user who is logged in is very easy. Simply change the permission level for the menu item from Public to either Registered (registered users and higher) or Special (authors and higher).

From the Menu Item Manager, click on the permission level in the Access Level column, as shown in Figure 6-64. If the item is set to Public, one click will change the permissions to Registered, whereas two clicks changes it to Special.

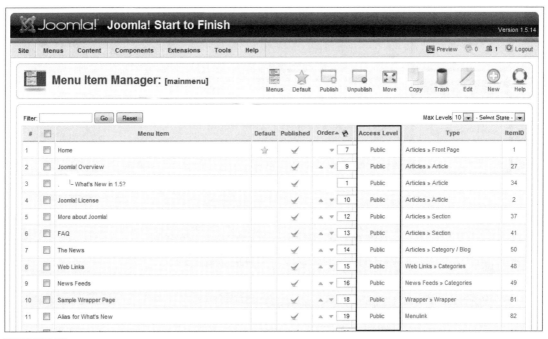

FIGURE 6-64

However, this sets only the *menu item* as available to registered users. The actual *content* behind the menu item might be set to public. Although there's no link taking you to the content from here, someone could possibly run a search and find the content that way.

Therefore, if you are building a registered user portion of your web site, make sure that all content — menu items and articles — is protected.

Creating Login and Related User Items

The following sections describe everything you need to create to support part of your web site protected by login. This includes adding a user registration form to the site, adding a login box, adding the reset and remind functionalities for resetting a password or reminding the user of their username, and including a form so users can change their password and profile.

Creating Registration

Before users can log into the site, they must register for it.

Joomla enables you to determine whether site registration is turned on or off in the Global Configuration, under System Tab ⇨ User Settings area. If Allow User Registration is set to Yes, then you'll see a link for Registration (called Create an Account) at the bottom of the login box on your site, as shown in Figure 6-65.

Clicking this link will take visitors to a registration page.

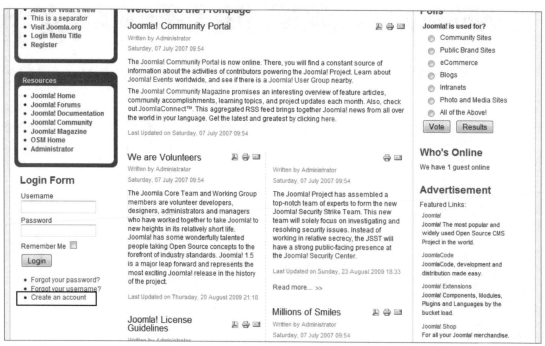

FIGURE 6-65

However, you might want to add a direct link to registration within your menu structure. That is doable through the Menu Item Manager for the menu to which you want to add the link. Click the New button, then User, Register, and Default Registration Layout, as shown in Figure 6-66.

FIGURE 6-66

Figure 6-67 shows the Default Registration Layout screen. There's not much to configure here. There is no Parameters (Basic), and Parameters (System) is exactly what you've seen before. Type in a menu title (such as Register or Site Registration), create an alias, assign a parent, and you're all done.

Creating a Login Link

If you're going to hide some information behind a login, then you must provide a login box. You can configure the login box either as a module (covered in Chapter 8) or as a link in a menu.

To create a login screen from a menu, go to the Menu Item Manager for the menu where you want the link (for example, the Main Menu). Click the New button, then choose User, Login, and Default Login Layout, as shown in Figure 6-68.

 If you create a registration page in the menu and then disable registration in the Global Configuration, a 403 error (access forbidden) appears when users click on the registration link. The registration link associated with any login boxes on the site will disappear automatically if you disable registration. Be sure to turn off any registration links you may have created if you decide to disable site registration.

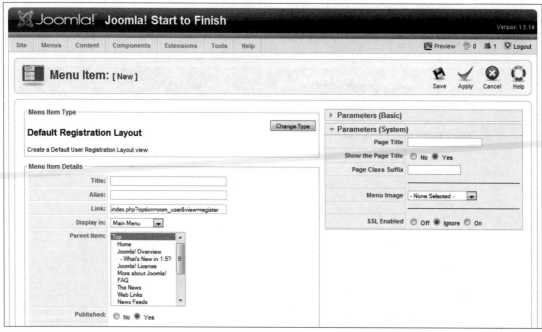

FIGURE 6-67

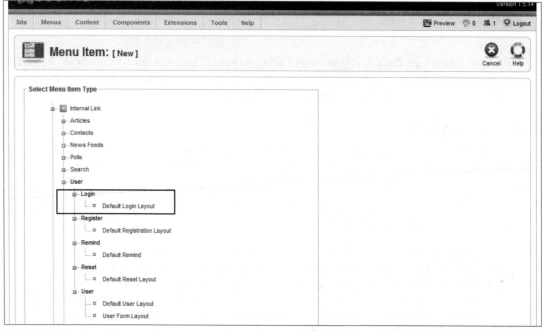

FIGURE 6-68

A Default Login Layout screen similar to that shown in Figure 6-69 appears.

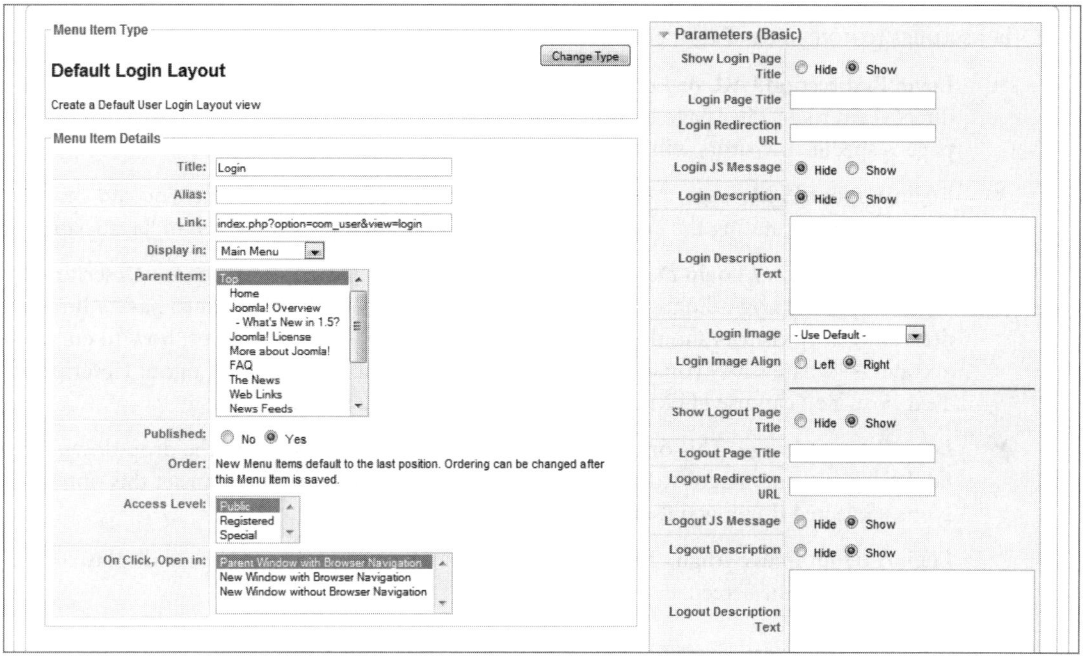

FIGURE 6-69

The Menu Item Details side should look familiar to you by now, so put in a menu title, an alias, if desired, and choose a parent item. In all likelihood, you want to leave the access level set to Public. After all, this is how you get the users logged in, so the login box should not be hidden behind a Registered or Special access level.

The page title for the login page is actually fairly confusing. Three items called "title" are associated with this page:

➤ **Menu Title.** You set the Menu Title in the Details side of the page in the Title box.

➤ **Login Page Title.** You set the Login Page Title (and whether to show or hide it) under Parameters (Basic).

➤ **Page Title.** The Page Title is set by default as Login. You can turn this on and off under Parameters (System) by setting Show Page Title to Yes (on) or No (off), and changing the text from simply Login to whatever you want by filling in the Page Title field.

This means it's possible to have, effectively, two titles for this page. The first would be the Login Page Title, set in the Parameters (Basic), and the second would be the Page Title set in Parameters (System). If you want no page title at all, set Show Login Page Title to Hide in Parameters (Basic) and Show Page Title to No in Parameters (System).

There is also a Logout Page Title and Show Logout Page Title. These work the same way as their login counterparts, except they show up as visitors are trying to log out.

Other settings to note under Parameters (Basic) include the following:

➤   **Login Redirection URL or Logout Redirection URL.** After visitors have logged in or out, direct them to another page of your choice. This field takes absolute or relative URLs. If no page is specified, visitors will be redirected to the home page.

➤   **Login/Logout JS Message.** After visitors have attempted to log in or out, you can show a pop-up window stating the success or failure of that attempt. (JS stands for JavaScript.)

➤   **Login Description / Login Description Text and Logout Description/Logout Description Text.** Under the Login/Logout Page Title and/or Page Title, if you want to have a little text describing why visitors should log in or log out, how to log in or log out, how to create an account — whatever — you can include this information in the Login/Logout Description Text box. You can use HTML in this text as well, if you want.

➤   **Login/Logout Image.** This option displays an image you choose from the drop-down menu (and it loads from images/stories). The default image is of keys. You can set this option to None xSelected if you want, and no image will show.

➤   **Login/Logout Image Align.** This option specifies whether the image should display on the left or right side of the screen.

The items under Parameters (System) are just like those you've seen before for articles, and they work the same way.

Creating the Remind and Reset Link

Everyone occasionally (or, perhaps, frequently) forgets a username or a password. Providing a "Lost Username" or "Lost Password" link is really helpful. These links are automatically built into the bottom of the login box, but you can also add them to your menu directly. Go to the New button in the Menu Item Manager and then click User. Choose either Remind and Default Remind to recover a username, or Reset and Default Reset Layout to reset a password.

As with the Registration options, there are no new options for Remind and Reset to explore. The left side of the screen has all the usual options (title, alias, access level, parent, and where the window should open) and the Parameters (System) panel has all the same options you've seen before.

Creating the User Form Layout Link

After visitors are finally logged in to the site, they might want to make changes to their profile. The User Form Layout enables visitors to set their name, email address, password, preferred front-end and back-end languages (assuming alternative languages are installed), user editor, and, if they're an administrator or higher, their help site. They can also set their time zone.

From the Menu Item Manager, click the New button. Choose User, User, and User Form Layout.

As with Registration, Remind, and Reset options, there are no new settings to explore on the User Form Layout screen. However, the User Form Layout is likely to be available only to registered users or special users, so be sure to set the access level accordingly.

If you're including any kind of social networking functionality on your web site (such as a forum, photo gallery where users can contribute photos, and so on), I strongly recommend that you include the User Form Layout as an option to registered users.

Creating Menus for Registered Users

Occasionally, you may want to have a menu that displays only when a user is logged in. As previously mentioned, you set the Access Level to Registered or Special for the content for that menu and its menu items. As an additional step, find the module that drives that menu, and set it to the same access level.

When public users visit the site, they will not see the menu. However, after the visitors are logged in, the menu will appear.

HIDING YOUR SITE BEHIND A LOGIN BOX

What if you're building an intranet web site with Joomla? Organizations use intranet web sites internally to share information among employees and/or volunteers. Generally, this type of site is out of the public view, yet potentially large numbers of people still need to access it.

An extranet is a site where you might share information with company or organizational partners, such as an external sales team, franchise owners, and so on (Chapter 14 discusses how the Kampgrounds of America, KOA, did this with their extranet site for franchise owners.) Again, the information should be kept from public view but still be easily accessible to those who need it.

In an organization with a board, you might have a special web site just for board members. This site allows board members to have their own behind-the-scenes conversation, perhaps recorded in a discussion forum, yet out of the public view.

In any of these scenarios, you might choose to hide the entire web site behind a login box. Here are the steps to set it up:

1. Create your sections, categories, articles, and menus, as usual.

2. Set all article and menu item access levels to Registered or Special.

3. Make sure the modules that drive all menus are set to the same Registered or Special user level.

4. Create a new menu. Do not set the corresponding menu module to appear on the site; it's probably not needed.

5. Create a single item for this menu, which is the login page. Make sure its access level is set to Public.

6. Use the Login Description Text to put some introductory text on the page, requiring login to see the site. Set the Login Redirect to the registered user home page.

And that should do it! When visitors go to the site, they should see a login box. They will have no navigation until they log into the site, at which point the navigation bars will appear.

CONSIDERING THE SECURITY OF REGISTERED USER INFORMATION

Now that you've created a section of your web site that's hidden behind a login, you might wonder how secure is the registered user/special user information? This is an excellent question. And, as always, the answer is, "It depends."

Let's consider a house for a moment. In all likelihood, your house has locks on its windows and doors. You may use those locks, or you may not use those locks. If you don't use them, the possibility exists that someone could easily walk in and take something. If you do use them, you significantly reduce that possibility. But if someone is really determined to get into your house, he certainly will. He could pick a lock, break a window, or even cut a hole in the wall to get in.

Any web site can be hacked. The obvious protections are to keep your site up to date with the latest Joomla security patches and patches for your extensions. Keep good usernames and passwords that aren't obvious or in the dictionary. Find a good host that's committed to security, and who may take a few more security measures on their server. This is like keeping your doors and windows locked in your house.

However, if hackers are really determined, they will find a way to get into your site. If they do, what happens if they steal the information they find there?

For most sites, this information is all publicly available. It just doesn't matter if the site is hacked, as the information is there because it's educating the public.

Certain pieces of information, though, are sensitive — Social Security numbers, credit card numbers, individual health and patient information, and so forth. If this information is hacked, it could be used for identity theft or in other crimes.

You have a responsibility, as a developer, to inform your client about this possibility, particularly when they talk about hiding information for certain users only. Make sure your client thinks through what might happen if the site is hacked. Is it devastating to the business? Does it leave the client (and you) open to lawsuits?

Joomla security is good, if you keep up with the latest patches to the core and to whatever extensions you choose to install. (See Chapter 2 for pointers for picking good extensions.) Still, think carefully about what information you're putting online.

7

Installing and Configuring Templates

WHAT'S IN THIS CHAPTER?

➤ Examining Joomla's core templates

➤ Assigning different templates to different pages

➤ Downloading and installing new templates

A Joomla web page is made up of several elements, some of which you've met already. The articles are the pieces that contain the content for a given page. They can have pictures, video, audio, or just words. The menus provide the buttons to click to get to the content. In later chapters, you'll learn about modules and components, which provide other types of functionality to the Joomla web page. Templates are the icing on this big cake — they are anything that makes your web site look pretty.

This chapter covers Joomla's default templates, how to assign different templates to different pages, and how to install new templates from other sites.

USING JOOMLA!'S DEFAULT TEMPLATES

Joomla comes with three templates by default. They're actually there as learning tools more than as templates you might use on a production web site.

If you choose Extensions ⇨ Template Manager, you can see a list of all installed templates for your web site, as shown in Figure 7-1.

 To see a thumbnail image of a template, simply mouse over the template's name.

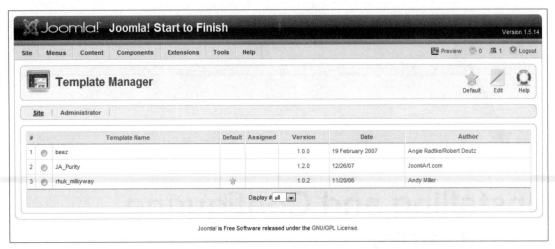

FIGURE 7-1

Note there are two tabs in the Template Manager: one for Site and one for Administrator. The Site tab refers to templates used on the front end of your site, whereas the Administrator tab refers to templates on the back end of the web site. Yes, it's possible to completely reengineer the way the back end of Joomla looks by changing its template! Only one administrator template comes with Joomla by default, called Khephri. There are a limited number of other Joomla administrator templates available for download at a variety of web sites. I recommend you stick with the Joomla default administrator template. It will make your support life easier as well. If you use different templates for different clients, you will have to remember which one they have installed. You'll also have to remember what the icons look like, where they're located, and how things look.

Let's go back to the Site tab. The default template is rhuk_milkyway (often just called Milkyway). If you click on the name of the template (or click the radio button next to its name and click the Edit button in the upper right), you can see some options for configuring this template, as shown in Figure 7-2. Milkyway is the template you've seen on the site all through this book.

Take a look at the template's Parameters on the right side of the screen. Color Variation is exactly what you would think it is — it changes the primary color scheme of the template. Change it to orange (or any other color) and click the Apply button (the big green check mark) in the upper right. Using Apply keeps you in this screen so that you can make more tweaks, but it applies your changes to the front end of the web site.

Now take a look at what happened by going to the front end of the web site and refreshing to see your changes. The titles and links are orange, but the background is blue.

That looks okay, but what if you could get the background to be orange, too? Fortunately, if you go back to the Template Manager Parameters screen, you can change the background color with the Background Variation drop-down menu. Click Apply, head back to the front end of the web site, and refresh. Getting better!

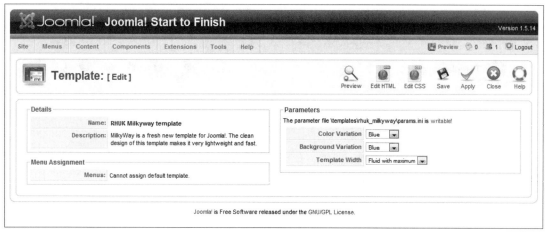

FIGURE 7-2

The Template Width drop-down menu of the Parameters area has to do with, intuitively, the width of the template. Small makes the template fit on an 800×600 monitor. Medium works with 1024×768 monitors. Fluid stretches the site to the full width of the browser window. Fluid with maximum makes the width fluid to a certain point, at which the site does not get any wider. Which is best? Of course, it depends. What monitor widths do your target audience use? Older computers have smaller monitors. If your target audience largely has newer computers, you could use one of the wider widths.

These parameters are unique to this template. They're created with some rather advanced template coding, and template developers have a lot of options for making these parameters. Some templates have several screens of parameters, whereas other templates might not have any parameters at all. The commercial templates might document which parameters do what, but the free templates seldom have any documentation.

ASSIGNING THE TEMPLATE TO SPECIFIC MENU ITEMS

Go back to the main Template Manager screen. If you're still in the Milkyway template's Parameters screen, click the Close button at the top right to return to the main Template Manager screen. If you're anywhere else on the site, choose Extensions ➪ Template Manager.

Note that the Milkyway template has a star in the column that says Default. This star indicates that when you create a new page and link it to the menu (which is how Joomla knows the page needs a template assigned), the Milkyway template is used on that page by default.

What if you want to assign a different template to a certain page or group of pages? You can assign templates to pages via the Template Manager.

For example, suppose you want to assign the Beez template to some of your pages. In the Template Manager, click on the Beez template name (or select the radio button and click the Edit button). The Beez template's Parameters screen appears, as shown in Figure 7-3.

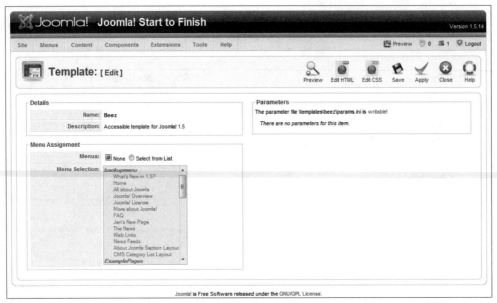

FIGURE 7-3

Note the Menu Assignment area in the bottom left, which currently is set to None. Change the radio button from None to Select from List, and then select Home from the Menu Selection box. Click the Apply button in the upper right, and go back to the web site home page on the front end and refresh it. It should look something like Figure 7-4.

FIGURE 7-4

Pretty radical change! Now click on any link in the main menu — the page changes back to the Milkyway template.

I most assuredly would not encourage you to have such a radical template change on your web site! Some kind of visual continuity should exist among all pages on your site, and it is clearly lacking in this example. You run the risk that visitors will not even be sure that they are on the same site when they go from your Beez home page to a Milkyway inside page.

However, occasionally you might have a home page that has a radically different layout, yet is visually continuous, with the inside pages on your site. Assigning a different template to the home page, in that case, might be a good plan.

Having more than one template on your site does have its drawbacks, though. There are maintenance issues. You might need to make changes in more than one location, if a logo or some type of style changes. You must also train your users to remember to assign the right template to their page. This can only be done from the back end of the site, not the front end, and it's an extra step your client must remember to do. Packing all your pages into a single template is ideal. Chapter 13, "Custom Templates," gives you pointers for doing this.

DOWNLOADING AND INSTALLING A TEMPLATE FROM ANOTHER SITE

One of Joomla's great strengths is its engaged and involved developer community, including its template developers. A Google search for "Joomla templates" pulls up dozens of links to sites where you can download templates for free or for fairly low cost.

Which is better — free or commercial? By now, you know the answer is, "It depends." If you are a beginning Joomla configuration specialist, you might do better with a commercial template with great support. Joomla Junkie, RocketTheme, Joomla Shack, and many others offer top-notch technical support with their templates.

Of course, for free, the price is right. Some of the aforementioned commercial developers also offer a few free templates that are well worth exploring. You can also download free templates from a number of other locations. However, when templates are free, sometimes they don't quite work right, or the styling is off, or they're incompatible in some browser or another. You'll want to have good technical chops to fix any problems that might arise with a free template — or you'll want to be able to walk away and pick a different template if the first one doesn't quite work for you.

 Templates are distributed as a zipped file. You don't want to unzip this file (unless the first zip contains documentation plus the template, and the template is bundled in there as its own zipped file). Keep it zipped, because this is how it installs on your site.

To install a template you've downloaded, do the following:

1. In the back end of Joomla, go to Extensions ⇨ Install/Uninstall, to get the installation screen, as shown in Figure 7-5.

You use this same screen for installing modules, components, plug-ins, templates, and languages. The installation process is the same for all of these items.

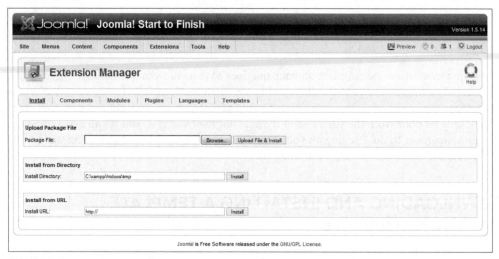

FIGURE 7-5

2. In the Upload Package File section, click the Browse button and browse for the zipped file on your computer. Select the file and click Open.

3. Click the Upload File & Install button to install the template to your site.

4. Choose Extensions ⇨ Template Manager; you should see your template in the list. Assign the template to whichever pages you want using the steps presented earlier in this chapter.

Alternatively, you can set it as the default template by choosing the radio button next to the template name and clicking the Default button in the upper right.

UNINSTALLING TEMPLATES

Once you've tried a bunch of templates on your web site, looking for the perfect match, you may decide you'd like to get rid of some of the templates that didn't work for you.

Getting rid of templates is very easy. Once again, go to Extensions ⇨ Install/Uninstall, and then switch to the Templates tab, as shown in Figure 7-6.

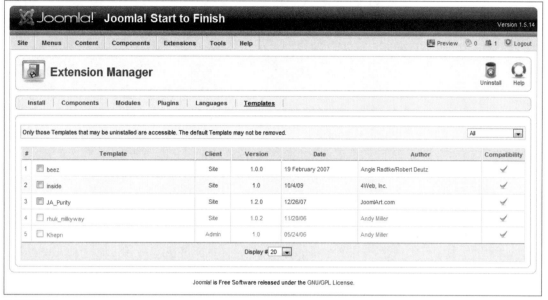

FIGURE 7-6

Place a checkmark after the template name you want to delete, and then click the Uninstall button at the top right.

Note that two templates are grayed out of the list. One is Milkyway, and the other is Khepri. These templates are the default templates for the front end and the back end of the site, respectively. You cannot delete the site's default templates.

Modules That Come with Joomla!

WHAT'S IN THIS CHAPTER?

➤ Configuring front-end modules: Breadcrumbs, Newsflash, Latest News, Random Image, Search, and Custom HTML

➤ Embedding modules in articles

➤ Configuring administrator modules

Modules are the little bits of text and functionality that appear, for the most part, on the perimeter of your web pages. Figure 8-1 shows the modules that appear on the home page of the Joomla site you've been working on.

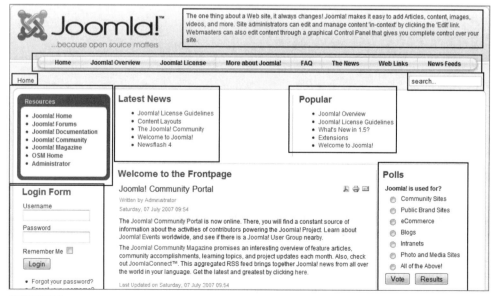

FIGURE 8-1

It has only two major items that aren't modules:

➤ The logo

➤ The story "Joomla! Community Portal"

Everything else is a module.

Modules are rather important in configuring your web page. Several modules come with Joomla by default. In this chapter, I described some of the most commonly used modules. You can also download thousands of modules, many for free, at `extensions.joomla.org`, the Joomla! Extensions Directory (JED).

CONFIGURING MODULES

Take a look at the Module Manager, as shown in Figure 8-2. You can access the Module Manager under the Extensions menu.

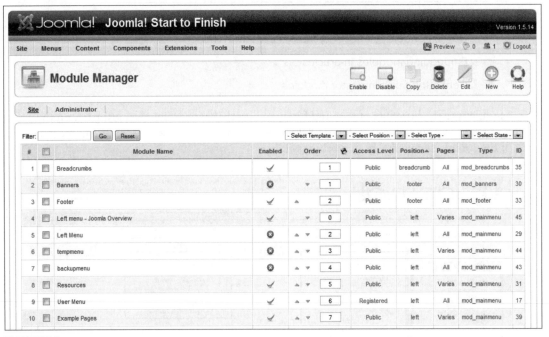

FIGURE 8-2

You are looking at the Module Manager for your site; that is, the modules that display on the front end of the web site. You can also see a tab for Administrator modules, which are covered later in the chapter.

If you have many modules on your site, you can filter them by using the Filter box (which essentially does a search among your modules). To the right of that are several drop-down menus. You can show all modules associated with a given template, a given position in the template, modules in a certain position, modules of a certain type, or all enabled or disabled modules (State drop-down menu).

A module position is a location on your web page where modules will display. You set up the positions in the template, where you give the positions a name. You can call module positions whatever you like, but generally, they're called by mostly descriptive names: left, top, bottom, footer, right, header, and so on.

> *Some developers will tell you that calling module positions by their location on the page (such as left or top) is incorrect. What if you want to move left somewhere else? In that case, it's no longer left. Technically speaking, they are absolutely correct. However, for most clients who will maintain the site, calling regions less descriptively (such as sidebar 1 and 2 instead of left and right) is not intuitive. I lean towards naming module positions as something that will make sense to my client, rather than a technically correct name.*

If the template has been coded correctly (see Chapter 13), all module positions you can choose from will show up as choices when you're configuring a module. You can also type in a name for the module. If you enter a name for a module position that does not exist in the template, that module will simply not display.

In the table that displays a list of your modules are many options you can sort by once again. Simply click the title header to sort by that column. By default, your modules are sorted as follows:

➤ **Module name** is the title you give the module.

➤ **Enabled** indicates whether the module is enabled (green check mark, the same as published) or disabled (red *x*, same as unpublished).

➤ **Order** works the same as the order functionality you saw in the Article Manager (refer to Chapter 5). Use the arrows or the blanks to reorder modules in a given position. If more than one module is assigned to a given position, the modules will display in the order they're shown in the Module Manager.

➤ **Access Level** sets the module to one of the three permissions choices: public, registered, or special. (See Chapter 4 for an explanation of these levels.)

➤ **Position** is the position in the template where this module displays.

➤ **Pages** indicates on which pages the modules display. Choices include all, none, or varies (that is, the module is assigned to specific pages).

➤ **Type** is the type of module (that is, breadcrumbs, banners, menus, and so on).

➤ **ID** is the ID assigned to this module in the database.

Additionally, note the following series of icons across the top right of the Module Manager:

➤ **Enable** sets selected (checked) modules from the list to enabled (published).

➤ **Disable** sets selected modules from the list to disabled (unpublished).

➤ **Copy** makes a copy of a single selected module from the list.

➤ **Delete** deletes a selected module.

➤ **Edit** takes you to the editing screen for a selected module. Clicking this icon is the same as clicking on the module title, which also takes you to the editing screen.

➤ **New** lets you create a new module, based on the modules that are installed for the site.

➤ **Help** provides contextual help for this screen.

Now take a look at some of the individual modules in the site. You can either create a new module, or if you have the sample data already installed, you can edit the existing module. The following examples use the sample data and show the editing of the existing modules.

If you want to create a new module, click the New button in the Module Manager. A screen appears listing all installed modules on your Joomla installation, as shown in Figure 8-3.

FIGURE 8-3

Choose the module of interest from the list (in this case, Breadcrumbs) and click Next. A configuration screen appears for the module you selected.

The Breadcrumbs Module

A *breadcrumb* is a navigational tool that's frequently used on very large web sites. If your site has a complex navigational structure, using a breadcrumb to help explain to visitors where they are in the site hierarchy makes sense. Typically, a breadcrumb displays the navigational path from the home page.

Breadcrumbs are not useful on very small web sites having just 10 pages or fewer, whereas they're quite helpful, and should be included, on web sites with 50 pages or more. In between? Use your best judgment. If the navigation is complex and deep, breadcrumbs are a very useful tool.

Figure 8-4 shows the breadcrumb on the What's New in 1.5 article on the web site.

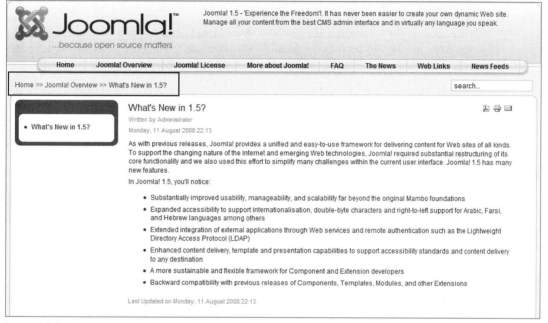

FIGURE 8-4

The links for Home and Joomla! Overview are both clickable, taking visitors back to those previous levels in the navigation hierarchy.

Take a look at the configuration screen for the Breadcrumbs module. If you have the sample data installed, click on the Breadcrumbs module item, or click on the New button and choose Breadcrumbs from the list. A configuration screen like that shown in Figure 8-5 appears.

 The left side of the screen shows parameters that are the same for every module you'll ever configure — they all have these same options. The right side of the screen varies with the individual module.

Starting on the left side of the screen are the following options:

➤ **Title** is what might show up on the top of the module, if you have enabled the title to show. Back in Figure 8-1, the text Latest News was on top of a bulleted list of items. Latest News is an example of a title. In this case, the title is set to Breadcrumbs. You must enter something in the Title field.

➤ **Show Title** asks whether the title should show on the web page. Note that the Breadcrumbs title is set to Yes, but you don't see Breadcrumbs as a title on the site. That's because the template is configured such that module titles don't show in that particular module position. You find out more about that in Chapter 13, "Custom Templates."

➤ **Enabled** means the module is set to show up on the web page or not (essentially, published or unpublished).

➤ **Order** indicates in what order the modules should display for a given position. You can set order here, or you can set it in the Module Manager itself, using the "Netflix" style ordering arrows, which are just like the ones you saw in the Article Manager.

➤ **Access level** indicates whether the module should display for everyone (Public), registered users only (Registered), or author-level users and above (Special). You can learn more about access levels in Chapter 4.

➤ **Menu Assignment** options indicate on which pages the module should display. It can display on all pages, no page, or a selected set of pages from the list.

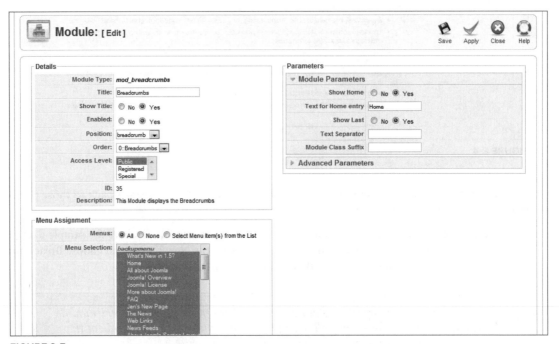

FIGURE 8-5

The right side of the screen offers parameters unique to the Breadcrumbs module. The following options appear under Module Parameters:

➤ **Show Home** refers to whether the word *home* should show up in the breadcrumb path. It does not refer to whether the breadcrumb should appear on the home page. You set that option in the Menu Assignment area.

➤ **Text for Home entry** refers to what text should appear where the word Home appears by default.

➤ **Show Last** indicates whether the last parameter in the breadcrumb path should show. In Figure 8-4, for example, the Show Last option would indicate whether What's New in 1.5 would show in the breadcrumb.

➤ **Text Separator** is some character or set of characters that separates each item in the breadcrumb list.

➤ **Module Class Suffix** has to do with CSS styling. Chapter 14, "Advanced Template and CSS Tricks" covers this topic.

In general, showing the Home link and keeping the text set to Home, as well as showing the last item in the breadcrumb path, is best. Most breadcrumbs on the web work this way, so not breaking that standard is best.

The Advanced Parameters contains a single item: whether the module should be cached. *Caching* means that a copy of the module in a given state is stored in Joomla, and it does not have to be calculated or created each time the page loads. This feature is handy if you have large amounts of traffic to your site. However, in general, most low-traffic sites can get away without caching. If your site is sluggish or overwhelmed with traffic, caching might be something to consider. (Or you might consider a new web host!)

The Latest News Module vs. the Newsflash Module

Although you may get the impression by their names that the Latest News and Newsflash have the same function, they actually do two different things.

Figure 8-6 shows both Latest News and Newsflash on the sample data home page.

FIGURE 8-6

The Newsflash module is located near the top of the page. It changes on refresh, rotating between a few articles.

The Latest News module is shown under the main navigation. It contains a bulleted list of article titles.

The Newsflash and Latest News modules are both in the sample data, and you can find them in the Module Manager in the top and user1 positions. Alternatively, you can create a new module for Latest News and another for Newsflash and see them in that way.

Newsflash

As shown in Figure 8-7, the Newsflash module displays one or several articles on the page. The "Randomly choose one article at a time" option makes this module a great candidate for a home page, because it rotates through some of the most recent news on the home page. Newsflash displays the introductory text in addition to the title and also displays a Read More link if you have it configured that way.

Take a look at the configuration screen for this module, shown in Figure 8-7. To get here, go to Extensions ➪ Module Manager, and then choose Newsflash from the list of modules.

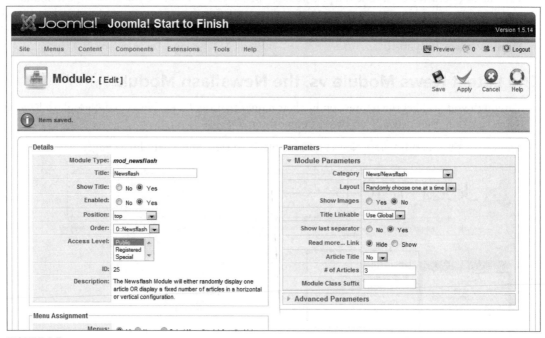

FIGURE 8-7

On the right side of the screen, look at the Module Parameters tab:

➤ **Category.** Choose the section/category pair from the drop-down menu. (Remember, you created sections and categories in Chapter 5.) This is the specific section and category from which Newsflash articles will come.

➤ **Layout.** You can lay your news items out horizontally, vertically, or they can randomly choose one from the list. Note that if you choose horizontal or vertical, the news articles will be laid out using tables.

➤ **Show Images.** Indicates whether images associated with the articles should be shown.

➤ **Title Linkable.** If you are showing the title for the articles, determines whether that title should link to the full version of the article.

➤ **Show last separator.** In between each article, an article separator appears in the HTML. You can style this separator, so that you could have a line or an image separating your articles. This option specifies whether the separator should appear after the last article on the list.

➤ **Read more... Link.** Determines whether the Read More... link at the end of the article shows or not. If you disable this option, you should show titles and make them linkable.

➤ **Article Title.** Determines whether the article title should display. Keep in mind this title is different from the module title, which you control on the left side of the configuration screen. Having the module title display, but not the article titles, and vice versa, is possible.

➤ **# of Articles.** Determines how many articles should display. If you've set Layout to "Randomly choose one at a time," then this field doesn't do anything — only one article appears.

➤ **Module Class Suffix.** This option has to do with CSS styling of the module and is covered in Chapter 14.

The Advanced Parameters area offers the same option for caching that is offered with the Breadcrumbs module. Remember that caching means that a copy of the module is stored for quick retrieval for some period of time (specified in the box), rather than creating the output of the module on-the-fly.

Latest News

The Latest News module displays a list of a configurable number of article titles, of a specific author, and from a specific section and category, if you choose. It can also just show the titles of the most recently published articles from anywhere on the site.

This type of functionality is great to show a series of titles, but it doesn't display any introductory text.

Figure 8-8 shows the Latest News configuration screen. To get here, go to Extensions ➪ Module Manager, and then select Latest News from the list.

The left side of the screen contains standard parameters, as described in "The Breadcrumbs Module" section. The right side of the screen contains the following parameters:

➤ **Count** indicates how many titles should show in the module.

➤ **Order** offers two choices. Recently Added First lists the article titles starting with the most recently created. Recently Modified First means that the most recently modified articles are listed first. A modified article is one that's been edited. This means that if you fix a typo in a two-year old article and your module is set to Recently Modified First, then this article would show first in the list.

➤ **Authors** lets you choose anyone as the author of the article, articles you added or modified, or articles you did not add or modify.

➤ **Front Page Articles** indicates whether articles that also show on the home page should also show in Latest News, or whether they should be hidden.

➤ **Section ID** means that you choose a given section to display. You will have to figure out its ID, a number you can find by going to the Section Manager (found under Content ➪ Section Manager). If you have more than one section you want to include, you can separate the numbers by commas. However, this method will mix up the articles within the different sections, still sorting options by the order.

➤ **Category ID** means that you choose a given category to display. You will have to figure out its ID, a number you can find by going to the Category Manager (under Content ➪ Category Manager). If you have more than one category you want to include, you can separate the numbers by commas. However, this will mix up the articles within the different sections, still sorting options by the order.

➤ **Module Class Suffix** is covered in Chapter 14.

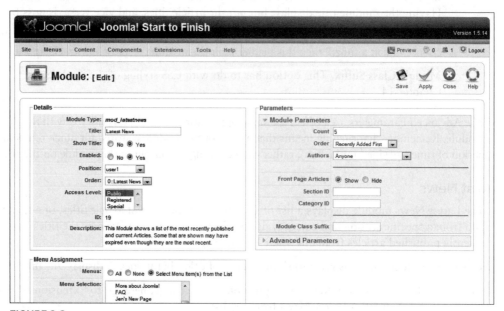

FIGURE 8-8

The Advanced Parameters area offers the same option for caching that is offered with the Breadcrumbs module. Remember that caching means that a copy of the module is stored for quick retrieval for some period of time (specified in the box), rather than creating the output of the module on-the-fly.

The Random Image Module

The Random Image module is a very handy addition to Joomla. Each time a page is loaded, the module chooses a random image from a given folder and displays it on the web site. The module does not rotate through the images, as a slideshow would (see the Appendix, which discusses how Front Page Slide Show is a great option for doing that).

To use the Random Image module effectively, your images should all have the same measurements. Depending on where you put the module, making the width and height of the images the same might make sense, or just making the width the same might work. If the width or height varies, note that content around the module may shift.

Unfortunately, the Random Image module does not offer the opportunity for an `alt` tag to be associated with the images, making this module somewhat less accessible than it could be. An `alt` tag is the text equivalent of the image. Therefore, using this module for a little "eye candy" on the web page — where it can show some pretty pictures that aren't really communicating a message that needs to be translated to text — probably makes most sense.

Figure 8-9 shows the Random Image module configuration screen, which you access by choosing Extensions ⇨ Module Manager, then selecting the New button followed by Random Image from the list.

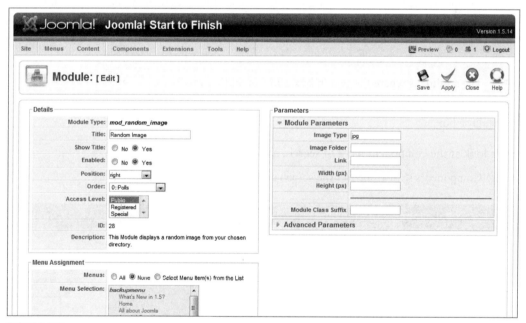

FIGURE 8-9

The right side of the configuration screen offers the following options:

➤ **Image Type.** The images should all have the same type of extension, either JPG, GIF, or PNG.

➤ **Image Folder.** This is the relative path to where the images exist in the site, somewhere in your images/stories folder, most likely. (If you'd like to give this a try, enter images/stories/fruit, which will direct the module to look in the fruit folder for some sample images. Be sure to set the image type to JPG as well.)

➤ **Link.** You can create a single link where all images link to the same location. This link can be relative or absolute.

➤ **Width (px)** and **Height (px).** These measurements should be the width and/or height of your images in pixels, respectively. If you have the same width but different heights, or the same height but different widths, specify the constant dimension only. As stated before, I recommend keeping at least one dimension constant.

➤ **Module Class Suffix** is explained in Chapter 14.

The Advanced Parameters area is as described previously.

The Search Module

The Search module, of course, is the little search box that visitors can use to search your web site. Search is an important module to include as your web site grows larger. If your site contains more than 50 pages, it should include a search, as some users prefer to use search to navigate the site for information. If your site is smaller than that, use your best judgment about whether it's really required for the site. You might consider how fast the site is growing, how often new content is added, and how often the site is being updated.

Search has two pieces in Joomla generally important to configuration:

➤ The **module** is where the search box appears on the web page.

➤ The **component** tracks what people searched for on the site — what they typed into the little box.

Take a look at the component piece of search, and then look at the module.

Choose Components ➪ Search, and the screen shown in Figure 8-10 appears.

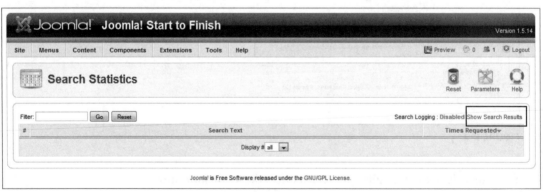

FIGURE 8-10

Currently, search results logging is turned off. This is the default, as logging what people are searching for is resource-intensive. Click on Parameters, in the upper right, and set Gather Search Statistics to Yes. Show Created Date, the other option, shows the created date for the articles in the search result if set to Show. Figure 8-11 shows these parameters.

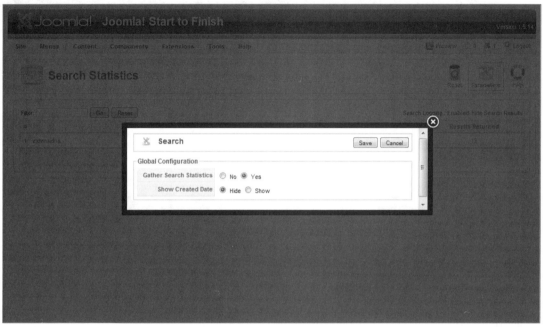

FIGURE 8-11

After someone has done a search, you'll see the keyword(s) the person entered, how many times it was requested, and how many results match, as shown in Figure 8-12.

FIGURE 8-12

Now return to the Search module, via Extensions ➪ Module Manager, as shown in Figure 8-13.

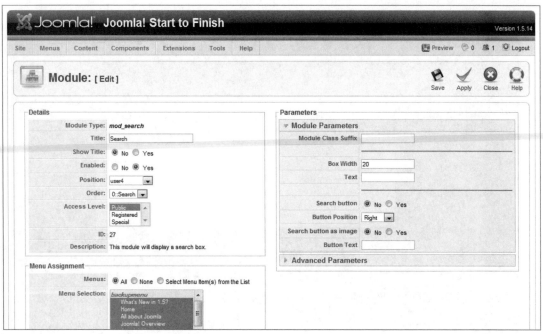

FIGURE 8-13

The parameters on the right side of the screen are as follows:

➤ **Module Class Suffix** is explained in Chapter 14.

➤ **Box Width** refers to the width of the search box. You can make the box larger or smaller by changing the number. Unfortunately, no matter how wide you make the box, only the first 20 characters are used in search. This limitation is hard coded into Joomla and requires several modifications to core code to change.

➤ **Text** is the text that appears inside of the search box. By default, that text is pulled from the language files.

➤ **Search button** indicates whether a button should show up next to the box. If you do not include a button, the user must know to press Enter to make a search happen. Including a search button is generally considered more usable and accessible.

➤ **Button Position** determines whether the button should appear to the right or left of the search box. For languages written left to right, like English, put the search button to the right of the box.

➤ **Search button as image** indicates whether the button is driven by HTML or whether it should be a clickable image. If you want an image button, you must first create it in an image processing program such as Adobe Photoshop or GIMP. Save the image as searchButton.gif and upload it into the images directory, into the folder called M_images. Unfortunately, if you upload this button via the Media Manager, it will rename the image searchbutton.gif, which is not the same name (capitalization counts!). You must FTP the image to the correct location on your web server to maintain the capitalization.

➤ **Button Text** is the text that will appear on the search button if you make an HTML button (that is, you don't include a button as an image).

The Advanced Parameters area offers the same option for caching that is offered with the Breadcrumbs module.

The Custom HTML Module

The Custom HTML module is one of the most useful modules in Joomla. What does it do? Pretty much anything you want! It's like a little article, in that it gives you a big box in which to type text and include links, images, and so on.

This module does not exist by default in the sample data, so create one from the Module Manager by following these steps:

1. Click the New button; the screen shown in Figure 8-3 appears.

2. Choose Custom HTML from the list by clicking on the title (or, alternatively, by selecting the radio button and clicking the Next button at the top right).

   Note that if you mouse over the text, text appears describing each of these modules.

3. In the screen that appears, as shown in Figure 8-14, you get to do whatever you want! Treat it as an article that can show up anywhere on your screen.

Having said this, keep any text short, because the text in modules typically highlights something on the page; drives the user's interest to another part of the site; or supplements information for a given article, section, or category. If what you have to say is long enough, consider making it into an article all on its own.

EMBEDDING MODULES IN ARTICLES

Modules are wonderful, but they are constrained to a module position on the web page. What if you want a module to appear in the middle of an article? Sometimes it can work quite well — think random images, donation buttons, and so forth.

Fortunately, Joomla has this functionality built in via the Load Module plug-in. See Chapter 10 for more about plug-ins, and about how this plug-in is specifically configured. For now, follow these steps for including a module in your article:

1. Create the module of interest. Assign it a unique position, such as *inset*, which causes the module to be set into the page. Assign the module to the page of interest. In this case, I've created a Random Image module, as shown in Figure 8-15. I'm planning on placing it in the What's New in 1.5 page on the site.

FIGURE 8-14

FIGURE 8-15

2. Create the article, or choose the article from the list in the Article Manager (under Content ⇨ Article Manager). Where you want the module to appear, include the following piece of code:

```
{loadposition inset}
```

where `loadposition` loads the module position, and `inset` is the name of the module position, which you already assigned to the module in the Module Manager. This is shown in Figure 8-16.

Provided the module is assigned the same position that's called in the article `loadposition` statement, and provided the module is assigned to that page, the module should show up in the middle of the article, as shown in Figure 8-17.

CONFIGURING ADMINISTRATOR MODULES

Seldom modified, but potentially quite handy, are the administrator modules. To this point, this chapter has addressed web site modules, modules that show up on the front end of the web site. But how about modules that show up on the back end?

Go to the Module Manager, and at the top left, choose Administrator instead of Site, as shown in Figure 8-18.

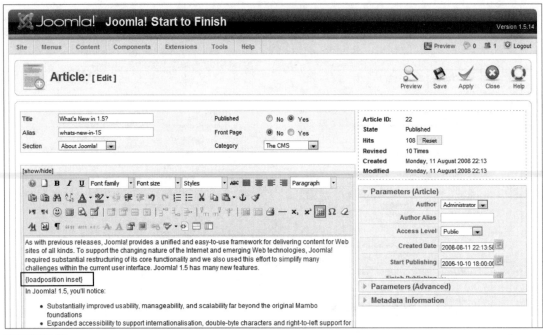

FIGURE 8-16

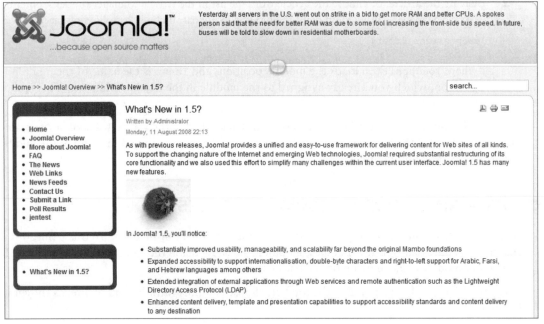

FIGURE 8-17

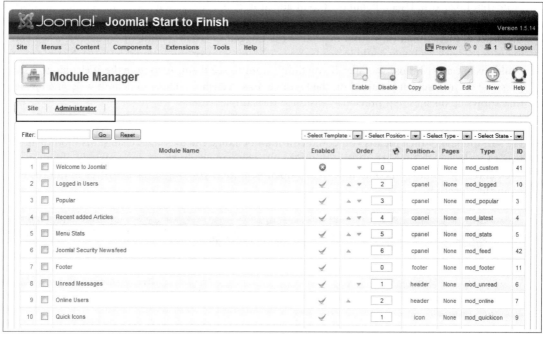

FIGURE 8-18

These modules drive the functionality within the Joomla administrator screens.

Most useful are the first few items, with the position of cPanel. These modules correspond with the accordion menu on the right of the back end control panel, as shown in Figure 8-19.

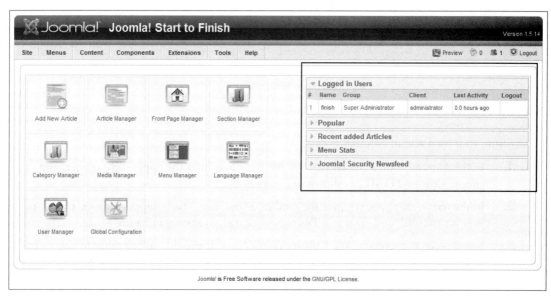

FIGURE 8-19

Note that Logged In Users, Popular, Recent added Articles, Menu Stats, and the Joomla! Security Newsfeed all correspond to modules here in the Administrator Module Manager. You could rearrange the order of these modules, so that instead of the Logged In Users coming up by default when you log into the back end, you could instead see your Menu Stats or the Joomla! Security Newsfeed. You could disable any of those modules if you didn't want to see them. Also note the Welcome to Joomla! Message on your screen (disabled on the Figure 8-16 screenshot). This is a default welcome message that shows up on sites that previously installed the sample data.

If you look at Figure 8-20 closely, you'll see that the Welcome to Joomla! message is a Custom HTML module, which means you could edit it and change the message. Using this module is a great way to include tech support information for your company right there, immediately obvious, in the back end of Joomla. You could link to any documentation you might have written about the site from that location.

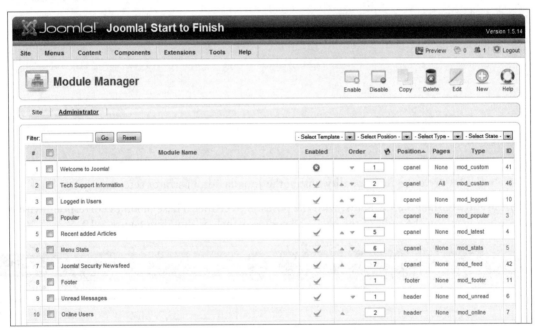

FIGURE 8-20

Creating your own admin modules is easy:

1. In the Admin Module Manager, click the New button in the upper-right corner, and then choose Custom HTML, as shown in Figure 8-21.

2. In the screen that appears, give the module a title, like "Tech Support Information," make sure it's enabled, and set it to a Position of cPanel, as shown in Figure 8-22.

3. Scroll down the screen to the Custom Output box. It should look familiar to you — it's the same box you use for inputting articles, and it's the same box you use for custom HTML modules for the front end of the web site.

FIGURE 8-21

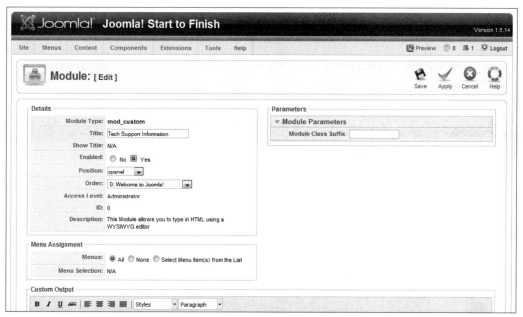

FIGURE 8-22

4. Enter some of your tech support information in this box, as shown in Figure 8-23.

FIGURE 8-23

5. Click the Save button in the upper-right corner.

Now go to the main menu and choose Site ➪ Control Panel and see what you get, as shown in Figure 8-24.

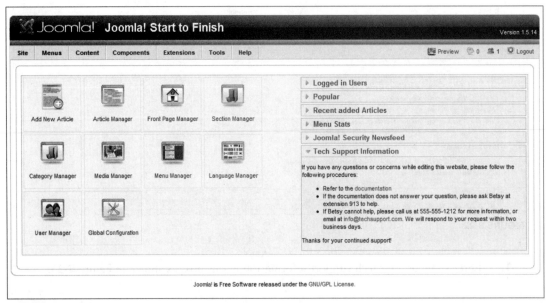

FIGURE 8-24

Note that, in this example, the module showed up at the bottom of the cPanel list of modules. You could reorder the modules in the Admin Module Manager and make it the first module on the list. Doing so would make it appear open when one arrived at the control panel for the back end of the web site.

In general, do *not* change too many of these admin modules! You could do some damage or disable needed functionality. Tread carefully, and if you're not sure what you're doing, don't do it.

Components That Come with Joomla!

WHAT'S IN THIS CHAPTER?

➤ Configuring contacts

➤ Configuring web links

➤ Configuring polls

➤ Configuring banners

A component is another type of extension. A component exists in the same area of the web page where the articles also go. Only one component can exist on each page.

Other components, such as banners and polls, are configured under the component menu. This is where you enter data about the poll or choose the banner images to display. Their display, however, happens via a module.

This chapter covers some of the most commonly used components that come with Joomla. Many other components are available for download. I list some commonly used third-party components in the Appendix, "Jen's Favorite Joomla! Extensions."

CONTACTS

The Contacts component provides an easy way to display contact information, including a contact form, about a given person, people, or an institution, on a web site.

The Contacts component is also excellent for quickly and easily adding a "Contact Us" page to a web site. The pre-programmed form lets site visitors complete a name, e-mail address, subject, and message, all of which are e-mailed to an address of the listed contact.

Figure 9-1 shows a typical contact page.

FIGURE 9-1

One of the major drawbacks to this contact form is that you cannot easily add more fields to the form. For example, if you want to collect the visitor's address and phone number, in addition to the default information, no straightforward way exists to add those fields to this form and make them connect with the PHP script that drives the form. If you want any fields that deviate from what Contacts offers, you are better off downloading a form-building component (see the Appendix for recommendations) and configuring it for your exact needs.

Another major drawback to the Contacts component is the abysmal HTML with nested tables that drives its layout. You should look into template overrides to clean up the HTML for this form. These are discussed in Chapter 14.

Configuring the Contacts Component

To configure the Contacts component, do the following.

Log in to the back end of Joomla and go to Components ⇨ Contacts ⇨ Categories, where you will find the Contact Category Manager. You must first create a category for your contact before you can create the contact. All individual contacts must be associated with a category, even if there's only one contact on your site.

To create a new category, click the New button in the upper-right corner of the Contact Category Manager. The Category [New] screen appears, as shown in Figure 9-2.

Items in this screen should be familiar to you, because this manager is very similar to an article's Section and Category Managers.

FIGURE 9-2

At a minimum, enter a title to create a category. Click Save to save this new category. Now, go to Components ➪ Contacts ➪ Contacts, or click the Contacts link in the submenu at the top of the Contact Category Manager.

At the top of the Contact Manager, click the New button to create a new contact. The Contact [New] screen appears, as shown in Figure 9-3.

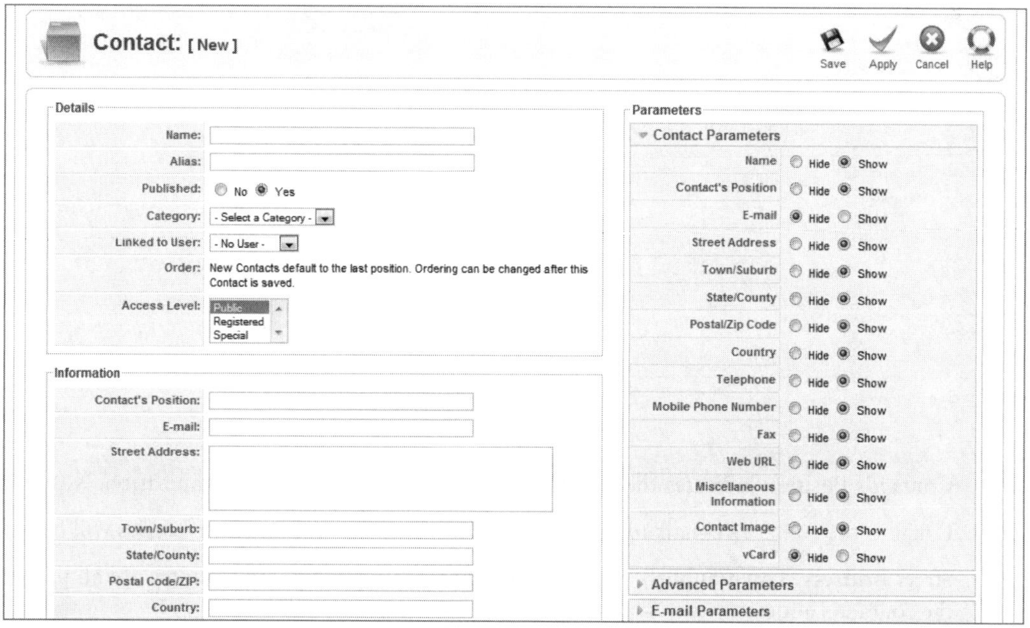

FIGURE 9-3

The minimum information required to create a contact includes Name and Category. All the other fields are not required. However, to show a contact form, you must also enter an e-mail address. If you do not include an e-mail address, the form will not show up on the page, even if you set it to display by clicking Show in the Parameters section.

Starting on the left side of the screen, under Details:

➤ **Name** is the contact's name. It also becomes the page title.

➤ **Alias** is used for search engine–friendly URLs with some configurations (see Chapter 4). Enter an alias for the name if you want.

➤ **Published** indicates whether this contact is able to show up on the web site or not.

➤ **Linked to User** is for linking a Joomla user to the specific contact, if you want.

➤ **Order** indicates the order in which the contacts will display in a category contact layout.

➤ **Access Level** indicates whether this contact is for the general public (public), registered users and higher (Registered), or Authors and higher (Special).

Scroll down to the lower-left side of the screen, in the Information block (see Figure 9-4).

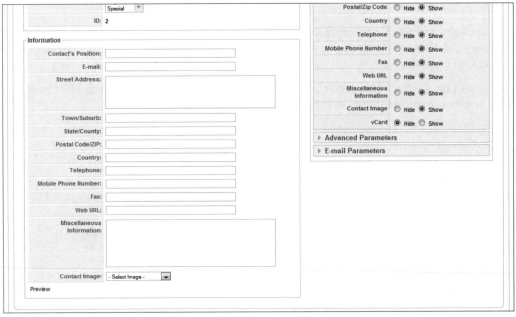

FIGURE 9-4

➤ **Contact's Position** indicates the contact's job title or position in the organization.

➤ **E-mail** is the contact's e-mail address. This is also where any contact form entries will be sent.

➤ **Street Address, Town/Suburb, State/County, Postal Code/ZIP,** and **Country** are all parts of the contact's address.

➤ **Telephone, Mobile Phone,** and **Fax** are all phone numbers that you may enter for the contact. There is no specific format required for entering numbers; that is, (555) 555-1212, 555-555-1212, and 555.555.1212 are all legitimate. However, if you're entering more than one phone number, such as both telephone and cell, typing all numbers in the same format for consistency on the web page is strongly recommended. If a contact has two telephone numbers, both may be typed in the same box and they will display on the page.

➤ **Web URL** is for including a URL. Make sure it is an absolute URL to the location, not a relative URL. If you do not put http:// in front of the URL, Joomla adds it for you. When clicked, this link will automatically opens the page in a new window.

➤ **Miscellaneous Information** is where you can enter any additional information you want about this particular contact. You may enter HTML in this field, and the HTML will be rendered on the site without being stripped out. This feature is helpful for including line breaks and spacing in the text in this particular field.

➤ **Contact Image** is for any image or photo you want to associate with this contact. The photo will display on the right side of the page. In Figure 9-1, this image is the "powered by Joomla" logo. When you upload an image for this contact, you must do it through the Media Manager. Upload the image to the images/stories folder (see Chapter 4 for more information).

Now take a look at the right side of the screen. Under Parameters, note the Contact Parameters section, as shown in Figure 9-5.

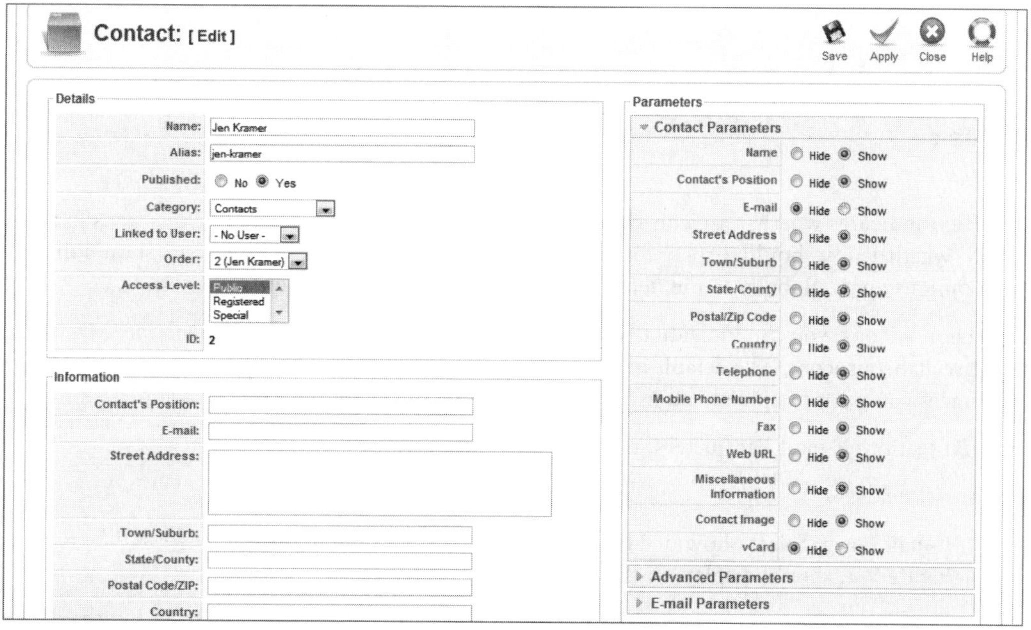

FIGURE 9-5

The Contact Parameters are a series of Hide/Show options for each of the items in the Information (lower left) section of this page. By default, E-mail and vCard are hidden, whereas all other items are set to show. vCard is the only option not covered in the Information section. A *vCard* is a format for importing a contact to a contact database, such as Microsoft Outlook.

Advanced Parameters are shown in Figure 9-6.

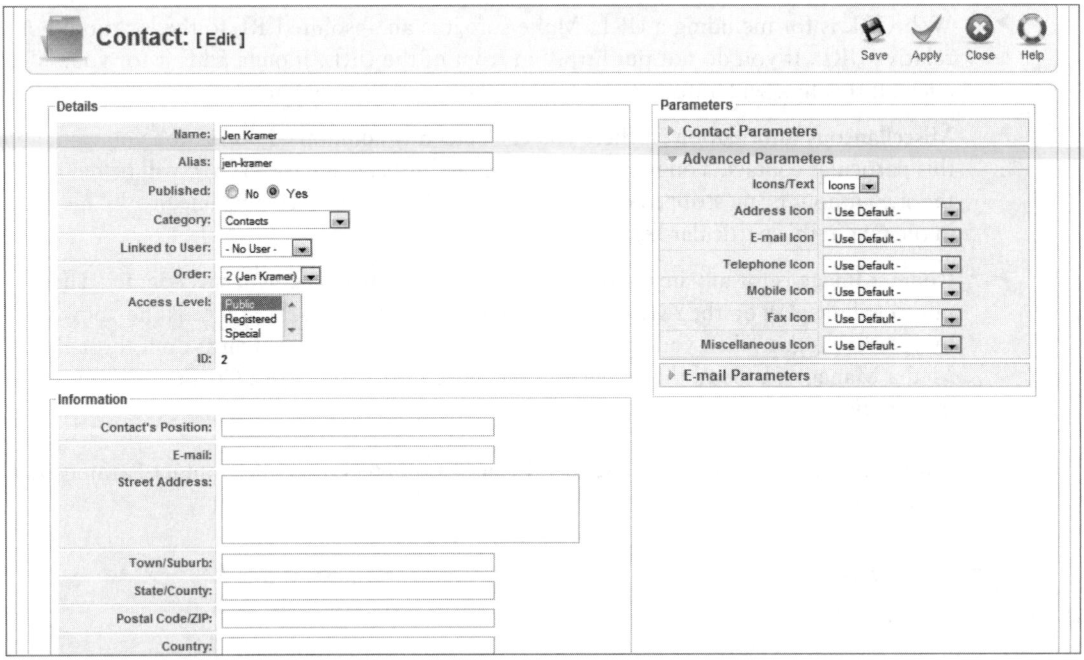

FIGURE 9-6

Icons/Text indicates whether an icon should appear on the page next to each of the items in this section, whether text should display instead, or whether neither of these indicators should display. These options apply globally to the fields listed in the Advanced Parameters section.

If you choose Icons, you can individually set those icons via Address, E-mail, Telephone, Mobile, Fax, and Miscellaneous icons. The default images are stored in the Media Manager in images/M_images. Any images you want to upload and use instead should be stored in that same location.

The final section, E-mail Parameters, is shown in Figure 9-7.

Here are its fields:

➤ **E-mail Form.** Select Show or Hide to indicate whether an e-mail contact form, like the one in Figure 9-1, should display on the page.

➤ **Description Text.** This field exists in the administrator screen, and it is stored in the database. However, oddly enough, this field never actually displays anywhere in any of the contacts views for the web site. I recommend you skip over this field.

➤ **E-mail Copy.** Select the Show radio button so that a copy of the message is sent to the email address entered as well as to the recipient.

➤ **Banned E-Mail, Banned Subject,** and **Banned Text.** Use these options to ban any e-mail address, subject, or text in the e-mail that contains specific words. Separate the words with a semicolon.

FIGURE 9-7

When you are done configuring the contact, click the Save button in the upper-right corner. The Contact Manager appears again.

Setting Contacts Parameters

Similar to articles (described in Chapter 5, "In the Beginning There Was Content), contacts also have parameters and a global system for setting and overriding them. The preceding section just described how to set up those parameters in an individual contact.

In the Contact Manager, notice the Parameters button in the upper right, as shown in Figure 9-8. When you click this button, you see the Global Configurations for contacts appears, as shown in Figure 9-9.

The Icons/Text area should be familiar to you, as should Enable vCard, Banned E-mail, Banned Subject, and Banned Text, further down on the page. You set these options for a single contact previously, but the Global Configuration allows you to set these options for multiple contacts at once.

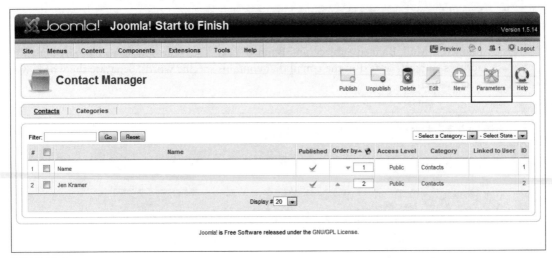

FIGURE 9-8

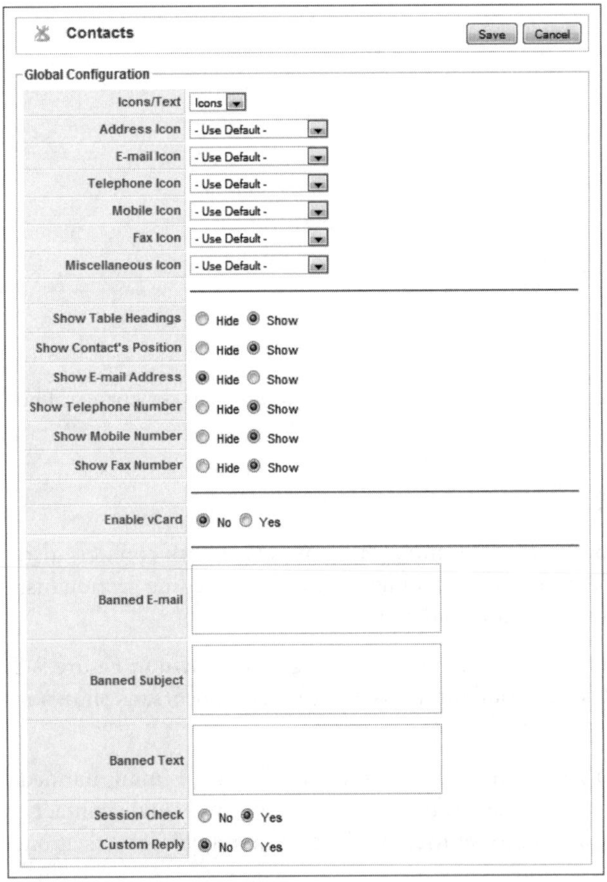

FIGURE 9-9

The second area, where you set preferences for showing/hiding table headings, contact position, and so on, has to do with the display as a Contact Category, not for the individual items in each contact listing. You learn how to link contacts to the menu in the next section.

Session check indicates that the form should check to see whether the visitor who completed the form had been to other pages on the site previously, including to the contact page itself. This is a way of reducing spam, as it's possible to submit the form without visiting the site.

Custom reply is a way of disabling the message that's generated when the form is submitted. If you are doing some custom programming, you might want to do this. Otherwise, don't change the setting, as your form will have no point — the visitor would fill it out, click Submit, and the contents would be lost immediately.

Linking a Contact to a Menu

Now that you've created at least one category and one contact (or you're working with the sample data), you can explore the options for making contacts appear on the web site.

Choose Menus ⇨ Main Menu (or any other menu of your choice). Click the New button in the upper right, and then choose Contacts from the list, as shown in Figure 9-10.

FIGURE 9-10

You have two choices:

➤ The **Contact Category Layout** displays a table of contacts, including some (but not necessarily all) of their contact information. Clicking through a link takes you to a page with their full listing. This feature is great if you have a number of people in a department, or a list of generic contacts in certain departments.

➤ The **Standard Contact Layout** displays a single listing on the page. This layout is great for a "Contact Us" page, if you want to display general organization information and direct the contact form to a generic address, such as info@mycompany.com.

Contact Category Layout

Figure 9-11 shows the screen for configuring the Contact Category Layout.

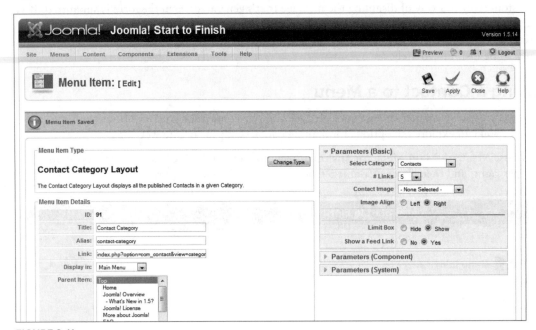

FIGURE 9-11

This section covers the settings on the right side of this screen. If you need help configuring the left side of the screen, which is the same for all types of menu items, refer to Chapter 6, "Menus."

The following options appear under the Parameters (Basic) tab:

➤ **Select Category.** Select a category from the list.

➤ **# Links.** Use this option to set how many links you want displayed on the page, before a visitor has to go to another page to see the rest of the choices. If you select "all" in this list, all contacts will appear on a single page, without any pagination.

➤ **Contact Image.** For this specific page (not the individual contacts), use this option to display an image from the list. You should upload the image to images/stories.

➤ **Image Align.** Aligns the image to the left or right side of the page.

➤ **Limit Box.** If you have more contacts than specified in # Links, the Limit Box option allows the list to expand to show more links.

➤ **Show a Feed Link.** This option displays a feed link on the page if specified.

Figure 9-12 shows how a Contact Category List looks with six contacts, with # Links set to 5 and Limit Box set to Show. The Limit Box is the Display # drop-down menu at the upper right of the table. The pagination on the bottom is present regardless of whether the Limit Box is set to Show.

FIGURE 9-12

Note the order of the contacts in this figure — there doesn't seem to be any! That's because contacts are always ordered by their list position in the Contact Manager. For example, if you want Jen Kramer to appear at the top of the list, you would need to use the ordering arrows to put her in that position.

Back to the menu configuration, take a look at the Parameters (Component) options, as shown in Figure 9-13.

If these items look familiar, it's because you've seen them at least twice. These are all the same options you saw in the Parameters screen from the Contact Manager. They override any of those Parameters settings for this one menu item. Pay special attention, though, to the second group of items, Show Table Headings, and so on. These options control which items will display in the table on the page, not in the individual contact listings. If you do not want to show the contact's position, for example, set this option to Hide, and that column will not appear on the Contact Category Layout page on the front end of the site. It will show up, however, in the individual contact listing, unless you've disabled it there.

Finally, the Parameters (System) options were described in Chapter 6.

Save your menu item by clicking the Save button, and then check the front end of the site to make sure everything appears as it should.

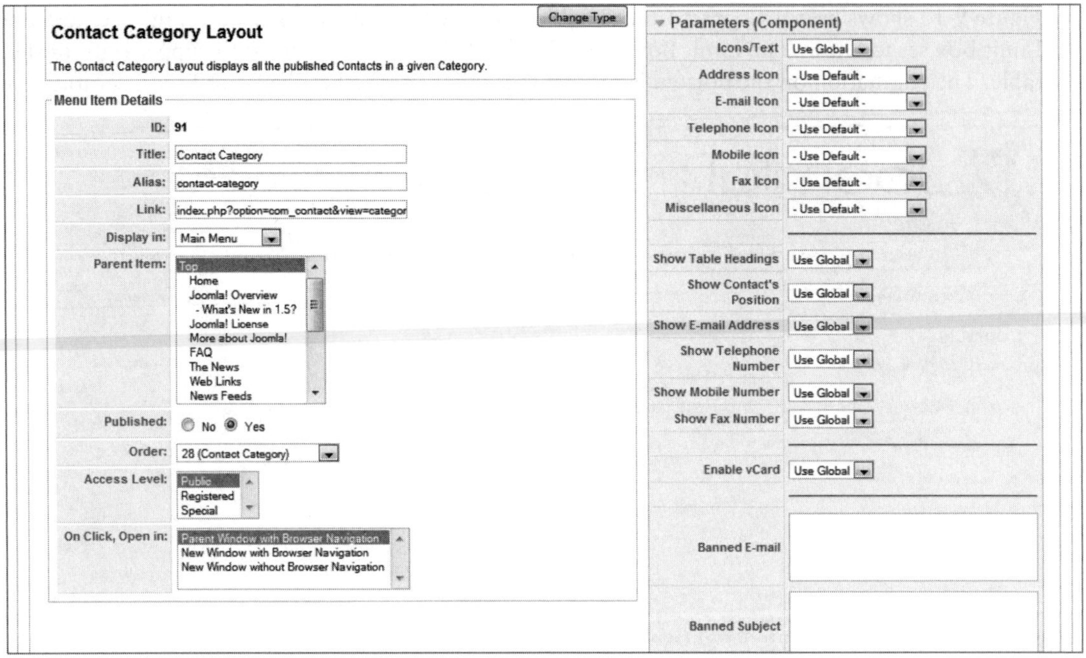

FIGURE 9-13

Standard Contact Layout

The Standard Contact Layout provides a link to a single contact's information. Figure 9-14 shows the screen for configuring the Standard Contact Layout.

This section covers the settings on the right side of this screen. If you need help configuring the left side of the screen, which is the same for all types of menu items, refer to Chapter 6.

The following options appear under the Parameters (Basic) tab:

➤ **Select Contact.** Select the contact to which you wish to directly link.

➤ **Dropdown.** This displays a dropdown of other contacts in the upper right corner of the screen. For a single contact page, I would recommend against using this, as it could be confusing to a visitor.

➤ **Show the Category in Breadcrumbs.** This will display the contact's category as part of the breadcrumb trail. If there is a single contact on the web site, I recommend against using this feature. Clicking the category name in the breadcrumb trail will take you to a Contact Category Layout page.

The Parameters (Component) and Parameters (System) options were described in the Contact Category Layout section and are configured in the same way.

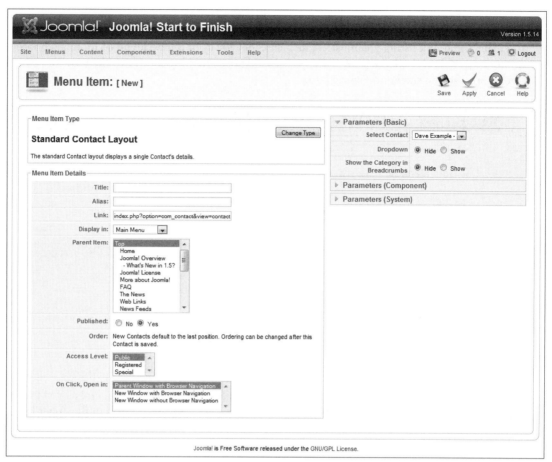

FIGURE 9-14

WEB LINKS

The Web Links component enables you to categorize and create links to other web sites. It is a good resource to use when you have many off-site links to include on your web site. Rather than having an article containing a laundry list of links, the Web Links component allows those links to be categorized and displayed in a more attractive manner. For example, you might use Web Links on an educational site, where you might want a list of links to reference materials or more information. It's also a great resource when you want registered users to contribute to a bank of links to other web sites.

You use the Web Links component to assign each link to a category. You can then display all of your categories or all the links within a category. You can include a description for each link if you want. Users who are logged in might also be allowed to submit more links for inclusion into the site.

Creating a Web Link Category

To create a web link listing you must create a category for it. In the back end of Joomla, choose Components ⇨ Web Links ⇨ Categories; you should see something similar to the Category Manager [Web Links] screen shown in Figure 9-15.

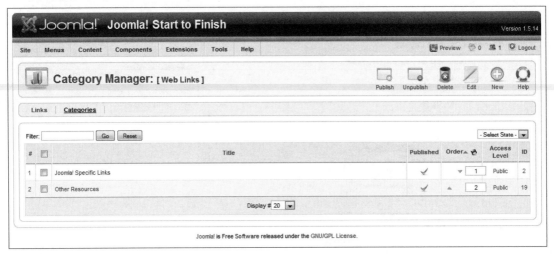

FIGURE 9-15

This screen is similar to many of the other category screens you've seen before, and as you might expect, it works the same way. To create a new category, click the New button in the upper right. The Category [New] screen appears, as shown in Figure 9-16.

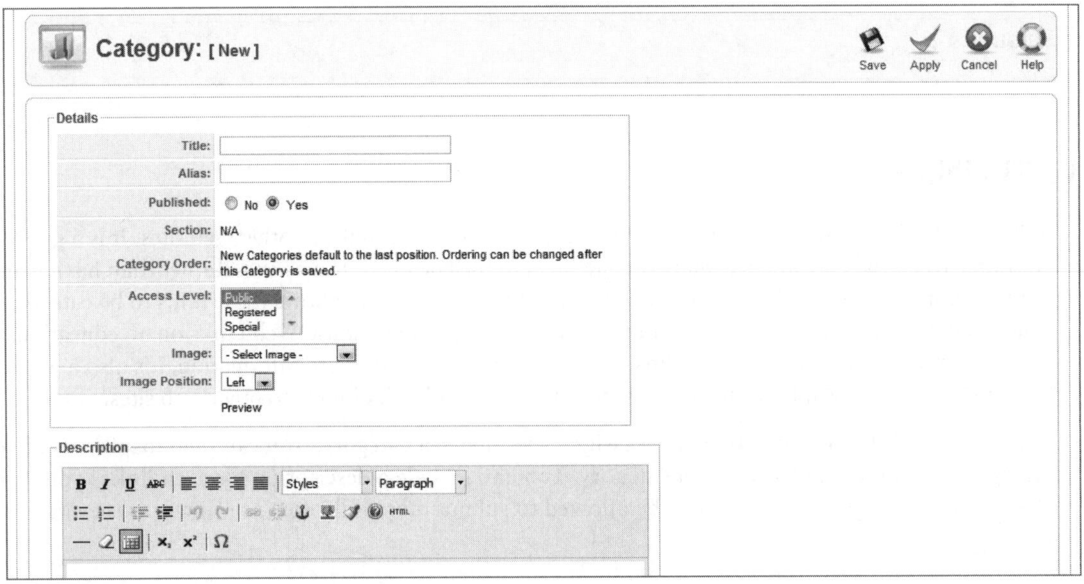

FIGURE 9-16

You must give the category a title. All other items are optional. As you've seen before, you can assign a picture to the category, as well as a description. Click Save when you are done here.

Creating a Web Link

After you've created at least one category, you can create a link in the Web Link Manager via Components ⇨ Web Links ⇨ Links, or via the Links link in the upper left, next to Categories, as shown in Figure 9-17.

FIGURE 9-17

To create a link, click the New button in the upper right. Alternatively, click on the link title (if you have the sample data installed) to see how a particular link is configured. Either way, the resulting screen looks like Figure 9-18.

The following options are available for configuration.

➤ **Name** is the name that will show up in the web links listing.

➤ **Alias** may be used in the web address for this page.

➤ **Published** indicates whether the link is able to show up on the site (yes) or not (no).

➤ **Category** refers to the categories you just created in the Web Links Category Manager. You must assign each link a category.

➤ **URL** is the URL for the link, which should start with http://.

➤ **Order** is the order of links in the list. You can also reorder links in the Web Link Manager via the Ordering column.

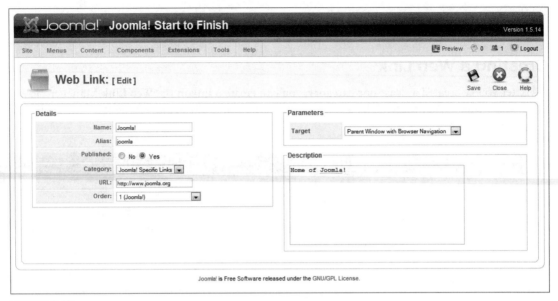

FIGURE 9-18

➤ **Target** indicates whether the link should open in the same window as your Joomla site (parent window with browser navigation), in a new window or tab (new window with browser navigation), or in a pop-up window (new window without browser navigation).

I recommend your offsite links go to the new window with browser navigation. Opening links that go offsite in a new window will keep your client's site open in a separate window or tab, so the visitor can return to the site later. Browser navigation refers to the Back, Home, Forward, and Refresh buttons commonly grouped together in a toolbar in the browser. If you open without browser navigation, you typically open a popup window, which generally is missing this toolbar in its display. Note, too, that you can configure the Target setting globally, which I cover in just a moment.

➤ **Description** is a description of this link. Although no editor is associated with this box, you can include HTML tags if you want.

When you're done, click the Save button to save your new link and return to the Web Link Manager.

Web Link Parameters

At the top of the Web Link Manager screen (Components ➪ Web Links ➪ Links), look for the button for Parameters, as shown in Figure 9-19.

Click this link and you will get the Parameters configuration screen, as shown in Figure 9-20, where you can globally set several web link parameters. I've also tagged some of the below items with its display on the front end in Figure 9-21, which shows the Category List Layout option for web links.

➤ **Description.** Use this option to show or hide the description shown in the Web Links Introduction box.

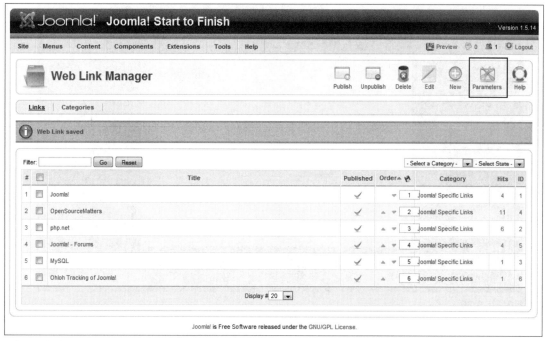

FIGURE 9-19

➤ **Web Links Introduction.** This introductory text shows up in the Web Link Category List. If you state the Description should show but do not put any text in this box, the following text appears by default:

We are regularly out on the Web. When we find a great site we list it.

If you do not want that text to show, and you don't want your own text to show either, set Description to Hide.

➤ **Hits.** This shows in the Category List Layout. This is a column indicating how many people have clicked on a particular link (1 in Figure 9-21).

➤ **Link Descriptions.** In the Category List Layout, this option displays a short description for each link (2 in Figure 9-21).

➤ **Other Categories.** In the Category List Layout, this option determines whether a bulleted list of categories should display underneath the web links table, as shown in 3 in Figure 9-21.

➤ **Table Headings.** In the Category List Layout, this option determines whether the table of links should have headings on the top for Web Link, Hits, and so on (4 in Figure 9-21).

➤ **Target.** This indicates whether the link should open in the same window as your Joomla site (parent window with browser navigation), in a new window or tab (new window with browser navigation), or in a pop-up window (new window without browser navigation).

➤ **Icon.** Use this option to set which image should show up on the Category List Layout page, if any (in Figure 9-21, the >> symbol, shown near 5).

FIGURE 9-20

FIGURE 9-21

Linking Web Links to a Menu

The Web Links component offers three layout options. To see them, go to Menus and choose the menu where you want to make the link (in this example, Main Menu). Click the New button in the upper right, and then choose Web Links. You'll get a screen similar to Figure 9-22.

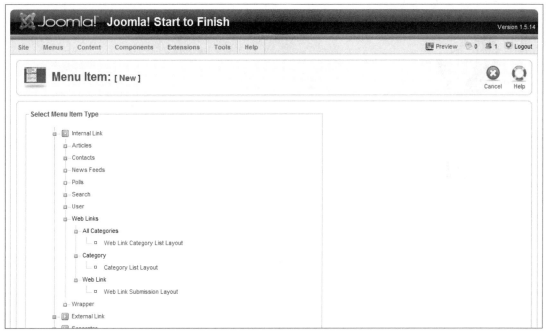

FIGURE 9-22

The Web Link Category List Layout produces a bulleted list of the categories for links, with how many links per category in parentheses after the name (see Figure 9-23).

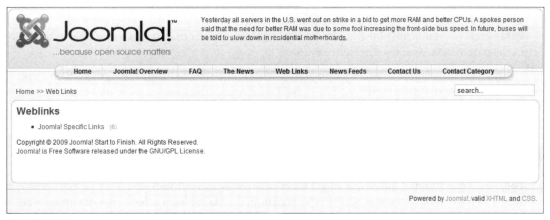

FIGURE 9-23

The Category List Layout lists all web links in a given category. You also get this view after selecting a category from the Web Link Category List Layout, as shown in Figure 9-24.

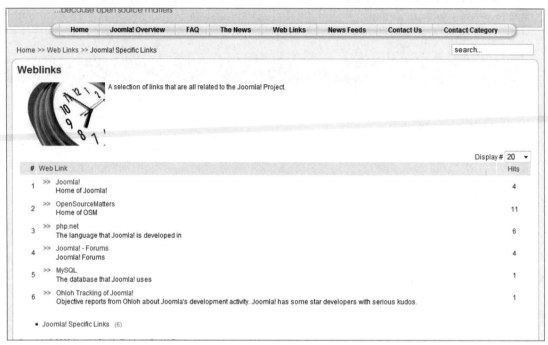

FIGURE 9-24

The final option, Web Link Submission Layout, links to a form for your front-end registered users so that they can submit a link suggestion, as shown in Figure 9-25. Note that this form is specifically for registered users. If you leave the menu setting to Public instead of Registered, the link will show, but users must log in to get the form.

All three of these layouts have exactly the same parameter sets. The Parameters (Basic) section has no options. Parameters (System) offers the same options already covered several times in the book. Parameters (Component) contains the same parameter settings that are also available in the Web Links parameters, as shown in Figure 9-26.

As you have seen before in other parameters settings (like Article Parameters), these Web Links parameters are the global settings. The individual menu settings override the global settings, and the individual link settings override both the menu and the global settings.

POLLS

Polls are a popular and quick way to get users engaged with your web site. They're most commonly seen and rotated on news sites, but they're occasionally available on other types of sites as well.

FIGURE 9-25

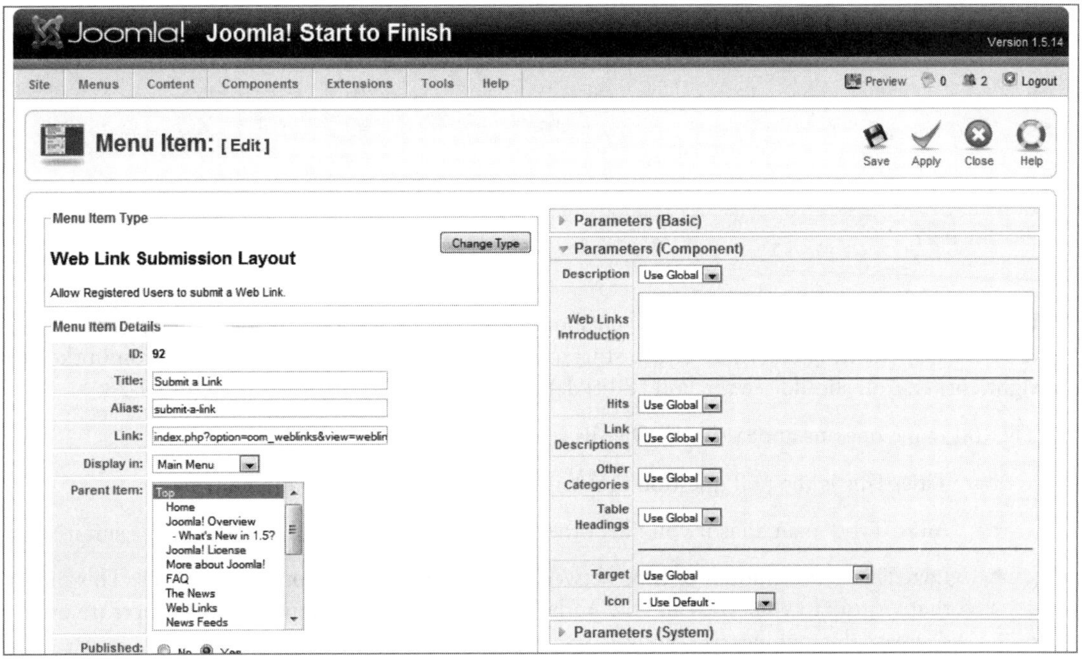

FIGURE 9-26

Remember that a poll is purely for fun. Respondents to a poll are self-selecting: They chose to visit your site, and they chose to vote. Results from these polls should not be extrapolated to what "everyone" thinks as a result. For example, polls that deal with politics frequently get skewed due to left-wing and right-wing web sites organizing their members to vote a certain way in the poll.

So, although polls are great fun, don't draw any big conclusions from the results! They're useful as a pulse of what people are thinking about today, and they're useful for engaging users.

The Joomla Polls component comes in two pieces:

➤ The **component** piece is where the poll question and its answers are configured.

➤ A **module** determines where that poll appears on the web site.

Configuring the Polls Component

To configure a poll question, choose Components ➪ Polls. The Poll Manager screen appears, as shown in Figure 9-27.

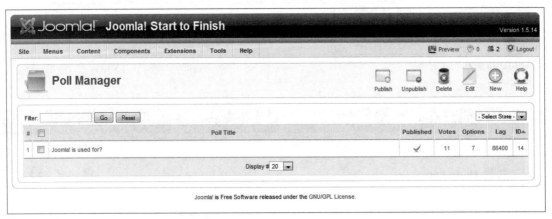

FIGURE 9-27

If you have the sample data installed, you should see a poll question already in place. You can edit it by clicking the title. Alternatively, to start a new poll question, click the New button in the upper-right corner. You should see the Poll [Edit] details and options, as shown in Figure 9-28.

The following options appear in the Details section:

➤ **Title.** This is the poll question that will appear on your web page.

➤ **Alias.** Type in an alias if you like; otherwise, leave it blank and Joomla will assign it.

➤ **Lag.** This is the amount of time between votes. 86400 is 24 hours, in seconds. This means that visitors to your site can vote in the poll once every 24 hours. You can increase or decrease this number as you like.

➤ **Published.** This setting indicates whether the poll can be displayed on your site.

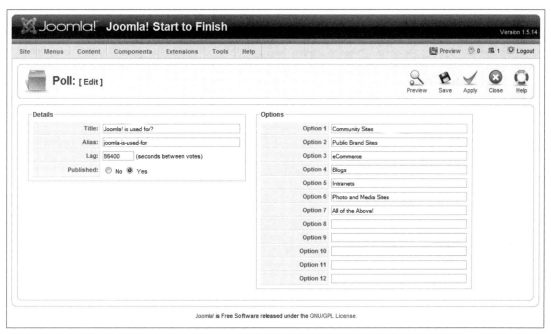

FIGURE 9-28

The right side of the screen contains an Options area, which are the potential answers to the poll question. It contains 12 blanks, so you can offer up to 12 options in your poll. Remember that you can only choose a single option for a poll answer, not several options, so if you want to offer "all of the above," you'll need to make it an option.

Just because there are 12 blanks does not mean you need to fill them all! I recommend you keep your poll to four choices or fewer. If you look at most online polls on large, heavily trafficked web sites, seeing more than four options is rare. If you do need to offer more than four possible answers, try to make the answers as clear as possible. As your visitors are offered more options, deciding which answer is right for them becomes more difficult.

Now that you have a poll question, you are ready to display the poll on the web site. Be sure to save your changes before leaving this screen.

Configuring the Polls Display Module

Switch over to the Module Manager by choosing Extensions ⇨ Module Manager. To display a poll on your web site, you need to create a Poll module. Click the New button in the upper-right corner, and then in the Modules [New] screen, choose Poll from the list (see Figure 9-29).

FIGURE 9-29

Configuring the module is easy because, as shown in Figure 9-30, only a few choices are available.

FIGURE 9-30

On the left side of this screen are the usual module choices and options, which I've previously described in Chapter 8.

On the right side under Module Parameters, pick your poll question from the Poll drop-down list. If your poll question is unpublished, it will not show in this drop-down list — only published questions will show. Chapter 14, "Advanced Template and CSS Tricks," covers the Module Class Suffix option. Advanced Parameters offers some caching options, which I covered previously for other modules in Chapter 8.

Save the module and check the front end of the web site. You should see the poll there in the assigned position and on the assigned page.

> *Note at the bottom of the poll, visitors can either vote by picking one of the answers, or they can view the results of the poll.*
>
> *You can also create a new menu item for the results page. A poll runs in a module, so you cannot make that its own page. (However, you can embed a module in an article. See Chapter 10, "Plug-ins That Come with Joomla!," for more details.)*

To create a results page in your menu navigation, choose Menus and the menu where you want the link. Click the New button, and choose Polls, as shown in Figure 9-31.

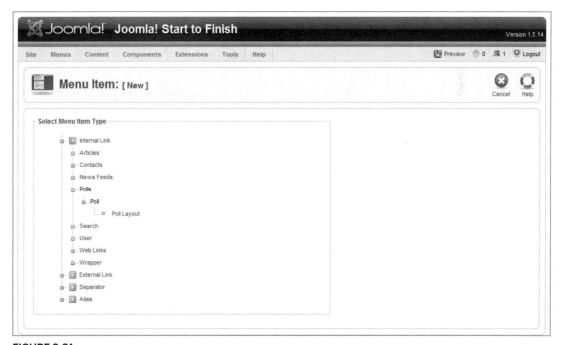

FIGURE 9-31

On the right side of the next screen, under Parameters (Basic), choose your poll from the drop-down list, as shown in Figure 9-32. Be sure to enter the title and other information on the left side of the screen as well (as covered in Chapter 6). Save when you're done.

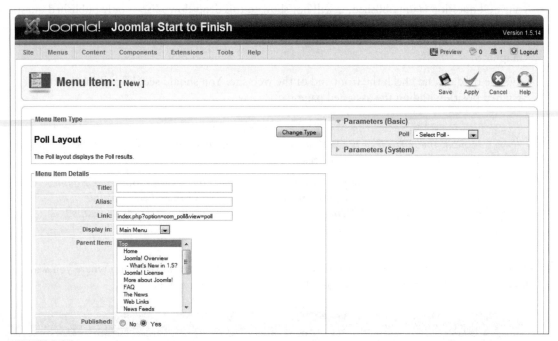

FIGURE 9-32

This process creates a menu item that enables visitors to see the results of the poll selected in the drop-down list. The results page also contains a drop-down list, where visitors can view the results of any other published poll on the web site, even if the voting is closed. Therefore, this type of menu link makes a great link for "past poll results," where visitors can see what other polls have run on the site previously and how voting turned out. Figure 9-33 shows a sample poll results page.

BANNER ADS

Love 'em or hate 'em, banner ads are a fixture in the web landscape. Joomla offers some basic functionality for running banner ads on your web site in the form of the Banner Ad *component*, where you configure the ads, and the Banner Ad *module*, which displays the ads.

I encourage you to think further about this component and module than just its ability to serve up banner ads. Essentially, the Banner Ad component and module (together, generally referred to as the *Banner Ad extension*) enable you to set up a series of random images, each of which can link to its own unique URL. You can track how many times each image has been viewed and how many times a clickthrough has occurred.

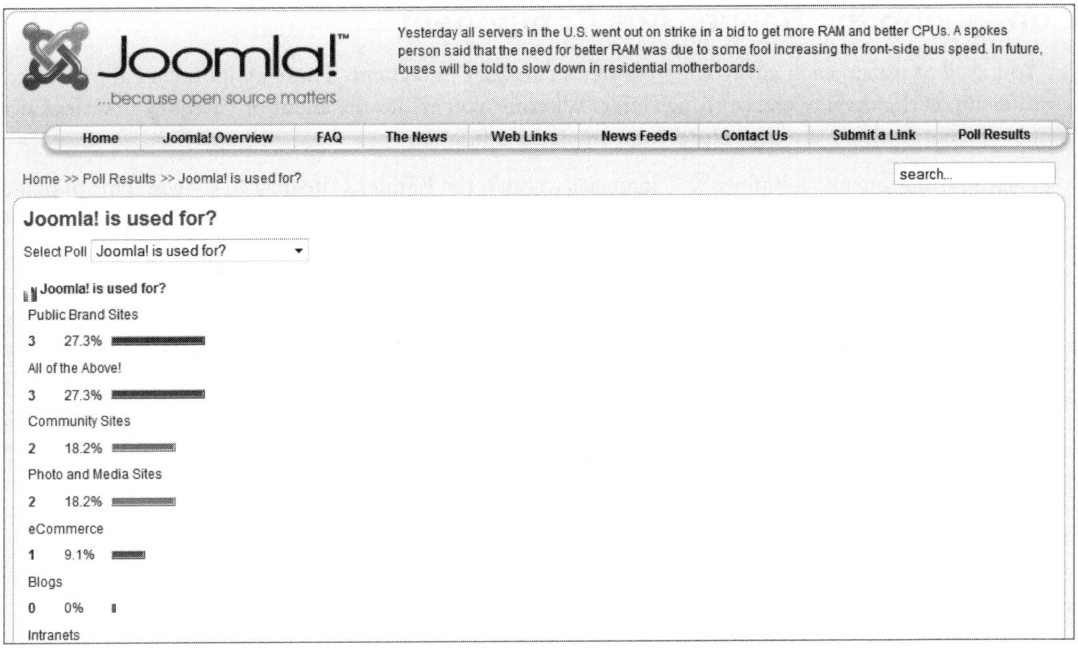

FIGURE 9-33

Unique URLs and clickthrough tracking separate the Banner Ad extension from the Random Image module. The Random Image module serves up images from a single directory, choosing one image at random, but all images have a link to the same location. You don't know how many times each image has been viewed or clicked on.

Therefore, the Banner Ad extension may be more useful to you, if you don't necessarily think of it strictly in terms of its advertising capability.

The Banner Ad extension is somewhat limited because it only shows images in GIF, JPG, or PNG format. It does not display Flash-based advertising. (You can force Flash banners to display via the Custom Banner Code field; more on that later in this chapter.)

If your client chooses to do banner advertising, you must determine what size the banners should be and use that size consistently. For example, if you have space for a 468×60 pixel banner ad, then all ads should be delivered at the same size. Your client should also specify where each ad should go on the user click.

As far as size of ads, technically speaking, you can choose whatever size you like. However, I recommend sticking with a standard dimension, so your clients can use their banner ads on multiple web sites. The Interactive Advertising Bureau (IAB, www.iab.net) sets these standard dimensions. To find out what the latest standards are, visit the IAB web site, where it lists the standard sizes for rectangles, banners, buttons, and skyscraper ads.

Configuring the Banner Ads Component

You need to assign each advertising banner a category and client. These assignments allow for some filtering on the display end of things later. Whether you create the client or category first does not matter, but both must exist before you can create a banner.

Choose Components ➪ Banner ➪ Categories to open the Banner Category Manager. This manager functions exactly like the other category managers you've seen. Click the New button to get a new category. Title is required, whereas other information is optional, as shown in Figure 9-34.

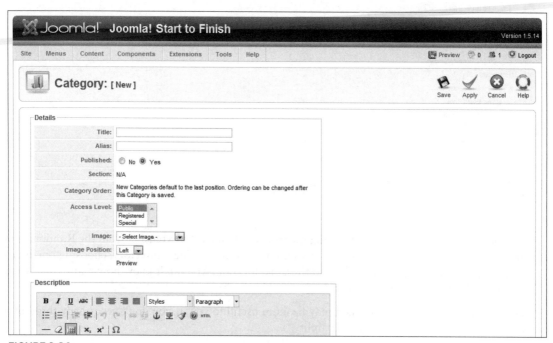

FIGURE 9-34

After you create the category by clicking Save, you need to create a client. Choose Components ➪ Banner ➪ Clients, or click on the subnavigation. Either one takes you to the Banner Client Manager (see Figure 9-35).

Click the New button to create a new client, as shown in Figure 9-36.

The following configuration options are available:

➤ **Client Name** is the client's name (that is, 4Web, Inc.).

➤ **Contact Name** is your contact's name at that location (that is, Jen Kramer).

➤ **Contact E-mail** is your contact's e-mail address.

➤ **Extra information** is a field where you can make any notes you want to about this particular client. These notes are not used anywhere in the banner ad extension, nor are they required.

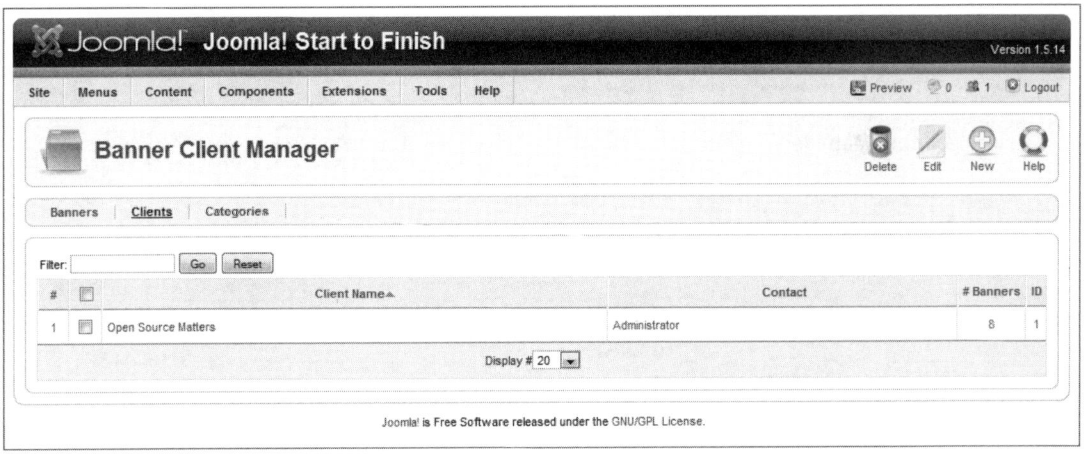

FIGURE 9-35

FIGURE 9-36

Save your changes to create the client.

Now that you have a banner category and a banner client, you're ready to create the banner itself. Choose Components ➪ Banner ➪ Banners, or use the breadcrumbs in the left corner of the Banner Client Manager to go to Banners, as shown in Figure 9-37.

To create a new banner, click the New button in the upper-right corner. You should see a Banner [New] screen similar to that in Figure 9-38.

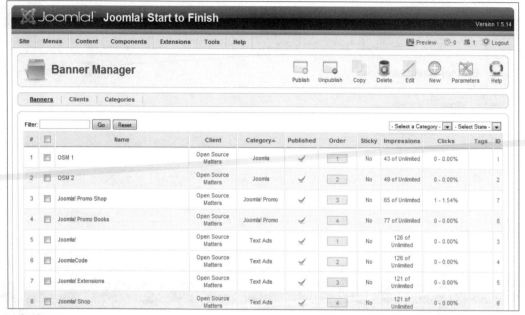

FIGURE 9-37

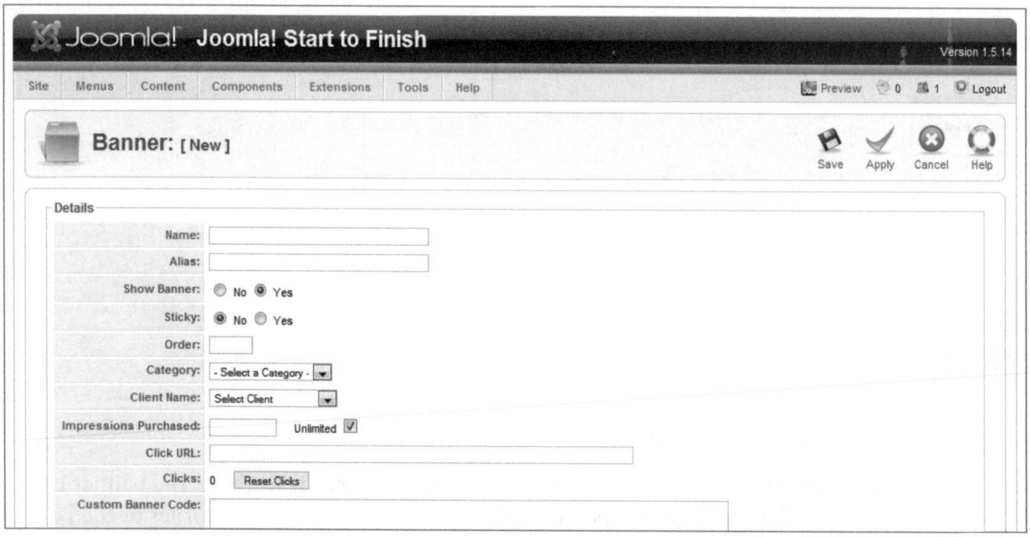

FIGURE 9-38

Set the following options for the banner and click Save:

➤   **Name.** Use this field to provide a name for this particular Banner. It will not display anywhere; it's just to describe this Banner so you know what it is.

➤ **Alias.** This is the alias for the Banner. Again, it is not displayed anywhere on the site.

➤ **Show Banner.** The option is the same as whether the Banner is published or not.

➤ **Sticky.** If a banner is labeled Sticky, it displays to the exclusion of any other banner in the category. If more than one banner is Sticky, those sticky banners will rotate to the exclusion of other banners in the category. Only when their impressions are used up and the banner becomes unpublished will the other non-sticky banners in the category begin to display.

➤ **Order.** Use this field to set what order the banner should appear in, if you are displaying the banners in order. Keep in mind that this option does not serve up the banners one by one to a specific web user. It serves up the banners one by one on a per-request basis, so it does not guarantee that the visitor sees every banner every time. For Order to work, you must also have it enabled in the Banner module.

➤ **Category.** Select a banner category from the drop-down list.

➤ **Client Name.** Select the banner client from the drop-down list.

➤ **Impressions Purchased.** If you are selling ads based on impressions, you can enter how many impressions should be delivered before the banner is unpublished. Note the Unlimited check box next to this option. This option allows the Banner to appear forever and never be disabled.

➤ **Click URL.** This URL is where the user goes when the banner is clicked.

➤ **Clicks.** This field shows how many times people have clicked on this Banner. The Reset Clicks button will set that number back to zero.

The screen continues in Figure 9-39.

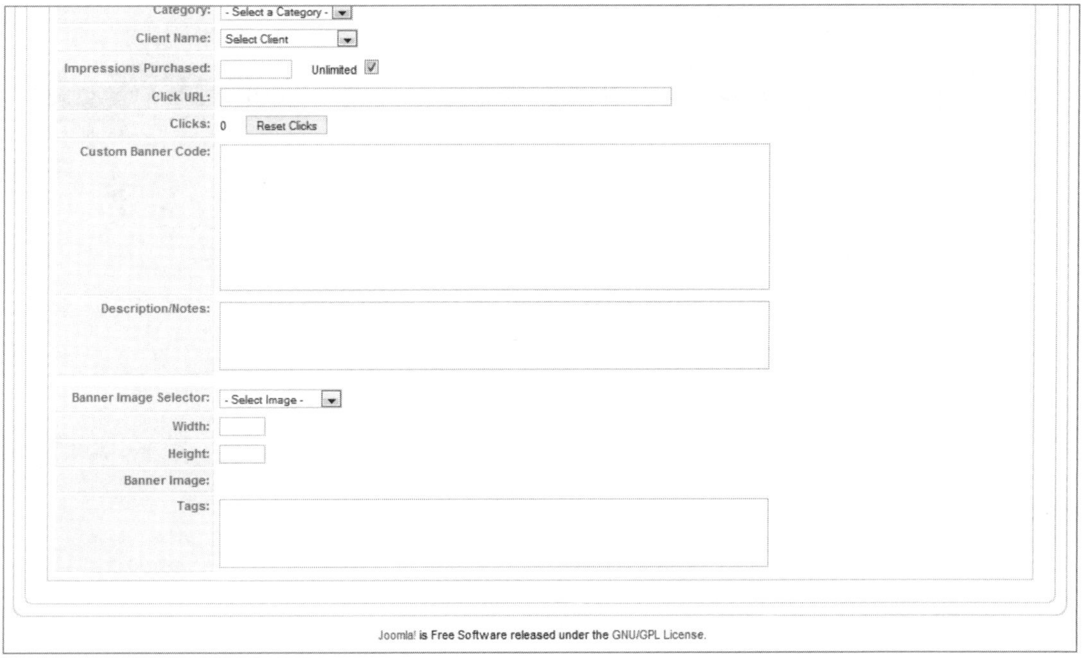

FIGURE 9-39

➤ **Custom Banner Code.** This option completely overrides any code Joomla generates for displaying the banner. This field is useful if you have a Flash (SWF)-based banner that you want to display. You need to generate the Flash display code on your own, but after you have it, you could paste it here.

➤ **Description/Notes.** You can make notes to yourself about this ad in this space.

➤ **Banner Image Selector.** This option sets which banner image is associated with this banner. Banners are stored in the Media Manager in the images/banners directory. You can upload your banner images via the Media Manager (covered in Chapter 4). After you choose a banner, a preview appears under **Banner Image**.

➤ **Width** and **Height.** These refer to the width and height of the image, respectively.

➤ **Tags.** Matching the content of the page with specific banners is possible, and the Tags option is how this happens. Assign some keywords here in the Tags field. In your articles, assign the same keywords in the Meta Keywords area. In the Banner Ad module, set Search by Tag to Yes (see the following section). The appropriate banner will display when the keywords between the article and the banner match.

Repeat this process for each banner. After your banners are configured, you're ready to configure the module to display those banners.

Configuring the Banner Display Module

The Banner Module displays all banners or a subset of banners on the web page.

Choose Extensions ➪ Module Manager, and click the New button in the upper-right corner. From the Modules list, choose Banner, as shown in Figure 9-40, and click Next.

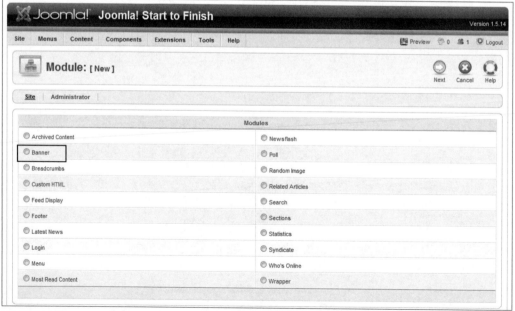

FIGURE 9-40

Now take a look at the module configuration screen, as shown in Figure 9-41.

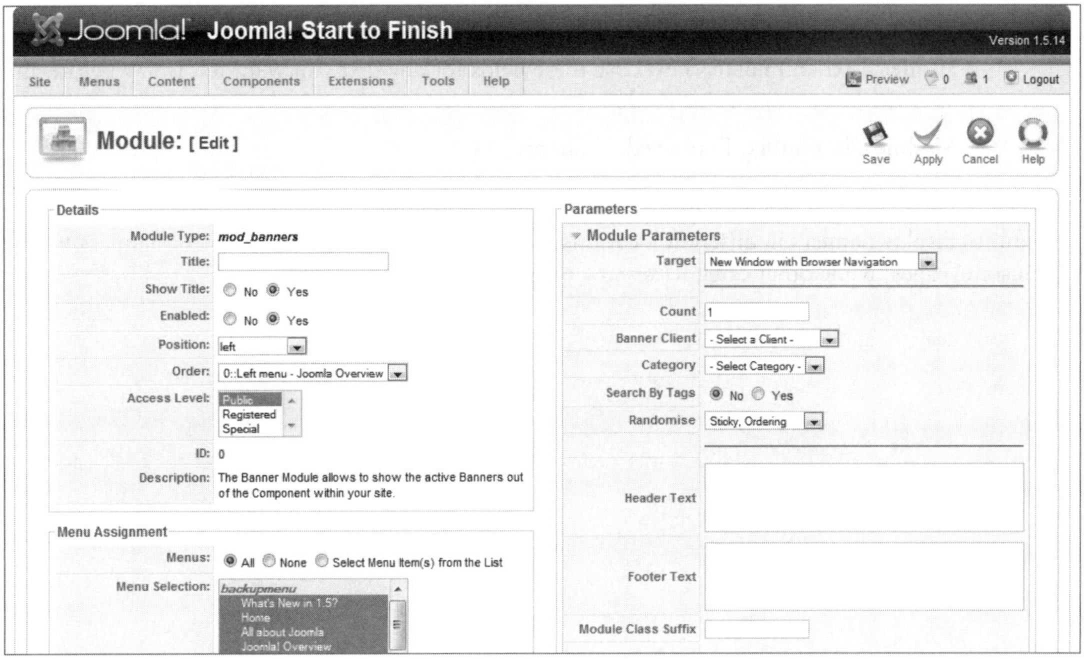

FIGURE 9-41

The Module Parameters are as follows:

➤ **Target.** This option determines whether the link, when clicked, should open in a new window with browser navigation, the same window with browser navigation, or a pop-up window (new window without browser navigation). I would stay away from no browser navigation in this application, since that takes away the end user's back button. If the banner links to a different web site, I recommend going with the new window with browser navigation. If you're opening a page on your web site, parent window with browser navigation would work fine.

➤ **Count.** Use this option to set how many banners should display simultaneously in this location. Generally, it's one, but you can have more than one.

➤ **Banner Client** and **Category.** These options serve as filtering mechanisms for your banners. You can display a specific client's banners with this module, you can display a specific category, or you could display a specific category and specific client together. You can also leave these options unset, which means they'll pull in banners from any client and any category.

➤ **Search by Tags.** I talked about this option in the preceding section. Enable it if you want to associate banners with certain keywords in articles.

➤ **Randomise.** Should banners display in a certain order, or should they display randomly? Sticky banners will display first, to the exclusion of any other banners. Sticky banners will display until they expire, and then ordering or randomization will take over. Ordering means the banners will display in the same order as shown in the Banner Manager. Randomization means that one banner is chosen randomly to be displayed.

➤ **Header Text** and **Footer Text.** Use these fields for any text you want to display before and/or after the banner(s) for this module.

➤ **Module Class Suffix.** Explained in Chapter 14.

Keep in mind that you can have more than one Banner module on your site — for example, if you want to display banners in different locations, or if you want certain categories of banners to show on some pages, while other categories show on other pages of your site.

10

Plug-Ins That Come with Joomla!

WHAT'S IN THIS CHAPTER?

➤ What is a plug-in?

➤ Plug-ins you might want to modify

➤ Choosing and installing a new editor

Plug-ins are another type of Joomla extension that typically work behind the scenes. They don't exist directly on a web page, like components and modules. Plug-ins power features such as the editor you use to edit articles, the "remember me" functionality in a login form, the cloaking of email addresses, and more.

Many plug-ins require no configuration or any special attention at all — they just work. But a few plug-ins do some things that might be of interest to you. One valuable improvement to Joomla via plug-in is changing your editor from the default TinyMCE to another editor, significantly improving Joomla's usability for your end-user clients as a result.

Leaving settings well enough alone in the plug-in configuration screens is best, because plug-ins can deeply affect the functioning (or non-functioning) of Joomla. However, in this section I walk you through a few plug-ins you might find useful to change.

THE REMEMBER ME PLUG-IN

This plug-in controls the Remember Me box on a login form. If the plug-in is enabled, the box appears on the form. If you disable the plug-in, visitors to your site will not have the Remember Me option on login.

Log in to the back end of Joomla, then choose Extensions ➪ Plugin Manager. The Plugin Manager screen appears, as shown in Figure 10-1.

FIGURE 10-1

Find the System – Remember Me plug-in in the Plugin Name list. It might be on the second page of your results. Click the title to edit it; you should see an Edit screen similar to Figure 10-2 appear.

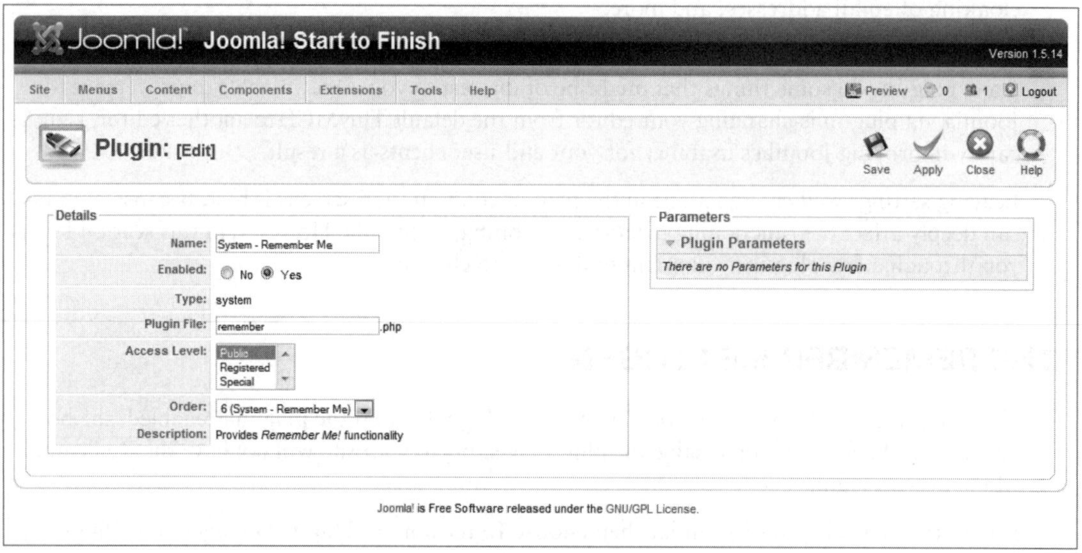

FIGURE 10-2

Like many plug-ins, this one has almost no settings to change (except, maybe, the name of the plug-in). The only thing you can do here is enable or disable the plug-in.

You might want to disable this plug-in if your site will run on a lot of public computers (for example, a public library site) and you do not want a "remember me" option to exist. If it doesn't exist, no one is tempted to tell the site to "remember me," and visitor accounts are more secure.

THE LOAD MODULE PLUG-IN

A more interactive and useful plug-in than Remember Me is the Content – Load Module plug-in, which enables you to include a module in the middle of an article. You use this extremely useful plug-in more in the coming chapters. Chapter 12 describes how to use this Load Module plug-in to configure your home page.

Find the Content – Load Module plug-in in the Plugin Manager and click the title to edit it. You should see a screen similar to Figure 10-3.

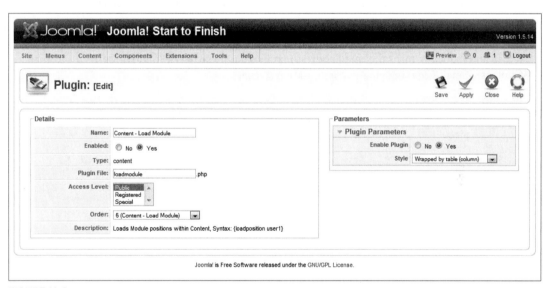

FIGURE 10-3

Note the plug-in description: "Loads Module positions within Content, Syntax: {loadposition user1}."

As the description states, simply put the syntax {loadposition left} anywhere in your article, and all modules assigned a position of left will load in that location in your article. I typically use the position "inset" in the article, as in {loadposition inset} because this tells me that the module is set into an article. But as always, you can call the module position whatever you want.

Note the Style drop-down menu on the right side of the screen. By default, a table is wrapped around the module, and if there's more than one module, the modules will appear in a column. However, tables aren't the ideal HTML for containing your module, as search engines and screen readers can have trouble with table code. I suggest using Wrapped by Divs for general use or Wrapped by Multiple Divs if there are going to be rounded corners in the module display.

Chapter 13, "Custom Templates," and Chapter 14, "Advanced Template and CSS Tricks," cover module formatting in detail.

THE EMAIL CLOAKING PLUG-IN

Email cloaking is a way of hiding an email address in the format of yourname@company.com from spammers. In the old days, you could make this text clickable by simply putting an HTML tag around the email address as follows:

```
<a href="mailto:yourname@company.com">yourname@company.com</a>
```

However, spam robots were then able to harvest these addresses. The idea behind email cloaking was to obscure the address, via JavaScript, from spam robots. Note that both the address that's typed in between the tags, as well as the `mailto:` part of the address, must be encrypted.

Email cloaking is turned on by default in Joomla. This means that simply typing an email address into the editor in your article activates the Email Cloaking plug-in to cloak the address with JavaScript. It also automatically turns the email address text into a `mailto:`-style link. Figure 10-4 shows the Content – Email Cloaking plug-in configuration screen.

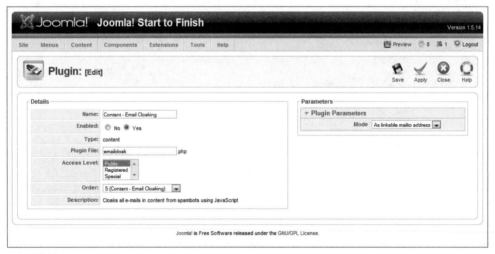

FIGURE 10-4

Note the Mode drop-down menu on the right side of the screen. It is set to the default, As Linkable Mailto Address, meaning that it takes an unlinked email address and turns it into a link. The other option is Non-linkable Text, which encrypts the email address but doesn't make it a link.

Disabling the Email Cloaking plug-in means that all email addresses will be available to be scraped up by spammers.

EDITOR BUTTONS

You might notice the three buttons at the bottom of the article editing window: Image, Pagebreak, and Read More, as shown in Figure 10-5.

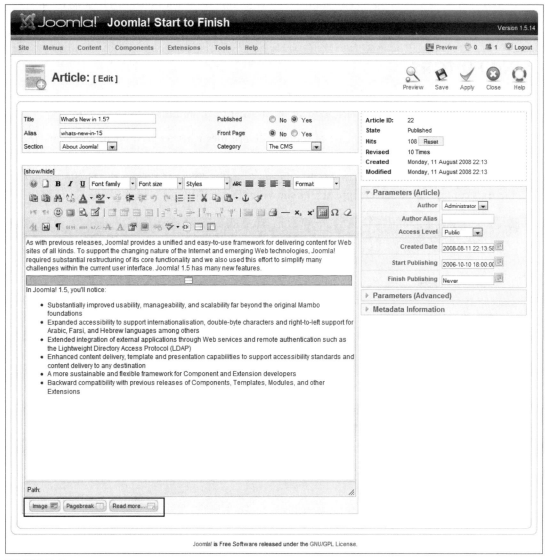

FIGURE 10-5

(There's actually a fourth button, Toggle Editor, but it is associated with TinyMCE, the default editor used in Joomla.)

The Image, Pagebreak, and Read More buttons are all controlled by their own individual plug-ins, called Editor Button – Image, Editor Button – Pagebreak, and Editor Button – Read More, respectively.

You can configure very few settings for these buttons in their plug-in screen. Essentially, all you can do is enable or disable them. However, this setting might be handy for controlling what your client can and cannot do in an editing environment. If you don't want your client to be able to create "read more" breaks or to break a long article into multiple pages, simply disable these buttons.

USING EDITORS

An editor is the tool you use to edit text in big boxes on your web site. That includes section descriptions, category descriptions, articles, custom HTML modules, and so forth.

The editor, which is at the very heart of Joomla, determines whether your client will think Joomla is easy and usable or hard and clumsy.

By default, Joomla comes with TinyMCE. Choose Editor ➪ TinyMCE from the Plugin Manager screen; its configuration screen appears, as shown in Figure 10-6.

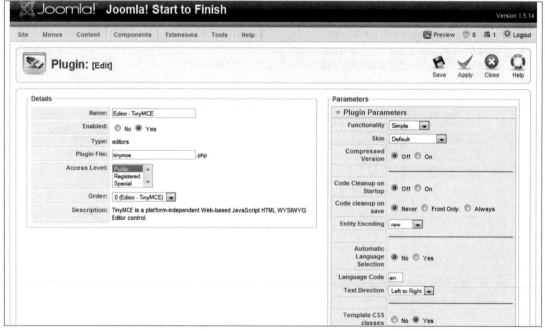

FIGURE 10-6

Note the first option in the Parameters section, Functionality. This option determines what kinds of editing tools are available for use.

If you choose Simple from the Functionality drop-down menu, the editor looks like Figure 10-7.

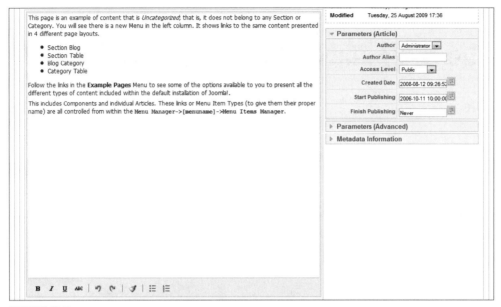

FIGURE 10-7

Note that the toolbar is very simple. It allows for bold, italic, underline, or strikethrough text; undo and redo; cleaning up messy code; and a bulleted and numbered list. The toolbar appears at the bottom of the editing window.

The Advanced Functionality setting offers several additional options, including alignment, styles (classes from a stylesheet), and format (heading tags, paragraphs, and so on), as shown in Figure 10-8.

FIGURE 10-8

The Extended Functionality setting offers the most options, as shown in Figure 10-9.

FIGURE 10-9

The biggest help in the Extended setting is the Paste from Word button, which I've marked with a box. This feature allows you to copy text from Word, then paste it into this window, and the Word markup will be stripped out. If you paste text from Word without using this feature, you're likely to include a lot of Word markup, which adds nothing to your page, bloats the code, slows down page load times, and occasionally breaks the page display.

However, you might not like the fact that now your client has the option to change the font family and font size, since it's likely you included article styling in your stylesheet. Fortunately, the TinyMCE plug-in configuration screen offers you the ability to toggle on and off each of these buttons and drop-down menus in Extended Functionality setting.

Figure 10-10 shows the TinyMCE plug-in configuration screen, and under Advanced Parameters, you can see that each toolbar item can be turned on and off if Extended Functionality is enabled.

Setting the Fonts option to Hide means that the font family and font size drop-down menus will not display.

One final configuration note about TinyMCE: Back in the Plugin Manager window for TinyMCE, under Plugin Parameters, you should pay special attention to your settings for Code Cleanup on Startup and Code Cleanup on Save, shown in Figure 10-11.

If you plan to keep TinyMCE as your editor, I recommend switching it to Extended Mode, if only for the Paste from Word functionality. You can turn off other functionalities in the plug-in if you don't want them. Personally, I would turn off fonts, which should be controlled in the stylesheet, not in the editor. If you give your client the option of styling text however they'd like, they probably will, and the professional look of your site will be lost over time.

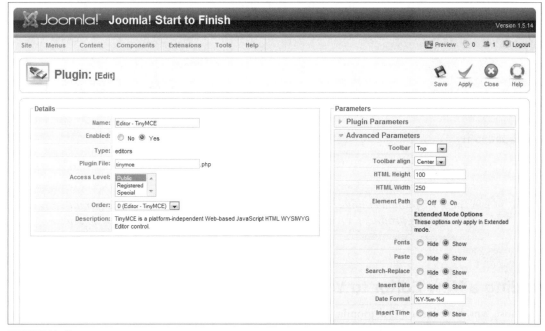

FIGURE 10-10

Enabling the Code Cleanup on Startup option means that when you open an article, category description, section description, and so on, TinyMCE will strip out code it considers incorrect or undesirable. Enabling Code Cleanup on Save, of course, means that same process happens when you save the item you're working on.

If you know what you're doing with HTML, you probably want to set Code Cleanup on Startup to Off. For Code Cleanup on Save, Never might be a good option. If you have users editing from the front end, the Front Only option might be good, particularly if you have a community contributing to your content, rather than just a few site editors.

Finally, towards the bottom of that parameter set, is a box for Prohibited Elements and Extended Valid Elements. These options offer a way to specifically reject or accept certain HTML tags. Note that applet is one of the prohibited elements, as it could be a security risk.

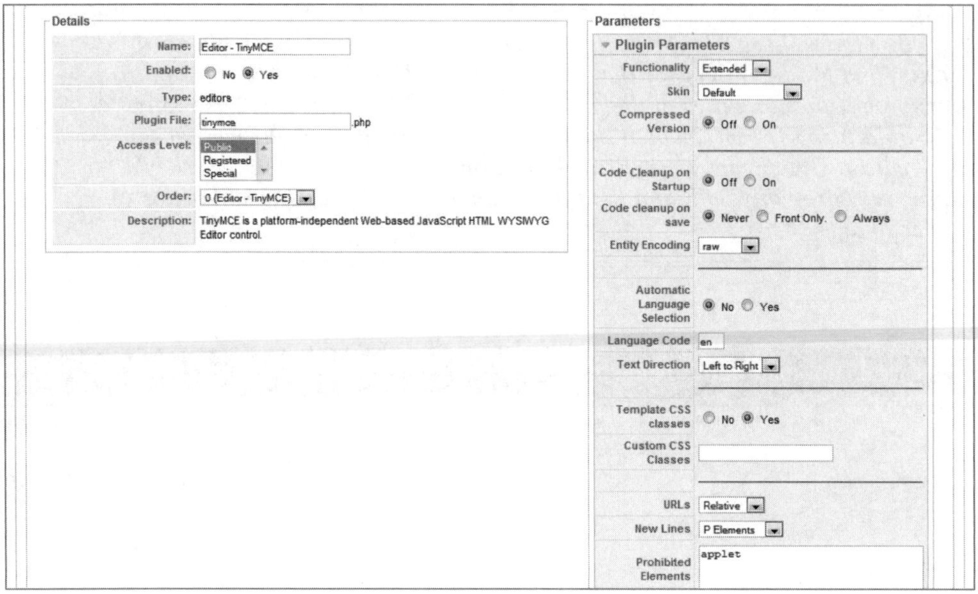

FIGURE 10-11

As in most Joomla configuration screens, rolling your mouse over the parameter name usually produces a tool tip that can help explain what each control does.

Adding a New Editor to Your Web Site

Those who have built a few Joomla sites eventually discover that they do not have to use the TinyMCE editor. The usability of this editor has improved over time, but many Joomla developers (including this one) have the opinion that TinyMCE lacks some specific functionality that would make it much easier to use.

For example, TinyMCE has no default way of linking one page in your Joomla site to another by simply browsing for the page. You must know the URL of the page to which you want to link, but most clients don't know this information and find that seeking it out is cumbersome to do. Other editors do have this linking capability, however.

You can look at most available editors in the Joomla Extensions Directory (JED) at `http://extensions.joomla.org/extensions/edition/editors`.

JCE, the Joomla Content Editor, is a free editor that has this linking functionality, the ability to paste from Word, and much more. It is what I install by default on sites I build.

Adding a new editor to your site is no different from adding a new module, component, or template. Follow these steps:

1. Download the plug-in. (JCE has both a component and a plug-in, which may be available bundled as a single download.)

2. Choose Extensions ⇨ Install/Uninstall, and upload the zipped file(s) via the Upload Package File dialog box.

3. Finally, if you want to assign the new editor to all users, choose Site ⇨ Global Configuration, and under the Site tab, set the Default WYSIWYG Editor to the editor you just installed (JCE in this example), as shown in Figure 10-12. This setting changes all users' editors to the editor you just chose.

FIGURE 10-12

Ideally, you should install this new editor before your client starts using Joomla to edit his or her site. Otherwise, your client might be a little upset that "everything changed" when you installed the new editor. (JCE is typically the second extension I install immediately after site creation, right after JoomlaPack, a backup utility. (See Chapter 15 for more information.)

If one user in particular wants a different editor — you, perhaps? — you can set it up in the User Manager (choose Site ⇨ User Manager). For this user, set his or her editor to something different. This setting applies to this user only and overrides what's set in the Global Configuration. Figure 10-13 shows the User Manager.

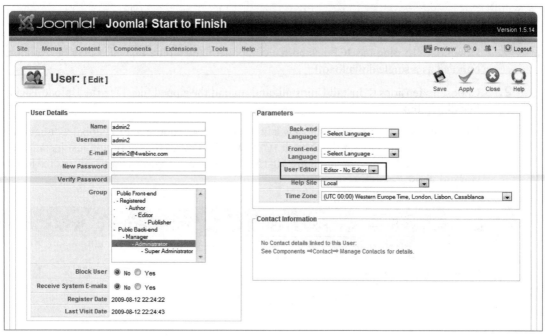

FIGURE 10-13

Note that the User Editor drop-down menu contains a No Editor option. This option is very handy if you know HTML. Sometimes just working in the code view directly is faster than using an editor, and the articles you want to edit load much faster when they don't have to load all the buttons and JavaScript that makes an editor work.

The editor is very critical as to whether your client will think Joomla is "easy" or "hard" to use. Spend some time evaluating editors for yourself, thinking about which tools will make your client's job the most straightforward to perform.

11

Adding Extensions to Joomla!

WHAT'S IN THIS CHAPTER?

➤ Installing extensions

➤ Configuring new extensions

You've had a good overview of all the great extensions included with Joomla. You should be happy, but of course, you're wondering: Where's the shopping cart? How about a slideshow? Can I add comments to my blog?

Fortunately, Joomla was built so that anyone can add to its structure quickly and easily via an extension. Extensions, as you've seen, include components, modules, and plug-ins. These are all different ways of adding functionality to Joomla without tampering with any core code. (Changes to core code could potentially be lost in a version upgrade.)

In addition to Joomla's extensions, more extensions are available via third-party developers. Some are free, whereas some cost a little money. (Most are in the $5–$45 range, though some cost more.) Some are well documented and come with great support, whereas others are undocumented and confusing. Some are well maintained and others appear to be abandoned. And some work, whereas others crash your system!

Extensions are available for download as a finished product. On occasion, though, you might want to add your own specific functionality to Joomla. You can write your own extension, or you can hire an engineer to write it for you. Writing extensions is beyond the scope of this book, but plenty of great books are available that describe the process in detail.

The Joomla Extensions Directory (JED) is located at `extensions.joomla.org`. Chapter 2 covers the JED and how to choose a great extension. This chapter addresses how to download and install a great extension.

INSTALLING EXTENSIONS

One of Joomla's "must-have" extensions is JoomlaPack. JoomlaPack is an Editor's Pick in the JED, has high ratings, and is generally viewed in a very positive light by the core development team at Joomla. You can read more about it at `http://extensions.joomla.org/extensions/access-a-security/backup/1606`.

I strongly recommend installing JoomlaPack for every Joomla site you build. JoomlaPack can make a backup of all files plus the database (or just the database), and it can put the backup in a file that can be downloaded for safekeeping. JoomlaPack also offers a restoration utility so that you can easily restore your site from the backup. This utility makes JoomlaPack very useful for moving a site from one host to another, in addition to making backups.

Figure 11-1 shows the JoomlaPack listing from the JED.

FIGURE 11-1

Note the buttons for Download, Support, and Documentation. The Download button lets you download the extension (or takes you to the page where you can download it). The Support button, in this case, takes you to the JoomlaPack forum where you can ask questions. The Documentation button takes you to some well-written documentation that explains the extension in detail.

Click the Download button, and find the link to download JoomlaPack Core for Joomla 1.5. (If your site is not in English, download JoomlaPack Plus, which contains additional translations.) You will download a zip file from the JoomlaPack Team server. Right now this file is called com_joomlapack-2.3.3-core.zip. The filename indicates it is a component by the com_ at the beginning. You will also see mod_ for modules and plg_ for plug-ins.

For some extensions, you might download a file with several bundled components. Occasionally, you have to initially unzip this file to get to the zipped file to install. However, your extension installation will always happen in the form of a zipped file.

After downloading the JoomlaPack extension, log in to the back end of your website and choose Extensions ➪ Install/Uninstall. The Extension Manager appears, as shown in Figure 11-2.

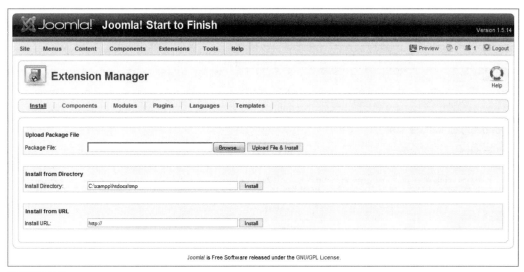

FIGURE 11-2

The Install tab offers three options. You can upload a package file (that is, a zip file) from your computer, you can install from a directory, or you can install from a URL. In most cases, you'll upload the package file. Click the Browse button, find the JoomlaPack zipped file on your hard drive, select it, and upload the file to the server by clicking the Upload File and Install button. You should get a success message, as shown in Figure 11-3.

For some extensions, you will only get the "install success" message on top of the Extension Manager screen, whereas other extensions provide additional information, as JoomlaPack does.

Before leaving the Extension Manager, take a quick peek at the other tabs for Components, Modules, Plugins, Languages, and Templates, as shown in the box in Figure 11-3.

These views in the Extension Manager show which extensions, templates, and languages you have installed. Some items are grayed out on the list. These items cannot be uninstalled. Figure 11-4 shows an example of the Components list.

To uninstall an item, select its radio button and click the Uninstall icon in the upper-right corner.

Should you uninstall non-essential extensions that are not in use? It depends! Suppose that you've installed a handful of photo galleries on a site, trying to find the best option for your client. You've decided on the one that will be used on the site. Cleaning up and uninstalling the other photo galleries you did not use is probably a good idea. They occupy disk space (particularly photo galleries), but more importantly, if they wind up having a security problem, you might forget they are on this site. (Keeping up with updates to third-party extensions is critical, because these can also provide a point for a hacker to get control of your site. See Chapter 15 for more information.)

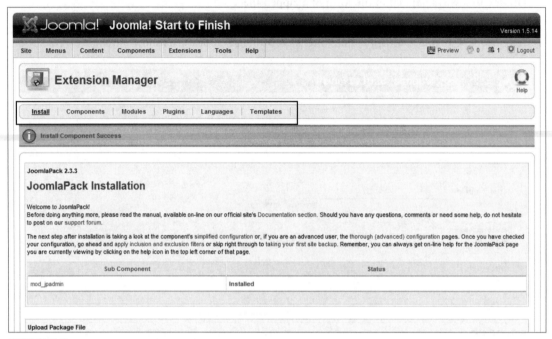

FIGURE 11-3

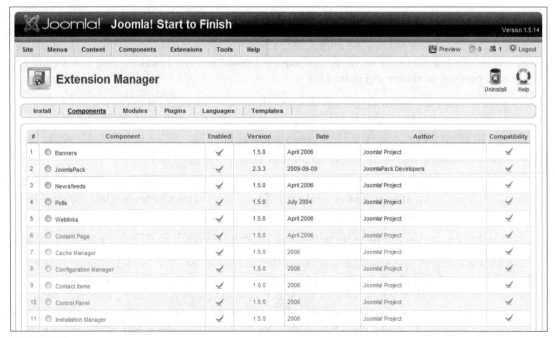

FIGURE 11-4

However, if the extension came with the initial Joomla installation, you might just want to leave it there, in case you want to use it some other time. Replacing the extensions that come with Joomla is difficult, and these particular extensions are kept up-to-date by the Joomla core team.

Also note the Compatibility column on the right side. This column indicates whether these extensions are compatible with Joomla 1.5 natively, or whether Joomla must run in legacy mode to accommodate those extensions. Now that Joomla 1.5 has been out for more than two years, you should try to stay away from legacy mode as much as possible — which should not be terribly difficult to do.

CONFIGURING NEW EXTENSIONS

After installing a new extension, you must configure it. In the case of JoomlaPack, some instructions appeared onscreen immediately after installation (refer to Figure 11-3). That's a great way to make it clear what the next step is after installation.

But all too often, an extension comes with no documentation or direction after installation. What should you do at that point?

Generally, a plug-in or module installs in an unpublished state. You must publish it (see Chapter 10 for plug-ins and Chapter 8 for modules) and assign it to a position in your template (in the case of a module, see Chapter 8) to see what settings are available and how to configure it. In the case of a component, you must link it to a menu (see Chapter 9) to see it and know what settings are available as you configure it. You can then start tweaking extension-specific settings. You'll just have to keep changing things and checking to see how it turns out, unfortunately.

I find that most extension developers who charge a small fee have reasonable documentation and tech support. After all, they are charging a fee for what they do, so you expect a bit more in return. You might find less support with free extensions, but that is certainly not always the case. JoomlaPack and JCE, of particular note, do an incredible job of supporting their free products.

Most developers have some type of technical support. Many developers offer a forum on their site, where you can ask questions and help others. These forums are successful only if you behave like a good forum user, politely asking for help and thanking those who do help you. These ground rules are also true for the Joomla forums at `forum.joomla.org`.

Here are some tips for being a good forum user:

➤ **Search the forum first.** Your first responsibility is to look through the forum posts to see whether your question has already been answered. Having many people ask the same question is common, and answering it over and over again is very frustrating to the developers. Do put in the effort before asking.

➤ **Have patience.** Don't expect an answer in five minutes or less. Some forums are very active, and response times are quick. Other forums are much less active, so give the developers a few days to answer your question. Developers might be on vacation in Tahiti when you write to them. (Well, it's a nice thought anyway. They are probably busy, like everyone else.)

➤ **Post your own answer.** This might sound silly, but if you find an answer to your problem, or if you figure it out, post an answer to your own question! By doing so, you are saving the developer time in the future. The more questions that have answers in the forum, the more useful the forum becomes as a tool for learning and resolving issues.

➤ **Share your knowledge.** After you understand what you're doing, pitch in and answer a few questions yourself. Understandably, when you're first learning, you may ask more questions than you answer. But you have a responsibility to give back to the community that gives you so much. This sharing is part of the heart of open source software. Answering questions frees up developers to do what they do best — creating more great software for people to use and enjoy.

➤ **Leave a review.** Note that if you've gotten your extension from the JED, you are encouraged to leave a review. Leaving feedback (particularly positive feedback) for the developers is always a big boost. Show your appreciation and leave thoughtful and honest reviews. Don't use the JED as an opportunity to trash the developer. By honestly contributing to the JED, you help others identify quality extensions that help to address their own problems. If you work with an extension that you don't like or doesn't work for you, try to de-personalize your criticism of the developer. Simply state what didn't work, what you did to try to get help, and what the outcome of that help was.

As a final note, some people are surprised that no documentation exists for parts of Joomla. The Joomla Project is always looking for clear documentation. You are welcome to register and edit the documentation wiki at `docs.joomla.org`. You can learn more about the Documentation Working Group and volunteer opportunities at `docs.joomla.org/Documentation_Working_Group`.

12

Home Page Tips and Tricks

WHAT'S IN THIS CHAPTER?

➤ Defining the home page

➤ Using the Front Page Manager and Front Page Blog Layout

➤ Creating your home page in an article

Steve Krug, in his must-read book, *Don't Make Me Think*!, says the home page is beyond your control. Every department and division wants a piece of it, preferably near the top and in an eye-catching way.

Despite the requests from all sides, your mission is to make the home page clear and concise. What exactly is this site, and why does it exist? What does it want from the visitor, or what does it want to do for the visitor? Why is this site better than the other guy's? All of this information must be communicated quickly and cleanly on the home page.

Clients often ask for news tickers, slide shows, photo carousels, Flash movies, and other things that blink and spin and move. They ask for blurbs for the latest news, the latest award, or the latest press release. They are so busy adding all this "interactivity" to keep the home page "fresh" that they forget about the basic message the home page should send.

➤ **Who is this company or organization?** Often this is communicated non-verbally via color and layout as clearly as a blurb about the company background. A site with rainbow bars and little construction men promising pages coming soon communicate something very different than a site with clean lines, concise text, and a few well-placed photos.

➤ **What will this site do for me, the visitor?** Perhaps the site offers a service (PayPal), the way to research and/or buy a product (Amazon), news and information (CNN), or the ability to network socially or professionally with friends and colleagues (Facebook, LinkedIn). Some sites provide enough information to make you want to visit their store or call for more information. Whatever your site is doing, it should be very clear from the home page.

➤ **What do I do now?** A complicated home page with a lot of features and functionality pull the site visitor in dozens of directions. Sometimes simple is so much better — for example, Twitter's home page (see Figure 12-1).

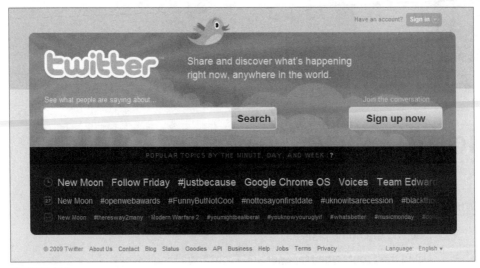

FIGURE 12-1

See the big Sign Up Now button? And the big Search box? It's pretty clear what you should do now when arriving on the Twitter home page. If you've been here before, there's a smaller Sign In box in the upper right. That's because the primary reason people will come to the Twitter site is to learn about Twitter and, hopefully, become new users. If you're already a Twitter user, you're more likely to go to your own page directly (for example, www.twitter.com/jen4web), rather than coming through the home page of the site.

Twitter's design doesn't work for all organizations, though. Not every organization serves the same target audience or has the same overall goals. When talking with your client about what should go on the home page, be sure to remember everything discussed in Chapters 1 and 2.

Above all, nothing has changed when you're on the home page as far as asking the question, "What problem does X feature try to solve?"

One of the most common requests I hear is for more interactivity. What is interactivity? Unfortunately, that's a term defined differently by every client I've ever worked with, so be sure you ask your client for their definition. Generally, what most clients are ultimately trying to convey with "interactivity" is that they are movers and shakers in their field, and there's a lot going on within the organization. I have found that when clients talk about interactivity, they're really talking about making the organization look interesting or compelling or perhaps bigger than they are.

A slideshow, for the sake of having pretty pictures that move, does very little for your client's web site. It's not necessarily solving a problem, other than perhaps providing something pretty to look at (frequently called *eye candy*). However, this is a frequent request for "interactivity." Unless your client has professional photos that fit what they do perfectly, a slideshow is just a distraction.

Likewise, including blurbs for "latest news" that change only a handful of times per year isn't necessarily smart either, unless you want to communicate that there isn't a lot going on within the organization.

Although some experts advocate for keeping the home page "fresh," in my experience, there are some clients for whom this simply will not work. They are either short of manpower to update the web site frequently, or they don't have much that changes in their organization. If your client fits this description, don't try to talk them into blogs they'll never update.

Know your client, and know what their capabilities are for keeping the site fresh. If they don't have the ability to write a regular blog post, if they don't have a lot of "latest news" or press releases, don't just throw up anything on the home page to make it look full and busy. Perhaps it's better to go the simple, clean route. Post some clear, concise text explaining the products and/or services the organization offers. Provide a clear way to access more information about those products and services via links. Include a few thoughtful photos that support the text, not just canned stock photography to make the page pretty. If you provide a compelling reason for people to investigate your site further, they will do so.

Finally, you might think about the home page last in your development process. Once you have the rest of the site clearly defined in terms of site map, type of content included, and types of extensions used on the interior pages of the site, then think about how the home page will communicate an abbreviated version of the site's message. Your client is likely to want to discuss the home page first. Remind them that by developing the home page last, they will have the best opportunity to refine their message to make the home page clear and compelling.

INTRODUCING THE FRONT PAGE MANAGER AND FRONT PAGE BLOG LAYOUT

Joomla tries to organize the insanity that is the home page by offering something called the *Front Page Blog Layout*. (No, it has nothing to do with an old Microsoft product from years ago.) This feature is essentially a blog layout for the home page, created via an option in the Menu Manager (see Chapter 6). The stories that appear in the blog, however, are specified on a case-by-case basis, by way of the Front Page option in the individual article's editing screen. You can get a list of all articles appearing in the Front Page Blog Layout via the Front Page Manager. The Front Page Manager is located under the Content menu in Joomla's back end.

Is this layout the best approach for your home page? It depends. Think of the Front Page Blog Layout as a tool in your kit, and perhaps it's the right approach for some sites. An alternative to the Front Page Blog Layout, using an article to lay out the home page, appears later in the chapter.

And by the way, although Joomla calls it a Front Page, I persist in calling it the home page. Consider these terms interchangeable in this chapter.

In all likelihood, you already have the Front Page Blog Layout in use on your web site. That's because when you install Joomla, even if you don't install the sample data, a single link is created — a link to your home page. That link is created with the Front Page Blog Layout.

Start by identifying the articles that you want to display on the home page. As mentioned earlier, the blog items are the articles you've flagged to show on the home page. In an individual article, you set the Front Page option to Yes, as shown in Figure 12-2.

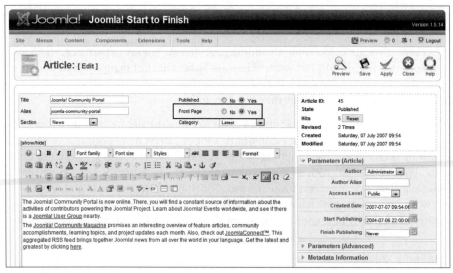

FIGURE 12-2

You can see all of these articles in one screen if you go to the Front Page Manager (see Figure 12-3), which you access by choosing Content ⇨ Front Page Manager.

The Front Page Manager gives you a quick look at all articles appearing on the home page. You'll notice this screen is similar to the Article Manager (covered in Chapter 5). The features here are essentially the same:

➤ **Title** is the title of the article.

➤ **Published** indicates whether the article is published (green check) or not (red X).

➤ **Order** indicates the order the articles will display in your blog, if you've chosen the Ordering option in the Menu Manager (explained later).

➤ **Access level** identifies items as registered, special, or public (covered in Chapter 4).

➤ **Section** and **Category** identify the section and category associated with each article.

➤ **Author** is the author for the article.

In the upper-right corner are icons for other actions. Check the box next to the article(s) you want to apply these actions to and then click one of the following buttons:

➤ **Archive** will archive selected articles. (See Chapter 5.)

➤ **Publish** and **Unpublish** will publish and unpublish selected articles, respectively.

➤ **Remove** removes an article from the Front Page Manager. It does *not* delete the article from the site. The article will still exist in the Article Manager, but it will no longer be displayed on the home page.

➤ **Help** gives help about the Front Page Manager.

To access the Front Page Blog Layout, locate your Home link within your menu structure. My Home link is in the Main Menu, which I can access by going to Menus ⇨ Main Menu, then clicking the Home link, as shown in Figure 12-4.

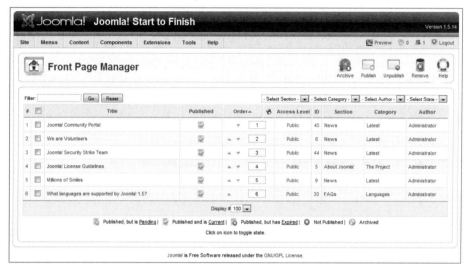

FIGURE 12-3

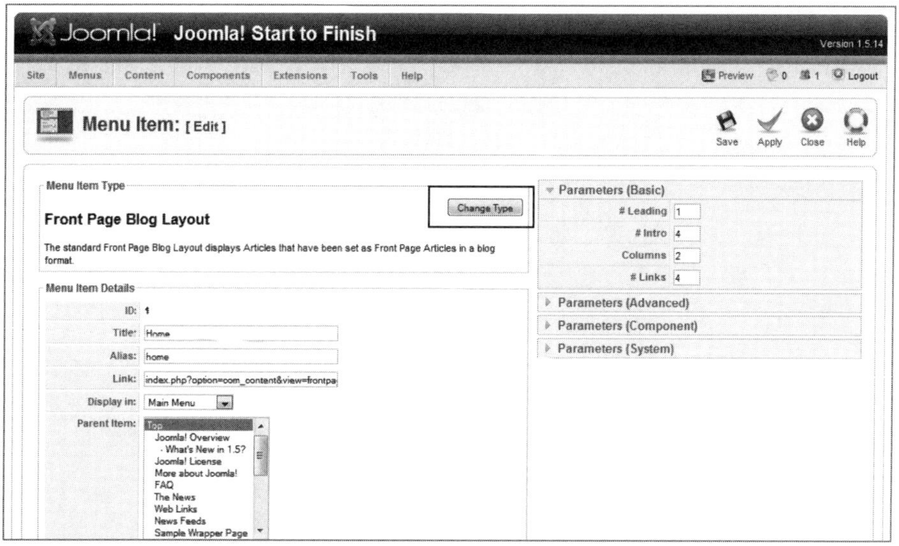

FIGURE 12-4

This screen might look familiar to you if you read Chapter 5, which covered blog configurations extensively. The parameters are the same as what you saw before in section and category blogs, and they're configured in the same way.

Do You Have to Use the Front Page Blog Layout?

But what if you don't want your home page to be in a blog format? What if you want something different?

You do not have to use Front Page Blog Layout at all. Note the Change Type button in Figure 12-4. This button allows you to change the type of home page layout to something else. For example, you could link directly to a specific article as the home page. Alternatively, you could link to a different component. For example, Staples, the office supply store, has a front page that looks very much like a site map. You could install a site map component and have that become your home page if you wanted.

Click the Change Type button, and you will see a screen similar to Figure 12-5.

FIGURE 12-5

This screen should look familiar to you. It's the same screen you see when you click the New button in the Menu Manager (covered in Chapter 6). It works the same way. Select the menu item type you want to use from the list, and configure it in the following screen.

Does Your Home Page Have to Say "Welcome to the Frontpage"?

Something you might notice on your Joomla home page is the title "Welcome to the Frontpage," which shows up in the text itself, as well as in the HTML title tag, as shown in Figure 12-6.

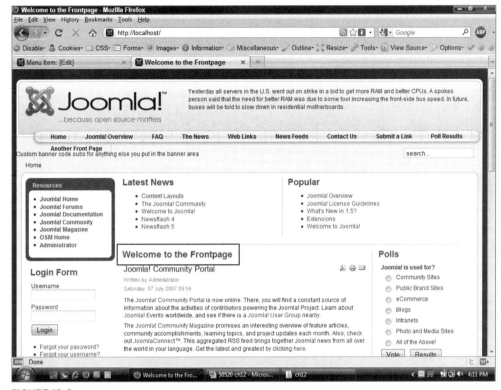

FIGURE 12-6

(The HTML title tag shows on the very top title bar of the screen next to the Firefox icon in this screenshot.)

Many people ask where this text comes from. In the Front Page Blog Layout configuration page, accessed via the Menu Manager by clicking on your Home link, under the Parameters (System) tab, note that "Welcome to the Frontpage" is actually the page title, and it's turned on by default. Turn off the page title, and "Welcome to the Frontpage" goes away, at least on the main page.

Note, however, that "Welcome to the Frontpage" persists in the HTML title tag. Although you have turned off the page title, it appears in the HTML title tag anyway. However, you can type something else in the Page Title field and have that text display in the title tag instead, even if it's not set to display on your page. Changing this text is a great way to get some good keywords into the HTML title tag, which is heavily weighted in search engines.

LAYING OUT THE HOME PAGE IN AN ARTICLE

Those of you who are familiar with HTML might want to take a look at the code generated by the Front Page Blog Layout. It's quite bloated, with a lot of nested tables. Also, this layout is limited to only articles on the home page within the component area. What if you want modules displaying in those spaces instead?

One trick I've used many times is to make an individual article my home page rather than using the Front Page Blog Layout. I cut way back on the code bloat using this technique. Of course, this option displays only a single article, right? Actually, you can include a layout in that single article, and then populate the various divisions on the page (whether you used table cells or divs) with articles or modules. Remember back in Chapter 10, "Plug-Ins That Come with Joomla!," which introduced the trick that allows you to use {loadmodule inset} to put a module anywhere on your page in an article? This is the perfect place to use that feature.

For example, look at *Brew Your Own* magazine, found at www.byo.com. Figure 12-7 shows a screenshot of the article editing screen for the home page.

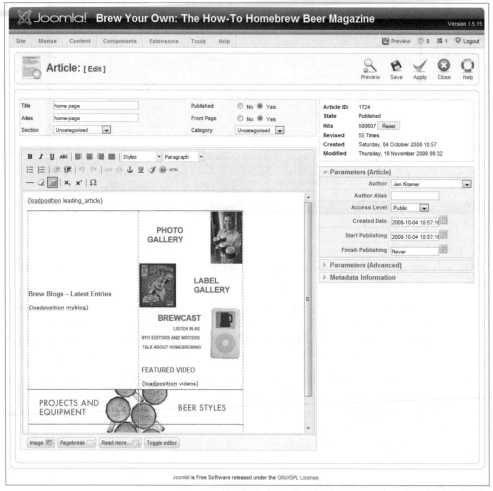

FIGURE 12-7

Compare this screen with the public home page, shown in Figure 12-8.

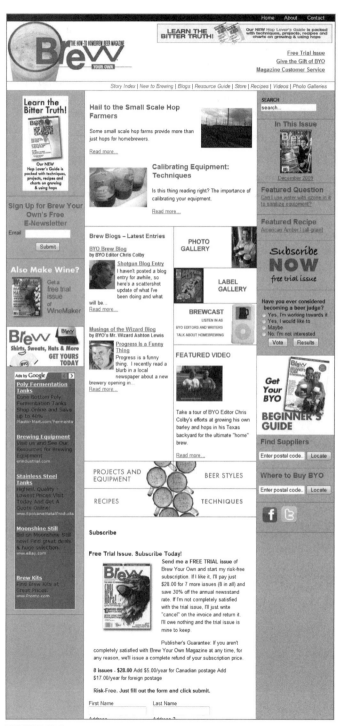

FIGURE 12-8

In Figure 12-7, the page starts with `{loadposition leading_article}`. This custom module displays a title, image, introductory text, and Read More link from two selected articles. This module is followed by the Brew Blogs on the left side. Note that it has a `{loadposition myblog}`, and it's loading some more custom modules that include the latest blog posts from the two bloggers. On the right are some static, hard-coded images to other areas of the site. This is followed by a `{loadposition videos}`, which loads a Newsflash module. It loads articles of a certain category in the position and displays their introductory text. Click the Read More link for the full article and embedded video.

This approach provides some great flexibility to display some good pieces of content, with exactly the formatting the client wanted to have.

Brew Your Own magazine maintains this site on its own, posting new editions of the magazine as they're released. Thanks to the modules provided and a lot of code behind the scenes, their job is relatively straightforward.

13

Custom Templates

➤ Prerequisites for building a template

➤ Creating a template from scratch

➤ Troubleshooting and debugging the template

After spending some time with Joomla and building a few sites, you might think about building your own template. After all, you can get exactly what the client wants for a design, plus a unique look for the site. Many people object to commercial templates on the grounds that "every site looks the same." Sites built with custom templates, however, look completely unique.

This chapter covers the background you need to build your own custom template, step-by-step instructions about how to build that template, and plenty of pointers about troubleshooting and debugging your template.

PREREQUISITES FOR CREATING CUSTOM TEMPLATES

Prior to this chapter, everything I've covered so far could be learned and completed by someone without a solid background in web design and development. However, to get the most out of this chapter and the next, you will need to know the following:

➤ **HTML.** HTML (Hypertext Markup Language) is the bedrock of the Web. All web pages, in their final format viewed in the web browser, consist of some HTML. HTML is a markup language, meaning you're identifying paragraphs, headings, lists, links, and more in a document. *HTML is not responsible for the display of the page.* That's left to…

➤ **CSS.** CSS (Cascading Style Sheets) is responsible for everything pretty: pretty colors, fonts, spacing, layouts, and much more. There may be one to several stylesheets pertaining to a given web page. You also must understand how CSS is handled differently by different web browsers and how to debug problems accordingly.

➤ **A tiny bit of XML.** You must understand at least enough XML to edit an existing document. You don't need to know how to write this document from scratch.

➤ **A little bit of PHP.** You need to at least know what PHP is, what it does, how it interfaces with the database, and how you can use it to your advantage on your site. Being a copy-and-paste whiz might be enough to get you by at a basic level.

➤ **Graphic design skills.** If you plan to create your own template, it should have a beautiful design. It should be as attractive, or preferably more attractive, than commercially available templates. If you can't produce a design more attractive than those of commercially available templates, you should just go with one of those. You'll have a better quality product. Or hire out the graphic design piece. The graphic designer needs to be an actual web designer as well, not just a print designer (see Chapter 2, "Choosing the Right Technologies to Solve the Business Problem," for more information).

➤ **Graphics production skills.** Even if you're not a designer, you should know the difference between GIF, JPG, and PNG images, how to produce those images, and how to change one large graphic into smaller graphics for your web page (a process called slicing). Typical software used for this step includes Adobe Photoshop, Adobe Fireworks, or the open source (and free) image-processing package called GIMP.

➤ **The plan.** Make sure you have a plan in place for the site map, extensions, and maintenance for the site before you start creating templates. All those items have an impact what you produce, so make sure you understand them before you decide on whether you want a blue or light blue background. (See Chapters 1 and 2 for more details.)

 As described in the following table, a number of excellent resources are available to help you enhance your web development skills. They range in price from free to several thousand dollars.

RESOURCE	DESCRIPTION	ADVANTAGE	DISADVANTAGE
Web sites	A zillion web sites promise they will teach you HTML, CSS, XML, and PHP.	Free! Zillions to choose from!	Free means no quality control, so who knows whether what they're telling you is right?
Books	A zillion books are available on these topics.	Cheap! Zillions to choose from!	You must be disciplined enough to read the book and try examples on your own time. No way exists to ask questions interactively.

RESOURCE	DESCRIPTION	ADVANTAGE	DISADVANTAGE
Training videos	Many book publishers and sites such as Lynda.com offer videos to train you.	Cheap! Increasingly available. Step-by-step instructions are valuable. It fits more learning styles.	You still must be disciplined enough to watch the movies and work through examples on your own. You typically have no way to ask questions.
Training courses	Commercial training is available on many topics, typically a one-day to one-week course. Some places, like the HTML Writer's Guild, offer wholly online classes over a six-week period.	They offer very quick learning and may be taught by experts in the field. The longer online courses typically have a homework assignment periodically, plus there's frequently an instructor answering questions on a discussion board.	Typically the one-day to one-week courses throw a lot of information at you very quickly, so there's little time to digest the information and really learn it. None of these courses offer degree credit. They are more expensive.
Courses in higher education (community college, universities)	Sign up for a semester-long class in topics of your choice.	Regular homework reinforces learning. Instructors are well qualified to teach the topics. Best learning outcomes for most people. You can leave with a degree, or you can just take a few classes. The degree may be useful in marketing or proving your skills. Courses may be offered wholly online or in person.	This option is the most expensive, but financial aid may be available. It also takes months to learn skills. You must complete an application process.

 Which plan is "best"? You guessed it: It depends. Think about your own learning style, personal self-discipline, and whether you need something to show at the end (like a degree or certification) to help guide your decision. If you don't need a degree, and you're motivated to learn, you might do fine with books or videos. If you need a homework assignment to keep you going, check out some of the longer online classes available. If the degree sounds like a good idea, by all means, enroll yourself at a community college or local university. Many schools offer web design and development degrees these days, and graduates are in good demand.

The best way to expand your Joomla skill set is to start by learning HTML and CSS. After you know those, tackle a topic a little more complicated like PHP.

For the rest of this chapter, I assume that you know HTML and CSS "cold" — that is, from a hand-coded perspective, not just how to generate HTML and CSS using a program like Adobe Dreamweaver. If you don't know XML or PHP, you learn how to pull those pieces together in this chapter. I also assume you know how to build a static HTML web page, either hand-coded or using a program like Dreamweaver.

WEB DEVELOPMENT WORKFLOWS

All web development projects follow a certain workflow. In the old days, with a static HTML site (that is, not hooked up to a database; not a content management system like Joomla), you did the following:

1. You landed a client. You discussed strategy and vision, and you developed a plan and a site map.

2. You discussed graphic design, went through several rounds of revisions, and built a Dreamweaver template.

3. You waited for your client to start delivering content. As you received content, you built out individual pages on your local computer.

4. After all the content was in place, you debugged the site in various browsers.

5. You posted the site to its final hosted location and then launched the site.

With Joomla, you can have a somewhat different workflow, which is arguably more efficient:

1. You land a client. You discuss strategy and vision, and you develop a plan and a site map (Chapters 1 and 2).

2. You set up a development area that enables you to build a site but keep it hidden from the general public. This area might be on your laptop or it might be in a hosted environment (Chapter 3).

3. In parallel, you do three tasks:

   a. You build sections, categories, and articles (perhaps using dummy content). You link these up to menus according to the site map (Chapters 5 and 6).

   b. You work with the client on the graphic design.

   c. The client works on compiling content (or the content writer works with the client to get content written).

4. You build the custom template and debug it (that's this chapter).

5. After the debugging is complete and the content is in place, you launch the site.

Because your Joomla site is no longer completely tied to its template and presentation, you can use a temporary template so you can get content in the site, and then switch to the real template when that template is ready. Provided that you use the same module positions (for example, what you want on the left, ultimately, has the same position in the temporary template), you will have very little work switching from one template to another.

For the temporary template, I recommend using a *wireframe* template, which is a very simple template done in black in white, with next to no styling. I like this template because it's crystal clear to the client that this template has nothing to do with the final look of the web site; it's just a temporary placeholder. You can download this example's wireframe template at the book's web site (www.wrox.com). Figure 13-1 shows a screenshot of the template.

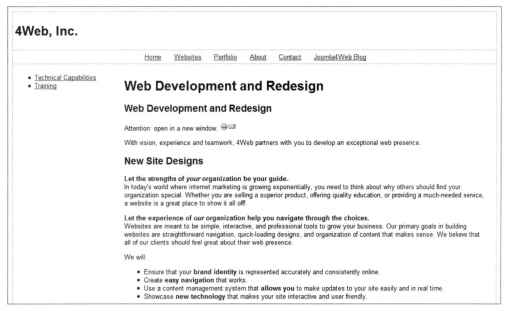

FIGURE 13-1

CREATING A CUSTOM TEMPLATE

Now that we've established that you've got a good background in HTML and CSS, and that you're not afraid to dabble in a bit of XML and PHP, we're ready to start building a custom template. At this point, you should have a finalized, approved graphic design for the site. That design was probably generated by a graphic designer (or you, if you have good graphic design skills). It should be an Adobe Photoshop PSD file, the native file format for Photoshop.

There are six major steps to creating a custom template. They should be completed in this order.

1. **Create a static HTML page.** You've probably done this before in your web development career. Convert the Photoshop design to a regular static HTML page.

2. **Insert Joomla codes.** Copy and paste in the codes that Joomla requires to show modules and components.

3. **Modify the XML file.** Modify a copy of an existing XML file to identify the images, stylesheets, and other files that make up your template so that it can be installed on your Joomla site.

4. **Create a favicon.** A favicon is the little picture that shows up next to the URL in some web browsers.

5. **Create a template thumbnail.** The template thumbnail is the little preview of the template you see when you roll your mouse over the template names in the Template Manager.

6. **Zip and upload the files.** Once all the preceding files exist, zip them together to create a package to install in your Joomla site.

Creating a Static HTML Page

After you've gone through the process of creating a graphic design for your client, the first step in creating a Joomla template is to build a standard HTML web page. Use standard markup to create left and/or right columns, a header, horizontal navigation, footer, and so on — whatever might be required for the design. If you were given one design for the home page and another design for the inside pages of the web site, start with the inside page design first. You can build the home page design later (either as a separate template or included in the same template; see Chapter 14 for details).

When creating this page, don't spend a huge amount of time working on the CSS piece of the design. Ultimately, Joomla will put in code for the modules, various components, menus, and so forth, and its HTML may not be the same as what you're using in terms of classes, IDs, and overall HTML structure. Joomla does want a very specific file structure when creating your template, however. I'll describe that structure below.

If you want to follow along, in this example I use Adobe Dreamweaver CS4. The program comes with some canned layouts, which are not pretty, but they're very functional. I'll show you how to use these canned Dreamweaver layouts to create a Joomla template. Adobe Dreamweaver is well worth buying, because it's an excellent HTML editor for those of you with a designer bent. A free, 30-day trial is available at www.adobe.com. If it's too expensive for your budget, or you're just a big open source fan, you might check out KompoZer, www.kompozer.net. It doesn't come with Dreamweaver's layouts and it's not as full-featured as Dreamweaver, but it does offer much of the functionality of Dreamweaver.

For those of you who want to follow along with the code, you can find the files for this chapter at www.wrox.com or www.joomlastarttofinish.com.

Open Dreamweaver, and get your static HTML page started!

1. Create a Dreamweaver site (by choosing Site ⇨ New Site). The root of your Dreamweaver site should be based on a folder called `templates` you created and saved on your desktop.

2. Inside of the folder called `templates`, make two more folders. Name one folder `images` (the word all spelled out, not `img`, no capital letters) and name the other folder `css` (again, all lowercase).

    As you might expect, all images for the template should be located in the `images` folder. Do not make subfolders; put all the images in the same folder. Likewise, your stylesheet should be located in your `css` folder. You will create one stylesheet for your template to start with. You can name this stylesheet whatever you like; I typically name mine `default.css`.

3. Create a three-column fixed, header and footer layout, with the stylesheet created as a separate document, as shown in Figure 13-2. Click the Create New File button when you're done configuring this screen.

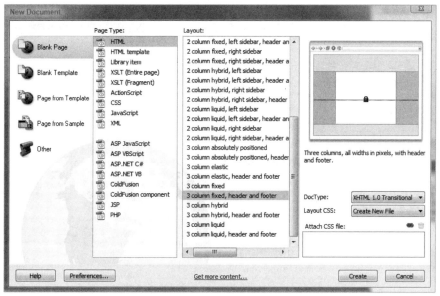

FIGURE 13-2

4. When Dreamweaver asks you where the stylesheet should be saved, name it `default.css` and save it to your `templates/css` folder, as shown in Figure 13-3. The page, with its layout, is created for you.

FIGURE 13-3

5. Save the HTML page as `index.html` so that you have a copy of the file you started with, as shown in Figure 13-4. This should be saved directly in the `templates` folder (not in a subdirectory). I am working in Design View in this screenshot.

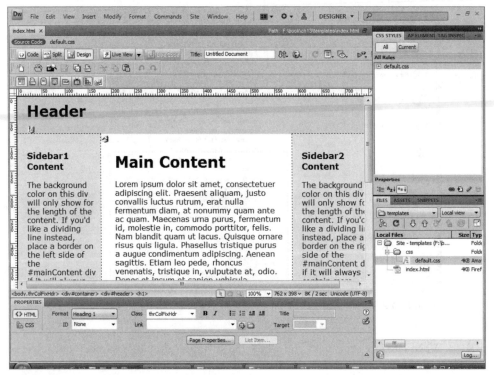

FIGURE 13-4

6. To have an example of an image to work with, remove the text that says "Header" and insert a logo instead. The logo should be located in the `templates/images` folder. You can insert the logo via Design View (as I did) or in Code View.

The page now looks like Figure 13-5 (Dreamweaver Design View). Be sure to pay attention to the Local Files panel on the right side, which shows the file structure for what you're building.

7. You've sweated long enough over this work of beauty. Open the file in a browser to see what it looks like. It should resemble Figure 13-6.

8. You are now done working with this document as index.html. Save the file, if you haven't already, and then resave the file with a new name, `index.php`.

With the static HTML page created, and with our copy of that page called `index.php`, you're ready to insert the Joomla codes that make this page a real Joomla template.

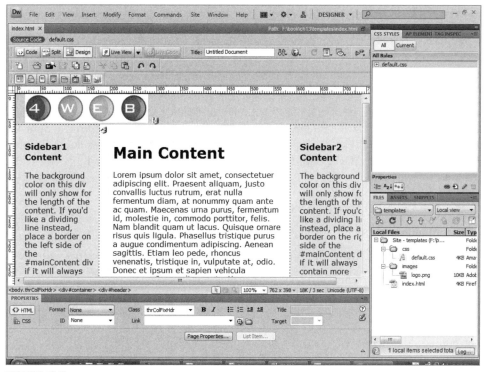

FIGURE 13-5

Sidebar1 Content

The background color on this div will only show for the length of the content. If you'd like a dividing line instead, place a border on the left side of the #mainContent div if it will always contain more content.

Donec eu mi sed turpis feugiat feugiat. Integer turpis arcu, pellentesque eget, cursus et, fermentum ut, sapien.

Main Content

Lorem ipsum dolor sit amet, consectetuer adipiscing elit. Praesent aliquam, justo convallis luctus rutrum, erat nulla fermentum diam, at nonummy quam ante ac quam. Maecenas urna purus, fermentum id, molestie in, commodo porttitor, felis. Nam blandit quam ut lacus. Quisque ornare risus quis ligula. Phasellus tristique purus a augue condimentum adipiscing. Aenean sagittis. Etiam leo pede, rhoncus venenatis, tristique in, vulputate at, odio. Donec et ipsum et sapien vehicula nonummy. Suspendisse potenti.

H2 level heading

Lorem ipsum dolor sit amet, consectetuer adipiscing elit. Praesent aliquam, justo convallis luctus rutrum, erat nulla fermentum diam, at nonummy quam ante ac quam. Maecenas urna purus, fermentum id, molestie in, commodo porttitor, felis. Nam blandit quam ut lacus. Quisque ornare risus quis ligula. Phasellus tristique purus

Sidebar2 Content

The background color on this div will only show for the length of the content. If you'd like a dividing line instead, place a border on the right side of the #mainContent div if it will always contain more content.

Donec eu mi sed turpis feugiat feugiat. Integer turpis arcu, pellentesque eget, cursus et, fermentum ut, sapien.

FIGURE 13-6

Inserting the Joomla! Codes

What makes your HTML page become a Joomla template are some special codes that you will insert at various points in the document. These codes allow the template to talk with the Joomla database and load in the right modules and components in the right places. Fortunately, you don't need to know these codes or memorize them. You simply copy them from one document to another.

In Dreamweaver, you'll need to flip index.php over to Code View (if you're not already there) to put these codes into place. If you do flip back to Design view (or if you're working in Split View), you'll note that the display will break. That's totally normal! Dreamweaver does not talk to Joomla or render these Joomla codes. Have faith that it will all come out well in the end.

You will insert the following four code snippets into your index.php file:

> ➤ **Head code**, which goes in the HTML head of the document

> ➤ **Module code**, which displays modules

> ➤ **Component code**, which displays the article (or component) associated with the page

> ➤ **Message code**, which displays any warning messages.

Head Code

The head code contains meta tags for keywords and descriptions, the HTML title for the web page, and links to stylesheets. The code looks like this:

```
<?php defined( '_JEXEC' ) or die( 'Restricted access' ); ?>

<!DOCTYPE html PUBLIC "-//W3C//DTD XHTML 1.0 Transitional//EN"
"http://www.w3.org/TR/xhtml1/DTD/xhtml1-transitional.dtd">

<html xmlns="http://www.w3.org/1999/xhtml"
xml:lang="<?php echo $this->language; ?>" lang="<?php echo $this->language; ?>" >

<head>

<jdoc:include type="head" />

<link rel="stylesheet" href="<?php echo $this->baseurl; ?>
/templates/system/css/general.css" type="text/css" />

<link rel="stylesheet" href="<?php echo $this->baseurl; ?>/templates/
<?php echo $this->template; ?>/css/default.css" type="text/css" />

</head>
```

I've put spaces in-between the lines so the code is a little more readable. Here are the line-by-line descriptions:

> ➤ Line 1 is a test (written in PHP) to find out whether Joomla is running. If it is, the program moves on to the next line; otherwise, it "dies" and returns the message "Restricted access." (You can change that message to anything you want, provided that you leave the quotes and other syntax in place.)

- ➤ Line 2 is a doctype declaration, which means that the page declares itself written in XHTML 1.0 transitional.

  For you standards geeks out there, you can pick whatever standard you like for your template, including XHTML 1.0 strict. Keep in mind that much of the rest of Joomla 1.5 is written to the 1.0 transitional standard.

- ➤ Line 3 is the opening HTML tag for the document. It also contains a language declaration, which is pulled from Joomla.

- ➤ Line 4 is an opening `head` tag.

- ➤ Line 5 is a Joomla-specific function, which says to find all information that normally goes in the `head` of the document and write it here. That includes a lot of meta tags and the HTML title, for the most part.

- ➤ Line 6 is a link to the Joomla core stylesheet. This contains some default styling for things such as errors, editors, and so forth. Including this link is a good practice.

- ➤ Line 7 is a link to your own stylesheet, `default.css`. You can copy Line 7 and modify it for as many additional stylesheets as you have.

- ➤ Line 8 closes the `head` tag.

In Dreamweaver, copy the entire `head` code and paste it into `index.php`. You will erase everything from the very top of the document down to the `</head>` tag. (If you flip to Design view after pasting the `head` code, that is when you'll notice that all styling is gone for the page. The path to the CSS file for `index.php` is no longer correct, so the page will look odd. This is normal. Keep working in Code view so you can paste in the next few Joomla codes.)

Module Code

Next, think about where you want modules to appear on this page. In all likelihood, with the design you created in Dreamweaver, you want modules in two places: in the left and right columns. If you're used to working with commercial templates, you might be thinking to yourself that this sounds amazing. A template with only two module positions? Remember that in custom coding, if the design doesn't require 25 module positions, you don't have to put them in. You only need as many positions as you'll use.

The module code looks like this:

```
<jdoc:include type="modules" name="top" style="xhtml" />
```

This code will find all modules that have a position of `top` and write them to the page at that spot with a `style` of `xhtml`.

The module position name can be whatever you like. It's nice if it's self-documenting. If the module position is going on the left side of the page, maybe "left" makes sense. If it's going to hold the search module and nothing else, perhaps you call it "search." You could call module positions "george" and "sally" if you want, but these types of names tend to get confusing, so I recommend the self-documenting approach.

Module styles come in the following six flavors (although you'll likely only ever use two of them):

➤ xhtml. A single, simple div wraps around the module.

➤ rounded. Four divs wrap around the module, enabling you to create rounded corners.

➤ table. An HTML table wraps around the module.

➤ horz. A single HTML table with one module per cell is created in a horizontal direction.

➤ outline. Great for debugging, this outlines each module position and writes its name in the corner.

➤ none. There are no surrounding divs or tables at all. However, if your module uses none, the title of the module will not be displayed, even if you have specified that the module title should display in the web page.

In all likelihood, you'll only ever use xhtml and rounded, but you should know the other positions exist, in case you encounter them in someone else's code. xhtml and rounded are standards-compliant, in that they use the div tag, a generic tag, for displaying the modules. table and horz both use HTML tables for display, which is discouraged due to code bloat. outline is useful only for debugging. none is not useful if you need the module title to display on the web page.

 If you forget to specify a style, or misspell the style, none *will be used as a default.*

You should copy the module codes for the left and right columns into your Dreamweaver document. The two module positions are left and right. The final code for each is as follows:

```
<jdoc:include type="modules" name="left" style="xhtml" />
<jdoc:include type="modules" name="right" style="xhtml" />
```

Component and Message Codes

The component code is where the content goes. It's also where any of the components will display, such as Web Links or Contacts.

The Joomla code for the component is as follows:

```
<jdoc:include type="component" />
```

This code can appear only once in your document, whereas the module code can appear as many times as you like.

You also want to include the code for a message. A message is typically an error message, or it could be a message stating simply that "your message has been sent" when completing the form on a contact page. (Contact pages and the Contact component were covered extensively in Chapter 9.) The message code is as follows:

```
<jdoc:include type="message" />
```

I typically put the message and component codes right next to each other — message first, followed by component, as follows:

```
<jdoc:include type="message" /><jdoc:include type="component" />
```

Copy and paste the message and component codes into index.php and save. Your code in index.php should now look like the following:

```
<?php defined( '_JEXEC' ) or die( 'Restricted access' ); ?>
<!DOCTYPE html PUBLIC "-//W3C//DTD XHTML 1.0 Transitional//EN" "http://www.w3.org/
TR/xhtml1/DTD/xhtml1-transitional.dtd">
<html xmlns="http://www.w3.org/1999/xhtml"
xml:lang="<?php echo $this->language; ?>" lang="<?php echo $this->language; ?>" >
<head>
<jdoc:include type="head" />
<link rel="stylesheet" href="<?php echo $this->baseurl;
?>/templates/system/css/general.css" type="text/css" />
<link rel="stylesheet" href="<?php echo $this->baseurl; ?>/templates/
<?php echo $this->template; ?>/css/default.css" type="text/css" />
</head>

<body class="thrColFixHdr">

<div id="container">
  <div id="header">
    <img src="images/logo.png" width="265" height="60" alt="4Web, Inc." />
  </div>
  <div id="sidebar1">
    <jdoc:include type="modules" name="left" style="xhtml" />
  </div>
  <div id="sidebar2">
    <jdoc:include type="modules" name="right" style="xhtml" />
  </div>
  <div id="mainContent">
    <jdoc:include type="message" /><jdoc:include type="component" />
  </div>
  <br class="clearfloat" />
  <div id="footer">
    <p>Footer</p>
  </div>
</div>
</body>
</html>
```

Save index.php again. You're done with it. The file now contains the head, module, message, and component codes, which you've copied and pasted into the index.php file.

Now it's time to create an XML installation file.

Modifying the XML File

The XML file is always called templateDetails.xml. (Be sure to note the capitalization; it's important.) It's used in the installation of a template and tells Joomla where to put all the files.

The XML file looks something like this (and is available to download at the book's web site, www.wrox.com):

```xml
<?xml version="1.0" encoding="utf-8"?>
<install type="template" version="1.5">
  <name>inside</name>
  <version>1.0</version>
  <creationDate>10/4/09</creationDate>
  <author>4Web, Inc.</author>
  <authorEmail>info@4webinc.com</authorEmail>
  <authorUrl>www.4webinc.com</authorUrl>
  <copyright>(c) 2009 4Web, Inc.</copyright>
  <license>GNU/GPL</license>
  <description>sample inside template</description>
  <files>
            <filename>index.php</filename>
            <filename>templateDetails.xml</filename>
            <filename>favicon.ico</filename>
            <filename>template_thumbnail.png</filename>
            <filename>css/default.css</filename>
            <filename>images/logo.png</filename>
  </files>
</install>
```

The following describes this file line by line:

➤   Line 1 states that this code is XML and that encoding is done by the UTF-8 standard.

➤   Line 2 says this code is a template installation (as opposed to a module or component, which also use XML files for their installation process), and the Joomla version is 1.5.

➤   Line 3 is the name of the template. It becomes the name of the folder and the name that displays in the Template Manager screen. I recommend using all lowercase letters and no spaces or funny characters (such as parenthesis, dollar signs, exclamation points, etc.) for this name.

➤   Line 4 indicates the template version.

➤   Line 5 is the creation date of the template. This template's date is set to October 4, 2009. You can set yours to 10/4/09, 4/10/09 (the European standard), October 4, 2009, 4 Oct 2009, or any other permutation you want.

➤   Line 6 is the author of the template, in this case, 4Web, Inc.

➤   Line 7 is the author's email address.

➤   Line 8 is the URL for the author's site or blog.

➤   Line 9 indicates the copyright holder.

➤   Line 10 indicates the type of license used for this template installation.

➤   Line 11 is the description of the template. From the Template Manager, when you select a template for editing, the description will show up on the left side of the screen.

The rest of the XML is a list of files that will be contained in the zipped package that you will create shortly to install the template (see the section, "Zipping and Uploading Files"). The files include the following:

➤ **index.php.** You created this in the previous section, where you saved `index.html` as `index.php` and added Joomla codes.

➤ **templateDetails.xml.** This is the name of the XML file.

➤ **favicon.ico.** This is a favicon, which you have not created yet.

➤ **template_thumbnail.png.** This is the thumbnail that shows up when you mouse over the template filename in the Template Manager and that you have not created yet.

➤ **css/default.css.** This is the stylesheet that you created.

➤ **images/logo.png.** This is the logo in your page.

If you had more than one stylesheet and/or more than one image, you would need to list those, line by line. Copy one line and paste it as many times as you have files, and then edit it.

For example, if you also had an image called `bkgd.gif`, you would modify the XML `files` section from the following:

```
<files>
            <filename>index.php</filename>
            <filename>templateDetails.xml</filename>
            <filename>favicon.ico</filename>
            <filename>template_thumbnail.png</filename>
            <filename>css/default.css</filename>
            <filename>images/logo.png</filename>
    </files>
```

to the following:

```
<files>
            <filename>index.php</filename>
            <filename>templateDetails.xml</filename>
            <filename>favicon.ico</filename>
            <filename>template_thumbnail.png</filename>
            <filename>css/default.css</filename>
            <filename>images/logo.png</filename>
            <filename>images/bkgd.gif</filename>

    </files>
```

If you also had an additional stylesheet called `navigation.css`, the XML files section would now look as follows:

```
<files>
            <filename>index.php</filename>
            <filename>templateDetails.xml</filename>
            <filename>favicon.ico</filename>
            <filename>template_thumbnail.png</filename>
            <filename>css/default.css</filename>
```

```
<filename>css/navigation.css</filename>
<filename>images/logo.png</filename>
<filename>images/bkgd.gif</filename>

</files>
```

You can download this XML file at www.wrox.com and edit the file for your template. Be sure to list all the files that are present in the `files` section of the XML document. If you include too many files, or not enough lines to describe the files, your template installation will ultimately fail.

Now you have your `index.php` file with all the critical codes, all your template-specific images, and all your stylesheets, and the XML file created and organized. Next you need to add a favicon and a template thumbnail (you call these out in the XML file, though neither exists yet).

Creating a Favicon

A *favicon* is that cute little 16×16 pixel icon that shows up next to the URL in a browser (assuming the browser supports favicon display, of course).

Because a favicon is so small, you should choose a simple design. Your photo may not work well, but the first letter of your name would be great. You want to create a square that contains the desired image.

After you've chosen a design, go to the web site www.favicon.cc. You can import an image, which the site will convert to a favicon for you.

Ultimately, your image should be called `favicon.ico` and you should put it in the root of your `templates` folder, with the `index.php` file. A favicon in this location overwrites the default Joomla favicon for those pages where the template is assigned.

 If you have multiple templates on your site, you must put the same favicon in each template folder for it to show up all the time.

Note that a favicon is *not* required. If you don't include it, the default Joomla favicon will show on the site. Favicons do add a little fun and interest, and they're used in bookmarking, which might make your site stand out in a list of bookmarks.

The final task is to create a template thumbnail, which was also called out in the XML document.

Creating a Template Thumbnail

The *template thumbnail* is the tiny picture that shows up when you mouse over a link in the Template Manager.

Essentially, you want to create a small 206×150 image and save it as a PNG file called `template_thumbnail.png`. It should be stored in the root of your `templates` folder, in the same location as `favicon.ico` and `index.php`.

I recommend displaying your HTML page, `index.html`, in your browser window and using it as the source for your template thumbnail. Take a screenshot, crop out the browser "chrome" (the stuff that appears around the browser window), and resize the image to 206×150 in your image processing software of choice (Photoshop, Fireworks, GIMP, etc).

Zipping and Uploading the Template Files

Now that you've created all the files, and listed them all in your XML file, you need to zip up everything into a single file. Be sure not to include index.html, because it's not listed in the XML file, and it's not needed as part of the Joomla template.

You can use any utility that creates a .zip file to zip the files. Some utilities come with Mac or PC operating systems, whereas others can be downloaded for free or for a small fee.

After you have the zipped group of files created, you can upload it to your Joomla web site. Choose Extensions ⮑ Install/Uninstall, and then Upload Package File. Browse for your zipped file and upload it, as shown in Figure 13-7.

FIGURE 13-7

If all goes well, you should get an Install Template Success message, as shown in Figure 13-8. Note also that the template description displays on this page.

Go to the Template Manager, choose the "inside" template from the list, and set it as the default template by clicking the Default icon in the upper right, as shown in Figure 13-9.

Take a look at the front end of the site. Oh no! As shown in Figure 13-10, it has a number of problems.

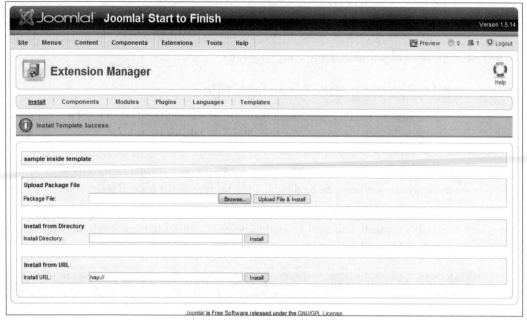

FIGURE 13-8

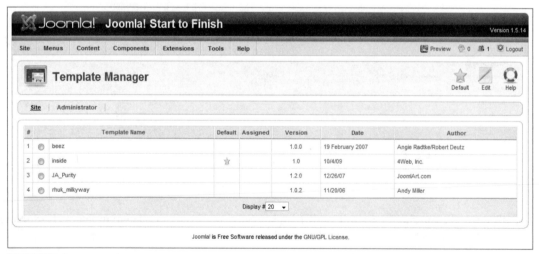

FIGURE 13-9

FIGURE 13-10

SOLVING COMMON TEMPLATE PROBLEMS

Well, clearly the template code is not quite finished yet. You've successfully uploaded it to the web site, and it's controlling the look of the web page. Unfortunately, it's not quite perfect yet, not on first upload. You have a few issues to fix.

Path Problems

Figure 13-10 shows the home page with a single article displayed. (This page is a new Joomla install without the sample data, with a single article in the site. Your site may look very different from this example.)

Note that no logo appears in the upper-left corner, only the `alt` text (as displayed in a Firefox browser; it may look somewhat different in other browsers). Remember that `alt` text is a text description of the image shown, located as an attribute within the `img` tag. There was a nice logo in the corner in the `index.html` file, so what happened to it?

The logo was included in the zipped file, but it's not displaying here. Typically, the problem in these kinds of cases is a bad path to the image. Now take a look at the path to the image in your template and fix it.

Go to the Template Manager under the Extensions menu, select the "inside" template and click Edit, and then click the Edit HTML button in the upper-right corner of the screen that appears. The Template HTML Editor opens with a screen of code, as shown in Figure 13-11.

The following line of code calls the logo:

```
<img src="images/logo.png" width="265" height="60" alt="4Web, Inc." />
```

FIGURE 13-11

Joomla interprets this path as http://www.joomlastarttofinish.com/images/logo.png. In other words, it's looking for the images in the wrong place. It's looking relative to the *root* folder of the site, not relative to the *templates* folder.

You need to tweak that path in one of three ways. Here is one solution:

```
<img src="templates/inside/images/logo.png" width="265" height="60"
alt="4Web, Inc." />
```

➤ **Positive:** Very quick and easy to code.

➤ **Negative:** It's hard-coded, so if you ever change the path to where the templates are stored, you will have to also edit the path to every image in the template.

Here is another solution:

```
<img src="<?php echo $this->baseurl ?>/templates/<?php echo $this->template; ?>
images/logo.png" width="265" height="60" alt="4Web, Inc." />
```

This solution uses two PHP variable statements. The first, `<?php echo $this->baseurl ?>`, puts in the first part of the URL for the site, which in this case is http://www.joomlastarttofinish.com. This URL is followed by the templates folder, which is then followed by the second variable statement, `<?php echo $this->template; ?>`, which means to fill in the folder in which this template is located. The final output for this path, then, is `http://www.joomlastartofinish.com/templates/` `inside/images/logo.png` — nearly the same path as was hard coded in the earlier example.

> ➤ **Positive:** It's a flexible path, so if you change the site to have a different web address, or you change the path to the folder where the template is stored, this code will accommodate those changes.

> ➤ **Negative:** It requires a little extra PHP to paste into the page, and may be a little more difficult to understand what's happening.

A third solution is a simple relative path:

```
<img src="templates/<?php echo $this->template; ?>/images/logo.png" width="265"
height="60" alt="4Web, Inc." />
```

> ➤ **Positive:** It's a flexible path, so if you change the path to the folder where the template is stored, this code will accommodate those changes. It also does not have an absolute URL, so perhaps this will load a little more quickly.

> ➤ **Negative:** Again, a little extra PHP is necessary.

Any of these solutions will work, so pick the easiest one for you.

Refresh your page, and the logo should now be visible, as shown in Figure 13-12.

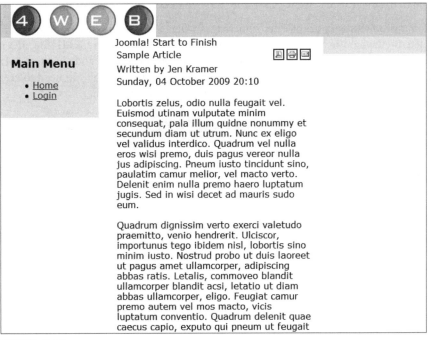

FIGURE 13-12

Wrong Page Title on Home Page

Another problem has to do with the page title. Remember that the title of this page, "Joomla! Start to Finish" is the Page Title, which was located in the menu item for Home. If you want to get rid of it, you must edit the menu item, as covered in Chapter 12.

Styling Problems

You'll no doubt notice that an awful lot of styling needs to happen. The article title, "Sample Article" is as large as the author line and date underneath. The icons for PDF, Print, and E-mail have ugly blue boxes around them. The font might be a little big. And on the right side, the start of a column appears, but there's nothing in it. If you had nothing to put in the right column, could you make the right column go away? And could you make it show up if you did have something to put in that right column?

All these problems are fixable. The article title, blue boxes, and font size are all controlled by CSS. The right column trick just takes a little fancy footwork. Chapter 14 covers coding an "optional" right column.

Template Installation Problems

Did your template not install?

Chances are you listed something in the XML file that wasn't in the zipped file, or you had an extra file in the zipped file that wasn't listed in the XML file. Be sure to check your list of files carefully.

Unfortunately, Joomla produces very cryptic error messages when something like this happens. For example, if you delete the favicon in your zipped file without mentioning it in the XML file, an error like the one shown in Figure 13-13 appears. You should either delete the line of code in the XML file calling for the favicon (in which case, the default Joomla favicon will display), or you need to create a favicon and include it in the zipped file in the location specified in the XML file.

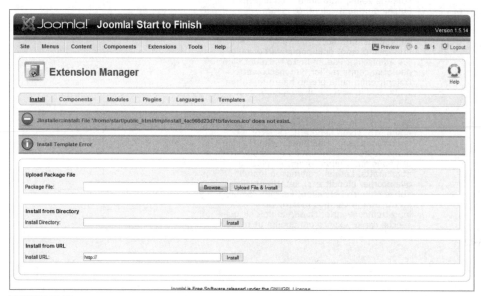

FIGURE 13-13

Another common problem you encounter occurs when you recycle the XML file into another template. Each template on a particular site must have a unique name. If you try to install a second template, but you forget to change Line 3 in the XML file (the template name), an error message appears that the template already exists.

If you want to try a second, third, or fourth time installing a template, remember that unless you uninstall the previous attempt, you might also get this error that the template already exists (even though the template did not install previously!). To uninstall a template, choose Extensions ⇨ Install/Uninstall, go to the Templates tab, select the template you want to uninstall from the list, and click the Uninstall button in the upper right, as shown in Figure 13-14.

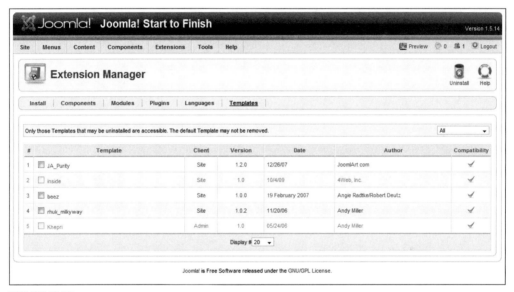

FIGURE 13-14

Be aware that you cannot delete your default template — that's why the "inside" template is grayed out in the list in the figure. You may also notice a template called Khepri that you may not have seen before. It is your back-end administrator template, which is set to the back-end default template.

Now that you know the basic mechanics of creating and installing a custom template, it's time to move on to making it pretty (okay, prettier). You do a lot of CSS editing in the next chapter, and you learn some fancy tricks with optional module regions as well (such as the optional right column I mentioned earlier).

14

Advanced Template and CSS Tricks

WHAT'S IN THIS CHAPTER?

- ➤ Conditional statements and optional regions
- ➤ Exceptions for the home page
- ➤ Template overrides
- ➤ Understanding suffixes
- ➤ Advanced templating examples

Now that you've built your first template, you are probably wondering about some more advanced tricks. For example, you have a right column in your template; however, on some pages, no modules are assigned to that area. You still have a right column with nothing in it. Wouldn't it be nice if that column could go away?

It can! With a little PHP magic, you can remove columns and do many other things to add sophistication to your templates. Throw in some cool CSS tricks, and you are on our way to a very professional-looking — and behaving — template.

This chapter is full of goodies for taking your templates to the next level. You'll learn how to incorporate multiple layouts in the same template, share stylesheets across templates, work with suffixes to do some very customized styling, and see a few examples of real sites using these techniques. As with the previous chapter, all files are available at wrox.com.

USING CONDITIONAL STATEMENTS AND OPTIONAL REGIONS

A *conditional statement* is one that tests to see whether something is true. If something is true, the code does one thing. If something is false, the code does something else.

An "optional region" is a term I borrowed from the Dreamweaver lexicon. In Dreamweaver, an optional region is a region in a template that can be enabled or disabled by someone setting up a new page based on that template. In Joomla, an optional region is a module position that exists if there's something to put in it; otherwise, it does not exist. Whether or not that Joomla module position exists is driven by a conditional statement.

Take a look at the totally awesome template that you created at the end of Chapter 13. Figure 14-1 shows the home page.

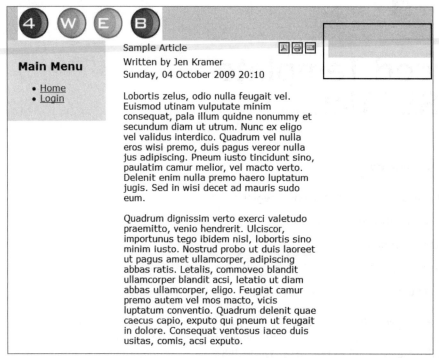

FIGURE 14-1

This design has many aspects that, no doubt, will trouble graphic designers. But note particularly in the right column the strange gray box that shows up. Where is it coming from?

Check the template code:

```
<div id="sidebar2">
  <jdoc:include type="modules" name="right" style="xhtml" />
</div>
```

The first line of this code says to start a div with an id of sidebar2. The second line writes in the modules assigned to this page for the right position, in the style of xhtml. Finally, the last line closes the div.

Computers frequently do exactly what you tell them to do. The best way to check what the computer is doing (and what you told it to do) is to view the HTML that makes up your web page via your browser's "view source" option. (Safari and Internet Explorer use the term "View Source," whereas Firefox uses "Page Source.")

I prefer using Firefox as my web browser. It offers great extensions for viewing your source, checking your standards compliance, tinkering with CSS, outlining regions, and much more. The extension I use all the time for this type of work is the Web Developer extension (`https://addons.mozilla.org/en-US/firefox/addon/60`). Others prefer Firebug (`http://getfirebug.com`). This chapter's examples use the Web Developer extension. To follow along, open up Firefox (or download and install it on your computer, then open it), and go to the above link for the Web Developer extension. Click the big green Add to Firefox button, and the extension will download and install within Firefox. You may need to restart Firefox to use the Web Developer extension.

In the Web Developer extension, you can click the View Source button, or you can choose View ⇨ Page Source. Scroll through the code to find the right column, a `div` with an ID of `sidebar2`. You will see the following:

```
<div id="sidebar2">

</div>
```

Notice what's happening here. As indicated by the empty second line, no module has been assigned to this page for the right column. Therefore, the PHP statement `<jdoc:include type="modules" name="right" style="xhtml" />` looked for modules for this page assigned the `right` position and found none. So, it wrote nothing to the page, thus the blank line. The problem with the original code is that the `id` of `sidebar2` has the following styling with it:

```
#sidebar2 {
      float: right;
      width: 160px;
      background: #EBEBEB;
      padding: 15px 10px 15px 20px;
}
```

Now what happens is that the `div` is written in, with the `padding` and a `background` color, which means that `div` shows up as a little gray box.

Remember, when you see four sets of numbers after padding, margin, *and various other CSS notation, you read them as top, right, bottom, left. Stay out of TRouBLe by remembering TRBL! Thank you to Eric Meyer, from whose books I've learned so much.*

So, the template is doing what you told it to do! It's writing in the `div` first, but then finding no modules to fill it. Instead, you need a little piece of code that says:

If at least one module is assigned to the right position, write in the modules and the `div` *that surrounds them. If not, do nothing.*

Fortunately, such a code snippet exists. Try changing your code as follows:

```php
<?php if ($this->countModules('right')) : ?>
<div id="sidebar2">
    <jdoc:include type="modules" name="right" style="xhtml" />
  </div>
<?php endif; ?>
```

What does the preceding say? A PHP tag always starts with an angle bracket (<), a question mark (?), and then php (<?php). It ends with a question mark and an angle bracket going the other way (?>). The code after the php in the tag says to count all the modules for the right position that are assigned to this page. If at least one exists, do what follows. An endif ends the statement. Obviously these directions are packed into a tiny little bit of code, but it works! Put it in your template and see Figure 14-2 for the results.

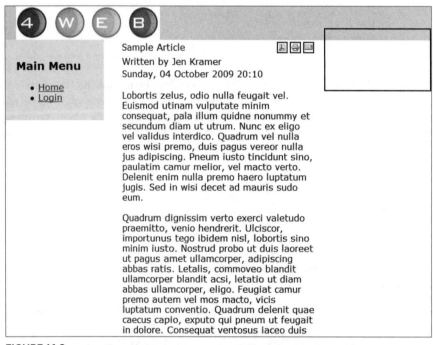

FIGURE 14-2

Hooray, the gray box is gone! If you check the code, you will see that no mention of any sidebar2 exists anywhere in the code.

"But wait," some graphic designers might say. "The text is still confined to the middle of the page. We want it to stretch into what was previously the right column."

You can do this, too. Make sure you know why that space exists. Take a look at the stylesheet, default.css. You can easily view it using the Web Developer extension in Firefox by going to its toolbar and selecting CSS-Edit CSS.

In the stylesheet, the left and right columns (IDs of sidebar1 and sidebar2) are floated to the left and right, respectively, whereas the main content (ID of mainContent) simply has big margins, as shown below.

```
#mainContent {
        margin: 0 200px;
        padding: 0 10px;
}
```

 Remember, when you see two sets of numbers after padding, margin, *and various other CSS notation, you read them as top/bottom for the first number, and left/right for the second number.*

Therefore, the mainContent ID is set to have a margin of 200px (pixels) on the left and right for every page on the web site. Now what you must do is have an exception to this styling rule. If no right column exists, you also do not want to have the right margin (or, more accurately, you want a much smaller right margin; otherwise, the text will run right to the edge of the page).

How could you do this? Likely, more than one answer exists if you know PHP, but I'm a simple HTML/ CSS designer. What I must do is assign one ID to the div that is currently called mainContent if the right column is present, but a different ID if no right column is present. This technique enables you to style that different ID to have a left margin of 200px and a right margin of something less, maybe 15px.

Let's take a look at the template code again, as it currently stands:

```
<?php if ($this->countModules('right')) : ?>
<div id="sidebar2">
    <jdoc:include type="modules" name="right" style="xhtml" />
  </div>
<?php endif; ?>

  <div id="mainContent">
    <jdoc:include type="message" /><jdoc:include type="component" />
  </div>
```

You want to change it to the following:

```
<?php if ($this->countModules('right')) : ?>
<div id="sidebar2">
    <jdoc:include type="modules" name="right" style="xhtml" />
  </div>
<?php endif; ?>

<?php if ($this->countModules('right')) : ?>
  <div id="mainContent">
<?php endif; ?>

<?php if (!$this->countModules('right')) : ?>
  <div id="mainContentNoRight">
```

```
<?php endif; ?>

    <jdoc:include type="message" /><jdoc:include type="component" />
  </div>
```

What does the preceding code say?

The first block of code you wrote earlier; it controls whether the right column will display. You haven't changed anything there.

The second block of code says, if right modules exist, then write the following HTML (a div with an ID of mainContent). You don't have to call a module position inside of your conditional code; you can actually do anything you want.

The third block of code is a little different. It's the same conditional statement, but a ! appears in front of $this. That means to take the opposite of the statement. In other words, count the modules assigned to this page for the right position. If no modules are assigned, write the following HTML (a div with an ID of mainContentNoRight).

This is all followed by the code for the Joomla message and the component, followed by the closing div. (I covered this in Chapter 13.)

Real PHP programmers would look at this code and say, "How verbose!" They would recommend making this code much shorter. Rather than having separate statements for the module and the start of the div, if right modules are present, you could combine the statements as follows:

```
<?php if ($this->countModules('right')) : ?>
<div id="sidebar2">
    <jdoc:include type="modules" name="right" style="xhtml" />
  </div>
  <div id="mainContent">
<?php endif; ?>

<?php if (!$this->countModules('right')) : ?>
  <div id="mainContentNoRight">
<?php endif; ?>

    <jdoc:include type="message" /><jdoc:include type="component" />
  </div>
```

Now you have only two statements. One thing happens if right modules are present, and another thing happens if they're not.

However, you can combine the statements even further. Rather than having two separate if statements, you could make a single one, starting with an if statement, and putting an else in the middle. This means evaluate the first statement. If it's true, do this; else, do this other thing, as follows:

```
<?php if ($this->countModules('right')) : ?>
<div id="sidebar2">
    <jdoc:include type="modules" name="right" style="xhtml" />
  </div>
```

```
    <div id="mainContent">

<?php else : ?>

    <div id="mainContentNoRight">
<?php endif; ?>

      <jdoc:include type="message" /><jdoc:include type="component" />
    </div>
```

The preceding code says to count all modules assigned to this page in the `right` position. If at least one module exists, write in a `div` of ID `sidebar2`, followed by the `modules`, and close the `div`. Next, start another `div` with an ID of `mainContent`. Otherwise (that is, if not even one module exists), write in a `div` with an ID of `mainContentNoRight`. Follow that by the Joomla `message` and the Joomla `component`, and close the `div` (which in this case is either the `mainContent` or the `mainContentNoRight` div).

Which block of code is "best?" Yep, it depends! Most programmers would tell you this last block of code is most correct, because it's streamlined into a minimum amount of code. However, if you don't understand it, and you're the developer, then that's not the right answer for you. Put in more `if` statements if that helps. You may be adding slightly to the overall overhead of your template by doing this, but for most sites, that really doesn't matter too much.

By the way, while you've been tweaking code, the front end of the site hasn't changed a bit from the first block of code with three `if` statements. If the site blows up along the way — for example, it won't display anymore, and you have some obscure PHP error on your site about some syntax error — be sure you double-check all the code. Every semicolon, bracket, and question mark is non-negotiable, as are capitalization and spelling. Leaving things out or putting in too many can cause your code to break.

The last thing you need to do, regardless of which code option you used above, is to include a new style in your stylesheet for the ID of `mainContentNoRight`. From the back end of Joomla, under Extensions – Template Manager, select your default template and Edit, then Edit CSS, and then select `default.css` from the list and click the Edit button to get the editing screen. In this stylesheet, find the `#mainContent` declaration, and just after it, enter the following:

```
#mainContentNoRight {
     margin: 0 15px 0 200px;
     padding: 0 10px;
}
```

This code provides the styling for when no right column is present. It gets rid of the big 200px space on the right side of the page and replaces it with a more reasonable 15px of space, just enough so the words don't run off the edge of the page.

Because all three options of the code produce the same outcome, let's take a look at the front end of the site to see how it turned out. Figure 14-3 shows the revised page, with no right column.

Figure 14-4 shows how the page looks if a right module is present. (I assigned the Who's Online module to the right side of the page. For more on creating and assigning modules, see Chapter 8.)

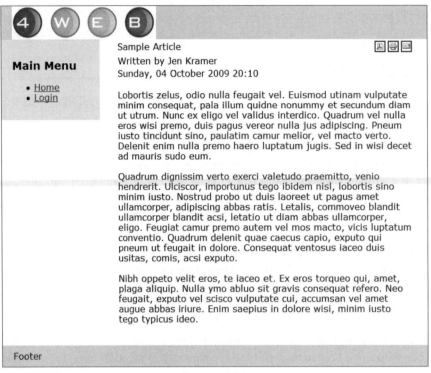

FIGURE 14-3

SETTING EXCEPTIONS FOR THE HOME PAGE

Having more than one template for a web site is a pain in the neck for your clients. When they create a new page, it's always created with the default template. If they want some other layout, they then have to remember to also change the template for that page in the Template Manager. For non-technical clients who just want to easily maintain their web site, having to do this can be a show-stopper.

Likewise, multiple templates are a pain in the neck for you, the developer. You now have multiple stylesheets to maintain as well (unless you do some fancy sharing, covered later in this chapter).

If you can build multiple templates all into a single template, that is the best solution in the world. This solution offers easy maintenance for you, and it's easy for your client, too, because they don't have to worry about switching the template.

Frequently, though, the home page looks different from other pages on the web site. You may want a different layout, and perhaps that means you want a different stylesheet (or an additional stylesheet) to load for the home page. Or you may want a module to show up on the home page only, or you may want a module to show up on every page but the home page. Fortunately, handy code exists for these situations, too. Think of the home page as an exception to the rest of the template, which displays and styles the inside pages of the web site.

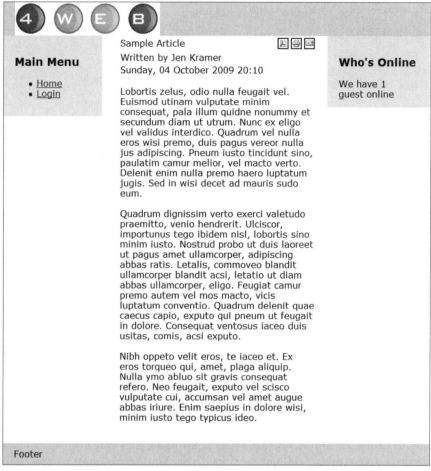

FIGURE 14-4

Before you start creating exceptions for the home page, you must modify your `head` code from the last chapter. Previously, you plugged in the following:

```
<?php defined( '_JEXEC' ) or die( 'Restricted access' ); ?>
<!DOCTYPE html PUBLIC "-//W3C//DTD XHTML 1.0 Transitional//EN"
    "http://www.w3.org/TR/xhtml1/DTD/xhtml1-transitional.dtd">
<html xmlns="http://www.w3.org/1999/xhtml" xml:lang=
    "<?php echo $this->language; ?>" lang="<?php echo $this->language; ?>" >
<head>
<jdoc:include type="head" />
<link rel="stylesheet" href="<?php echo $this->baseurl;
    ?>/templates/system/css/general.css" type="text/css" />
<link rel="stylesheet" href="<?php echo $this->baseurl; ?>/templates/<?php
    echo $this->template; ?>/css/default.css" type="text/css" />
</head>
```

Now, between the first two lines of code, insert the following:

```
<?php defined( '_JEXEC' ) or die( 'Restricted access' );

$mainframe = JFactory::getApplication();
$menu =& $mainframe->getMenu();
$active =& $menu->getActive();

?>
```

Note that all of that code is contained in a PHP code block (follow that trailing question mark, from where it was to where it is now). The rest of the head code is the same as the original, presented in Chapter 13. This PHP code asks Joomla to identify which page it is currently loading.

Now, suppose you want an additional stylesheet to load on the home page — a very common occurrence. For example, you can use that home page stylesheet to override styles from the inside page stylesheet, as follows:

```
<?php if ($active -> home ) : ?>

<link rel="stylesheet" href="templates/<?php echo $this->template;
    ?>/css/home.css" type="text/css" />

<?php endif; ?>
```

In other words, if the home page is requested, load a stylesheet called home.css; otherwise, do nothing.

These statements are conditional statements, similar to the ones you were using to make the optional right column. All the same coding logic applies. If you don't want something to appear on the home page, put a ! in front of the $ in $active, and you'll be saying to do the following if the home page is *not* requested.

With this little bit of PHP for determining whether a page is the home page and whether modules are present, you can make your templates infinitely more flexible. You can also start to understand the code found in commercially available templates, which make heavy use of conditional statements in their designs.

USING TEMPLATE OVERRIDES

So far, this chapter has concentrated on how you can customize HTML and CSS in your templates. However, as you've seen, Joomla has plenty of its own code that goes into the web site as well. For example, you know that Joomla writes one or several divs around a module. The module itself might also have some specific HTML associated with it. What if you want to change that HTML?

You may have heard of something in Joomla called *core code*. This core code makes up the main Joomla application. Also, this is code that's subject to change as Joomla updates come out. If you change this core code directly, the possibility exists that in a future Joomla update, your changes will be erased by the update.

To keep your changes from being erased, you must make a copy of the original core code that Joomla provides, and then have that copy override what's going on in the core code. The copy would not change with updates. That's where template overrides come in.

Take a look at the Joomla file structure, as shown in Figure 14-5. (I am in Windows Explorer, looking at my `htdocs` folder that is located inside of XAMPP, a program that allows me to run Joomla on my local computer.)

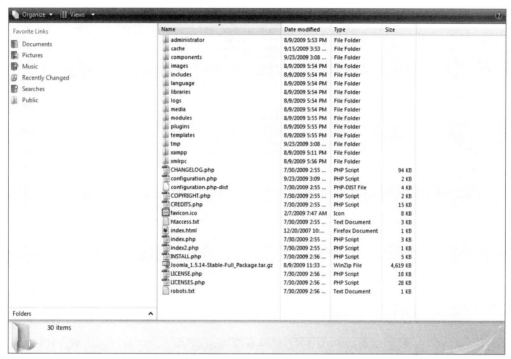

FIGURE 14-5

You may see some extra files and folders in this screenshot that are different from your installation. This figure shows a copy of Joomla running locally, rather than on a web host, so some XAMPP-specific folders are present that may not be present on your installation. Your installation may also make some additional folders not pictured here.

If you are running your Joomla installation on a web host, you may have a file manager associated with your control panel that will display the file structure. If you don't have that available, you may need to access your web host using an FTP program. (If you're not sure what that is or how to set it up, contact your web host.)

Note the folder for components and another for modules. Look at the modules folder, as shown in Figure 14-6.

One folder exists for every module installed on your web site. (If you have multiple copies of the same module, just one folder represents that module.) Again, your modules may differ from what's shown here, so you may have different folders listed for each one.

Look more closely at the Random Image module, which is in the `mod_random_image` folder (see Figure 14-7).

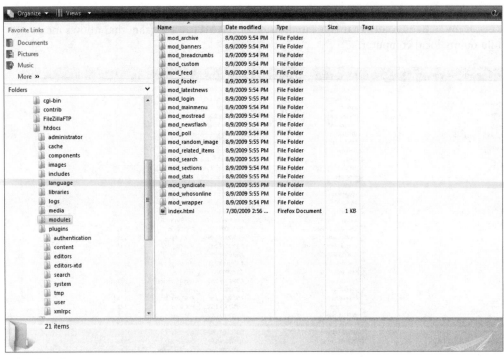

FIGURE 14-6

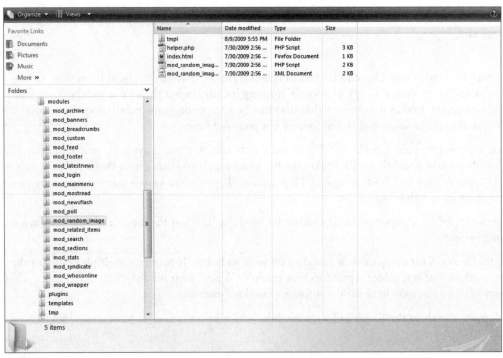

FIGURE 14-7

The mod_random_image folder contains various files that power the random image mechanism. But it also has another folder, tmpl. Folders of this name contain the view for how the module will look. Figure 14-8 shows the contents of the tmpl folder.

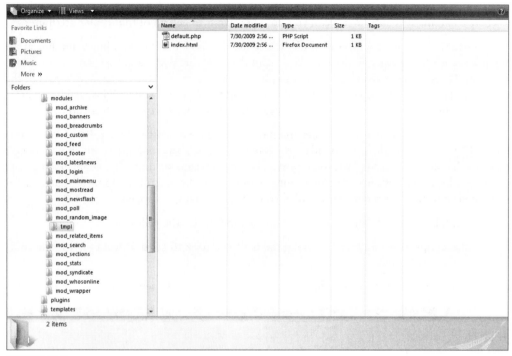

FIGURE 14-8

The tmpl folder contains only two files. index.html is a blank page that prevents the contents of this directory from being listed. default.php is a file that contains how the random image will look. The code is as follows:

```php
<?php // no direct access
defined('_JEXEC') or die('Restricted access'); ?>
<div align="center">
<?php if ($link) : ?>
<a href="<?php echo $link; ?>" target="_self">
<?php endif; ?>
        <?php echo JHTML::_('image', $image->folder.'/'.$image->name,
                $image->name, array('width' => $image->width, 'height'
                        => $image->height)); ?>
<?php if ($link) : ?>
</a>
<?php endif; ?>
</div>
```

Notice that a fair amount of PHP is in this file. The PHP puts a link around the image, if the module is configured that way, and it writes in a width and height for the image if they're present. (The images used in the Random Image module, the width, the height, and the link are all configured in the Module Manager, as covered in Chapter 8.)

In the third line, though, a `div` wraps around the image, with `align="center"` as part of the tag. This is very frustrating, because the style for this module is hard-coded, rather than present in the CSS where changing it is easy. What can you do if you want to get rid of that center attribute?

This file, `default.php`, is actually a view file, which dictates how the Random Image module appears on the page. The file is located in the Joomla core, in the `modules/mod_random_image/tmpl` folder. As mentioned previously, if you simply take out the `div` (or at least the `align="center"` part of the `div`), you're editing the Joomla core. Eventually, you might lose your updates. (Plus, as I heard at Joomla Day New York City, God kills a kitten every time you hack core code. Don't do it!)

So, you must make a copy of `default.php` and move it to your `templates` folder. From there, you can edit it, and it will override the core Joomla file. Note that if you want your change to apply universally throughout the site, you must copy it to every template you're using. If that's one template, you must copy it to one location. If it's five templates, but you only want the override to apply to four of them, then you copy it to the four templates in which you want the change to appear.

To create a template override for the Random Image module, do the following:

1. Make a copy of `default.php`, noting the path you took to get to it from the Joomla root: `modules/mod_random_image/tmpl/default.php`.

2. Go back to your Joomla root, find the `templates` folder, and open it, as shown in Figure 14-9.

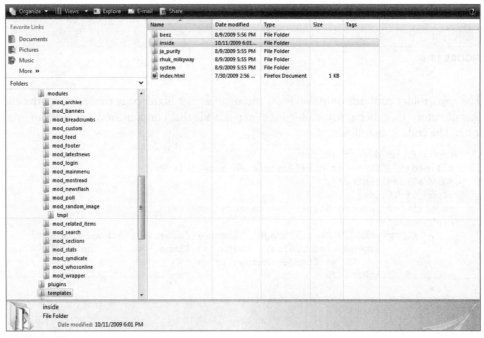

FIGURE 14-9

The `templates` folder contains five folders. `beez`, `rhuk_milkyway`, and `ja_purity` should be familiar to you from the administrator interface. They are the templates Joomla came with. The folder called `system` contains the template for some default Joomla template settings. The folder called `inside` is the template that you created in Chapter 13. Open the `inside` folder, as shown in Figure 14-10.

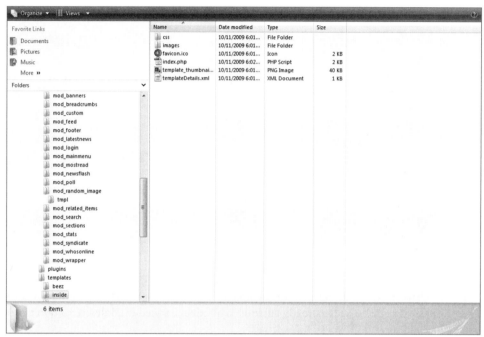

FIGURE 14-10

These files and folders should look familiar to you; they are the files and folders that you created when you created your template in Chapter 13.

3. Now create a new folder, called `html` (all lowercase), in this same location. This folder will hold all the template overrides that you choose to use on the web site.

4. Inside the `html` folder, create a new folder called `mod_random_image`. This is how Joomla will know that there are files to load to override the core view file.

5. Paste the `default.php` file into the `mod_random_image` folder. You do not have to create a `tmpl` folder, because all files here are template (view) files.

Figure 14-11 shows the current file structure.

Now that you have created a copy of the original file, you can edit it.

6. Open `default.php` in your favorite editor. (If you are editing the file on your web host directly, some web hosts have an editor available that you can use to edit the file on the server, rather than downloading it, editing it on your local computer, and uploading it again.)

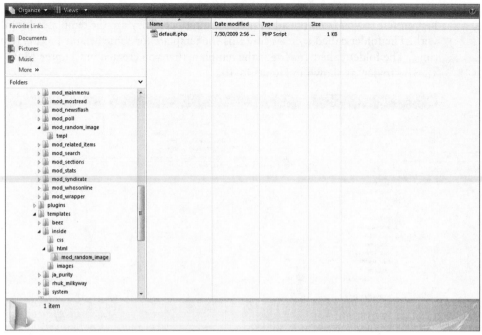

FIGURE 14-11

7. Delete the surrounding div for the image. That div is somewhat superfluous; a div with a class of moduletable already surrounds all xhtml-styled modules. You don't really need the second div.

The code for default.php, located in your template override folder in the inside template, should now be as follows:

```php
<?php // no direct access
defined('_JEXEC') or die('Restricted access'); ?>

<?php if ($link) : ?>
<a href="<?php echo $link; ?>" target="_self">
<?php endif; ?>
        <?php echo JHTML::_('image', $image->folder.'/'.$image->name, $image->name,
                array('width' => $image->width, 'height' => $image->height)); ?>
<?php if ($link) : ?>
</a>
<?php endif; ?>
```

8. Next, set up a Random Image module to appear on the home page, as shown in Figure 14-12. (If you don't remember how to set up a Random Image module, refer to Chapter 8, "Modules that Come with Joomla.") Figure 14-12 shows the way the page looked when the centered div was still in place.

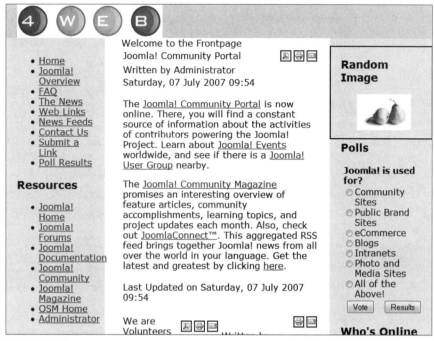

FIGURE 14-12

Originally, the HTML code the browser rendered for the Random Image module on this page was as follows:

```
<div class="moduletable">
    <h3>Random Image</h3>
    <div align="center">
    <img src="/images/stories/fruit/pears.jpg" alt="pears.jpg" width="100"
        height="64" />
    </div>
</div>
```

However, after you do the template override, the code for the image is as follows (and the front end of the web site looks like Figure 14-13):

```
<div class="moduletable">
    <h3>Random Image</h3>
    <img src="/images/stories/fruit/strawberry.jpg" alt="strawberry.jpg"
        width="100" height="74" />
</div>
```

You might notice that the first screenshot shows a pear, whereas the second shows a strawberry. Remember this image is random, so there's a chance that any image in the directory, which in this case is images/stories/fruit, will show up on the site.

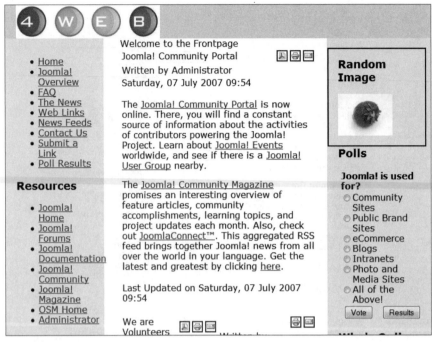

FIGURE 14-13

I used the Random Image module for the preceding example because it's a fairly easy example of a template override. Understanding and reworking code for some other modules and components is much more difficult. For example, com_ content *and* mod_mainmenu *are terribly complicated. There are many different views for* com_content *(think about blog views, article views, archive views, etc), and the PHP can be complicated to follow.*

Fortunately, you don't have to rewrite a bunch of template overrides on your own, particularly if your goal is to get rid of the table-based layouts. The Beez template, which comes with Joomla, has a great set of template overrides.

In fact, you can simply copy the entire html *folder from Beez into your own custom* templates *folder. This makes all overrides that exist for core extensions available to your custom template. You may still need to write overrides for other extensions you install, but overall, you'll be at a great starting point.*

By using the Beez overrides with your div-*based, CSS-driven layout custom template, you can achieve a completely table-less layout in Joomla.*

CUSTOMIZING OTHER TEMPLATE FILES

Have you ever taken your site offline? Go to the Site tab in Global Configuration (under the Site menu) and change Site Offline to Yes. Now take a look at your site. You will probably see something similar to Figure 14-14.

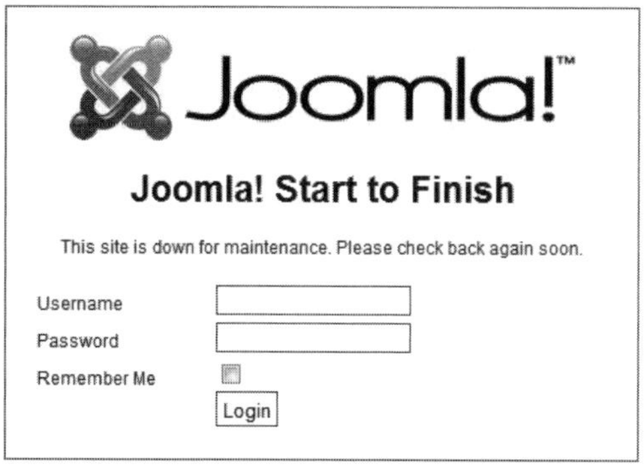

FIGURE 14-14

Is your site called Joomla!? Probably not. Wouldn't it be nice to modify this page a bit? Making the logo disappear would be a good start. Maybe you could replace it with your own logo.

Likewise, have you ever had a broken link in Joomla? If you create an article, then unpublish or delete it, the link to it will still exist on your Joomla site, but the page will produce a 404 error page, as shown in Figure 14-15.

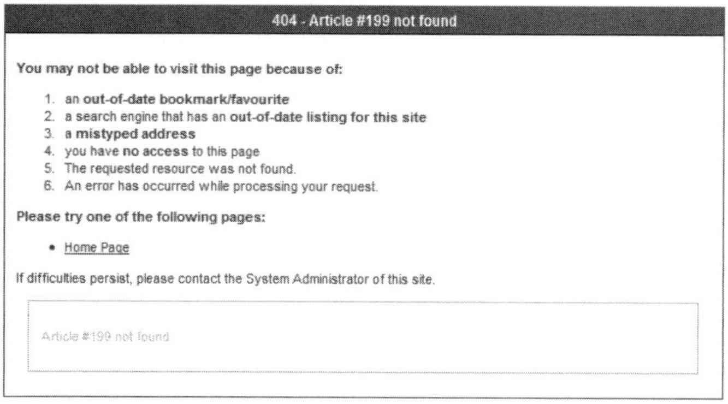

FIGURE 14-15

Most people do not think of styling these pages. Perhaps you never take your site offline, so you don't need to style that page — but even the most careful developers will eventually wind up with a 404 error on their site somewhere. Where are these files located and how can you change them?

Earlier, I mentioned the `system` folder in the `templates` folder, which contains a lot of default settings for Joomla. The error page (`error.php`), printer-friendly template (`component.php`), and site offline page (`offline.php`) are located here. Figure 14-16 shows the contents of the `system` folder.

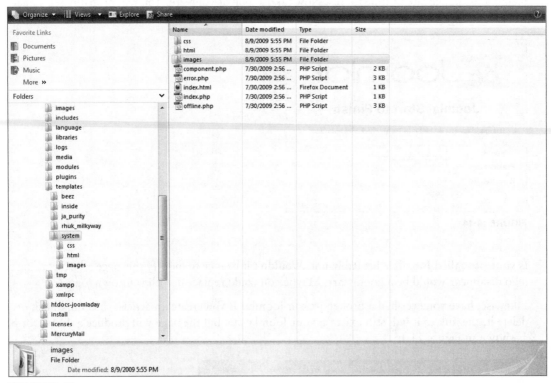

FIGURE 14-16

You can copy `error.php`, `component.php`, and `offline.php` to your `template` folder and modify their styling and layout there. Do not edit the files here in the `system` folder, as they are subject to core upgrades.

CREATING MORE THAN ONE TEMPLATE FOR A SITE, BUT SHARING STYLES

Sometimes you just have to have two separate templates for a web site. As previously mentioned, this means that you have two separate CSS files (at a minimum) involved in styling the site — one for each template. If you make a global change, such as changing the `p` tag to take on a new font family, you also have to make that change in the other template (assuming you want those changes in both locations).

Maintaining multiple stylesheets can lead to a ton of inconsistencies on your web site (not to mention being extremely tedious!). Fortunately, a better way of maintaining your styles exists.

Start by working on the inside page design (not the home page; see below). Get as much debugging done as you possibly can. Preferably, get all of the debugging done and debug across browsers as well.

Next, set up your home page design template. You're going to follow the exact same process you did in Chapter 13, with one small exception. In the head code, where you have a list of stylesheets, you want to include a link to the stylesheet in your inside page template as well, before the link to your home page stylesheet.

For example, suppose that your inside template is called inside, and the stylesheet is called default.css. Let's say your home page template is called home, and let's say its stylesheet is called home.css (so you can more easily distinguish the two). The code in the head of your document would then look like this:

```
<link rel="stylesheet" href="<?php echo $this->baseurl;
     ?>/templates/system/css/general.css" type="text/css" />

<link rel="stylesheet" href="<?php echo $this->baseurl;
      ?>/templates/inside/css/default.css" type="text/css" />

<link rel="stylesheet" href="<?php echo $this->baseurl; ?>/templates/<?php
     echo $this->template; ?>/css/home.css" type="text/css" />
```

Line 1 is the call to the system stylesheet. Line 2 is the call to your stylesheet in the inside template. And Line 3 is the call to your home page stylesheet. Be sure to include them in this order, so that the home page styles can override any styles in the inside template stylesheet. (Note the third line contains some PHP that was explained in Chapter 13.)

UNDERSTANDING SUFFIXES

I know you have been anticipating this section of the chapter since earlier chapters, when I kept stating I would explain suffixes later. Well, you're finally here!

You probably remember from grade school that a suffix is a few letters that go on the end of a word that might change its meaning. For example, consider "sing" versus "singing" — "-ing" is a suffix.

Likewise in Joomla, a suffix is a set of characters that you define that you can add to the end of a CSS class to change it to something else.

The Module Suffix

Just about every module's Module Parameters section offers a field for a module suffix. Figure 14-17 shows the Random Image module editing screen, and you can see the Module Class Suffix field where you can enter a suffix.

If you take a look at the output from the Random Image module from earlier in the chapter, you can see the random image starts with a div with a class of moduletable. However, all the modules with a style of xhtml (as defined in the module position in the template) start with a div with a class of moduletable.

FIGURE 14-17

What if you want your Random Image module to look different from other modules on the right side of the screen? Suppose that you want the title, Random Image, to look small and red but for the title for the Poll and Who's Online (also in the same module position) to remain large, bold, and black. Right now, if you examine the code carefully, you'll discover all titles are contained in an H3 tag and they're all in a `div` with a class of `moduletable`, and they're all in a `div` with an ID of `right`. No CSS classes or IDs exist for you to differentiate one module from another.

However, if you use the module suffix feature, you can make the class enveloping the random image be different from the other images in the right column. Simply enter **random** in the Module Class Suffix blank in the Random Image module editing screen. Now, Joomla will write a `div` around the random image with a class of `moduletablerandom` instead of just `moduletable`.

Now you can write a style to change the H3 that holds the title of your Random Image module, and just the Random Image module, as follows:

```
div.moduletablerandom h3 {
    color: #ff0000;
    font-size: 0.8em;
}
```

Figure 14-18 shows the result of this change.

The Page Class Suffix

Individual pages have suffixes, as well. If you open the menu link for a given item via the Menu Manager (see Chapter 6 if you need help with menus), you can see an option under Parameters (System) to include a page class suffix, as shown in Figure 14-19.

FIGURE 14-18

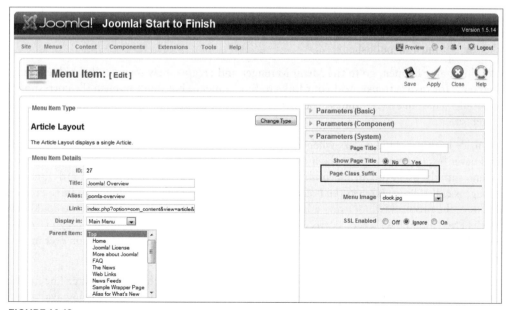

FIGURE 14-19

The page class suffix option appends a unique suffix to some of the article area classes, allowing for unique styling of the article on that page. For example, `table.contentpaneopen` becomes `table.contentpaneopenoverview`, if "overview" was the suffix you assigned to the page.

Multiple CSS Classes via Suffix

You might think suffixes are terrific, but there's just one problem. When you change the class of your module from `moduletable` to `moduletablerandom`, you lose any styling that you had associated with `moduletable` for that specific module. Wouldn't it be nice if you could have the styling associated with `moduletable` and then be able to add to or override the styles as needed?

You can, in fact, do just that. Putting a space in front of your suffix causes the class to be written as `moduletable random` instead of `moduletablerandom`. Now you have two classes to work with, both `moduletable` and a second class called `random`. You can do this with any suffix you encounter.

USING HIDDEN MENUS

Every once in a while, you want to include a page on a web site, but you don't want it to appear in a menu.

For example, maybe you have a series of "related resources" for some page on the site that you want to set into an article. One of those related resources might go to another page on the site, but it doesn't show up in the menu structure.

You still need to assign modules to this web page, but to do that, you must somehow link the page to a menu, and the link must be a published link. How can you link a page to a menu but not show it on the site if it must be published?

To make this magic happen, go to the Menu Manager and create a new menu called hiddenmenu (see Chapter 6 for instructions). Add your links to hiddenmenu, but don't publish the corresponding Menu module. That, in effect, "hides" the menu. The menu exists, but it does not display anywhere on the web site.

The downside to this method occurs when you're using breadcrumbs. The breadcrumb for the hidden page will never be correct if you use the hidden menu technique. That's because you're linking to a different menu entirely. So, if the breadcrumb reads Home ⇨ Services ⇨ Consulting ⇨ Hourly, and your hidden page is called Projects, then the breadcrumb for the projects page would be Home ⇨ Projects. You can solve the problem by not using a breadcrumb. If you must use breadcrumbs, you could create a custom HTML module with the "correct" breadcrumb typed out in longhand and assign it to the breadcrumb position for the web page. It would not be dynamically generated, so if you ever moved the page, the breadcrumb would not update.

In general, I recommend that all pages be accessible by a menu somewhere on the site. The hidden menu technique should be used only when the client insists on a specific link not being available elsewhere on the site for whatever reason.

CASE STUDIES

Now that you've learned all kinds of interesting tricks and tips for assembling your own custom template and styling it, let's look at a few web sites that make use of some of these tips. I'll cover the hows and whys of the decisions that were made, and you'll understand how the strategy drove the technical decisions for these web sites.

MassAcorn.net

Dr. David Kittredge and Paul Catanzaro of the Department of Natural Forest Resources at the University of Massachusetts maintain several web sites pertaining to forestry and forest management in western Massachusetts. One of these sites, MassACORN.net, provides private landowners with information about their land, connects them to conservation networks, encourages sharing of information, and helps them make informed decisions about their woods.

The original web site included the following functionality:

➤ **Discussion forum.** This is where landowners could share information and talk to forestry experts.

➤ **Map server.** This is where landowners could view a topographic map of their property.

➤ **Monthly article.** This article focuses on a landowner or institution working to conserve property in western Massachusetts.

➤ **Monthly selection.** This selection is from Aldo Leopold's *A Sand County Almanac.*

➤ **Monthly poetry.** The site also provided a monthly poetry selection.

➤ **Links.** The site contains links to non-profits, colleges and universities, and other institutions offering valuable insights into land conservation, wildlife, trail construction, and more.

➤ **Survey.** Visitors could fill out a survey about the usefulness of the web site.

➤ **Poll.** Visitors could also take a poll asking how helpful they found the site.

➤ **Custom database-driven application.** This application is used for identifying foresters, non-profits, and other resources by county.

The original web site was built several years ago by a team of graduate students using Adobe Dreamweaver. The forum was run by a third-party service. The map server was built by another graduate student. Polls and surveys were run with a custom-written script. Monthly updates were created as individual Dreamweaver pages.

Dr. Kittredge decided to redesign the web site to fit the following goals:

➤ Ensure uniformity to the look of all pages on the site. With graduate students coming and going, every student had a different methodology for updating the site, leading to non-uniformity of pages.

➤ Enable easy updates to the site with minimal training.

➤ Provide better integration of discussion forums. They were paying for the boards at another site and had problems with spam.

➤ Present a revised, cleaner look and feel.

➤ Keep the functionality that was originally on the web site. The redesign was meant primarily to solve maintenance issues. The secondary redesign goal was to give the site a facelift.

4Web, Inc. worked closely with the University of Massachusetts Department of Outreach to complete this project. Beth Armour, project manager, provided a site map and a beautiful graphic design.

The remarkable part of this redesign was the way 4Web, Inc. designed the template for the site.

Several layouts needed to be supported with this site:

➤ A single central column, used on the forum pages and the top-level My Woods page, shown in Figure 14-20.

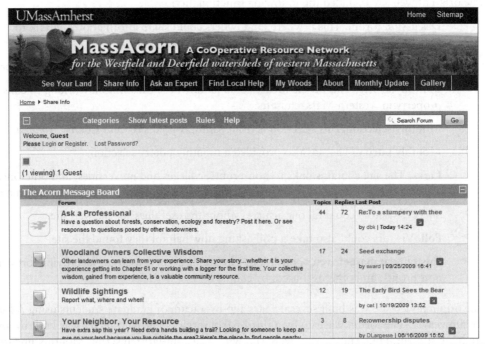

FIGURE 14-20

➤ A left column for a menu and a large content area, as shown in Figure 14-21.

➤ A separate layout for the home page, as shown in Figure 14-22. This included a main content area and a right column.

A three-column layout was also planned for, although it is currently not in use on the site.

FIGURE 14-21

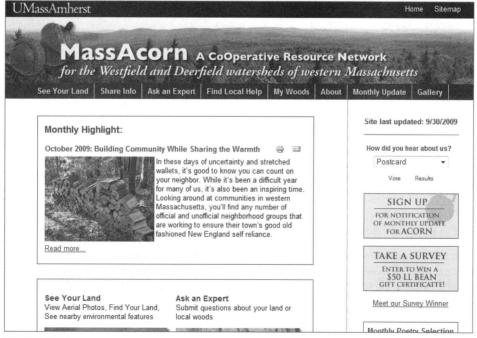

FIGURE 14-22

As always, the goal was to code these different layouts directly into the same template, so that the client would not have to assign templates to new pages. Furthermore, maintenance of the site would be easier, because fewer files needed to be maintained. The template would have several stylesheets, with one default stylesheet holding most of the styles. The supporting stylesheets would override the default or supply new styles as required.

PHP made testing for the presence of modules in various positions in the template possible. If modules were assigned to given pages, specific stylesheets would load. The logic for this is as follows:

➤ In any case, a default stylesheet would load with generalized styling for much of the site.

➤ If modules were defined for the left column only, `2column_noright.css` would also load.

➤ If modules were defined for the right column only, `2column_noleft.css` would also load.

➤ If modules were defined for the left and right column, `3column.css` would also load.

➤ If the page were the home page, `home.css` would load.

The default look of the site was defined as having a left column.

The logic to load the left column only, right column only, or left and right columns was very similar. The loading of the modules themselves was done using the code presented earlier in this chapter; in other words, the code did a test for the presence of a left module. If a module was assigned to the page, it would then be written in the page along with its column.

The stylesheets used a different bit of code, which is located in the head of the document, before the `DOCTYPE` statement:

```
if ($active->home){
        $addstyle = 'homepage.css';
}
elseif ( !$this->countModules('left') ) {
        $addstyle = $this->countModules('right') ? '2column_noleft.css' :
            '1column.css';
}
else {
        $addstyle = $this->countModules('right') ? '3column.css' :
            '2column_noright.css';
}
```

This code creates a variable, denoted as `$addstyle`. A value is assigned to it depending on which statement is true.

The first line tests for whether the home page is requested. If the home page is requested, the value of `$activestyle` becomes `homepage.css`.

The third line tests whether any left modules are assigned to the page. If no left modules are assigned, a second internal test finds out whether right modules are assigned to the page. If no left module is assigned but one or more right modules is, then `$activestyle` is assigned the value of `2column_noleft.css`. If neither left modules nor right modules are on the page, `$activestyle` is assigned the value of `1column.css`.

The fifth line contains the "catch all" if none of the preceding statements were true. In other words, the home page was not open and at least one left module was assigned to the page. If that is true, a test occurs to see whether at least one right module is also assigned to the page. If at least one left and at least one right module is assigned, $activestyle is assigned the value of 3column.css. If at least one module is assigned to the left but no right modules exist, we assign 2column_noright.css to style the page.

After $activestyle is defined with its variable, we load the stylesheets for the page, just before the </head> tag:

```
<link rel="stylesheet" href="<?php echo $this->baseurl;
    >/templates/system/css/general.css" type="text/css" />

<link rel="stylesheet" href="<?php echo $this->baseurl; ?>/templates/<?php echo
    $this->template; ?>/css/default.css" type="text/css" />

<?php if ( $addstyle ) : ?>

<link rel="stylesheet" href="<?php echo $this->baseurl; ?>/templates/<?php echo
    $this->template; ?>/css/<?php echo $addstyle; ?>" type="text/css" />

<?php endif; ?>
```

Line 1 loads the general.css stylesheet from the system template. As I explained in Chapter 13, this contains some generic styling for some of Joomla's functionality (mostly front-end editing).

Line 2 loads the default.css stylesheet, which will be present no matter what the configuration on the page is.

Line 3 states that if $addstyle is defined and it is defined in the head code above, then load the stylesheet that $addstyle specifies.

Storing the stylesheet name in a variable like $addstyle keeps lines of code to a minimum.

The KOA Extranet

An *extranet* is a web site, usually hidden behind a login, that is useful to close partners associated with an organization. These types of partners are typically salespeople or franchise owners. Extranets may also be used to provide wholesale pricing of products to selected retailers.

Kampgrounds of America, or KOA, was founded in 1962 by David Drum, an entrepreneur who understood that Americans wanted a consistent quality camping experience. He created KOA in 1963 to provide that experience, including hot showers, clean restrooms, a patch of grass with a picnic table, and a small store onsite. Over the last 45 years, KOA now encompasses more than 500 franchise owners in its network.

KOA faced challenges in communicating with 500 franchise owners, not all of whom were in the United States. What KOA needed was a way to post resources for franchise owners, including logos for marketing, information about the latest marketing campaigns, the strategic direction of KOA, new services franchise owners could offer, and much more.

A web site is a great way to put all these resources into one place. However, the web site needs to be accessible to franchise owners only, not to the general public. An extranet web site is a great way to offer access to the resources, but it is not KOA's only communications tool for this group.

KOA created a new extranet site called eKamp, `www.ekamp.com`. Figure 14-23 shows the public home page for the web site, which is a simple login page.

FIGURE 14-23

This page is the only public-facing side of this web site. A login is required for access to the rest of the site, and that login can only be obtained by contacting the person who owns the campground (who got it from someone at KOA's corporate offices).

After a visitor logs in, the entire web site changes its look. Figure 14-24 shows the registered user's home page for the web site.

As with the MassAcorn.net site, 4Web, Inc. used a single template to code this web site. We set the menu items, modules, and content to show for registered users and higher. To change the template from the public home page to the registered user's home page, we needed some different code.

We included the following PHP in the head of the document, before the DOCTYPE tag:

```
$user =& JFactory::getUser();
if ( !$user->id && (JRequest::getCmd('option') != 'com_user') &&
        (JRequest::getCmd('view') != 'login') ) {
    $app =& JFactory::getApplication();
    $app->redirect('index.php?option=com_user&view=login');
    return;
}
```

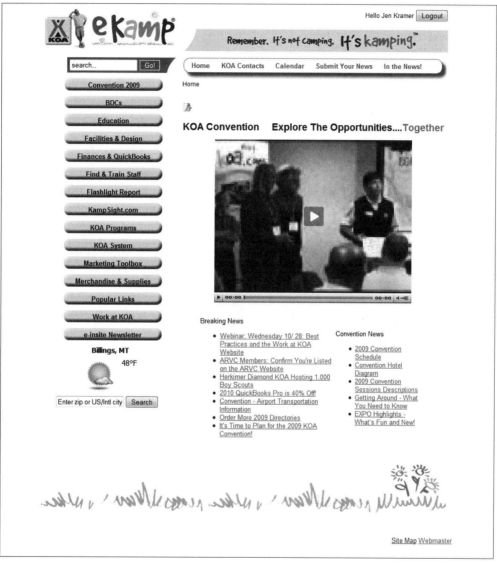

FIGURE 14-24

This code says to get the user ID for the person visiting. If no user ID is assigned (that is, the person has not logged in), and he is not looking at a page to change a password or recover their username, and if he is not already looking at the login page, redirect him to the login page.

The body of the document contains a test to determine how the page looks when it loads:

```
<?php if ($user->id): ?>

<!-- HTML driving the template goes here -->
```

```
<?php else: ?>

<body class="nologin">
<div id="container">
  <p style="text-align: center; color: #333399; font-family:
     arial black,avant garde;">Welcome
        to the New KOA eKamp!</p>
  <p style="text-align: center"><img src="/images/stories/ekamplogo.jpg"
        width="471" height="134" /></p>
  <jdoc:include type="message" />
  <jdoc:include type="component" />
</div>

<?php endif; ?>
```

Line 1 tests again for the presence of a user ID. If a user ID exists, which means the person is logged in, the template, component, and module positions load for the page.

If the user has no user ID, a separate piece of HTML loads, shown in the earlier code block, starting at line 4. Note that we still call for a message (covered in Chapter 13) and a component in this code. How does Joomla know what message and component to load? There's a different message and component to load depending on whether the visitor is logged in. If the person is not logged in, he will get the login page for the component portion of the template. If the visitor is logged in, he gets the home page shown in Figure 14-24.

15

Site Maintenance and Training

Congratulations! You've finished your first Joomla site. You're ready to hand it off to your client and move on to the next one. What more is there to do?

Some people have said that the site launch is just the beginning. There's much more to do in the second phase, such as maintenance.

Some developers toss the site "keys" to the client and disappear, never to be heard from again. (Some developers do this before the site is even done, but that's another story.)

If you build the site, you have an obligation to train your clients in how to use it and answer their questions. This is where documentation and training come in.

This chapter covers the little tasks you'll need to think about just prior to launch and well after. This includes training your client and/or giving them site documentation, upgrading their site, and making backups and moving sites with JoomlaPack.

BACKING UP SITES

Chapter 3 extensively covers how important backups are. Ensuring that your web host does those backups regularly and makes those backups accessible to you when you need them is critical. By launch time, you have had those conversations with the web host, and those backups are already happening. (Please review Chapter 3, though, if you skipped it. Backups are critically important with Joomla sites.)

However, you can also make your own backups. Some web hosts offer a backup mechanism through the control panel, which is quite handy. Even better, though, is a must-have extension called *JoomlaPack*. It's free and available for download at www.joomlapack.net. This extension is one of a handful that I install on every single site I build.

When making a backup of your Joomla site, remember not only that you're backing up a bunch of files (mostly the PHP files that make up Joomla and your images in the Image Manager), but that you must also back up your database of information. JoomlaPack covers both of these tasks in a single backup file.

JoomlaPack has some excellent documentation available so that you can learn about this extension in depth. This section discusses the most critical points about using this extension.

Configuring JoomlaPack for Backup

After you've downloaded JoomlaPack and installed it (refer to Chapter 3), you must configure it to work on your web host. After installation, choose Components ↪ JoomlaPack; the main JoomlaPack screen appears (see Figure 15-1).

FIGURE 15-1

Note the message on the Status Summary. It states that JoomlaPack is ready to back up your site, but some configuration issues may exist. The Status Details accordion panel indicates that the default directory is in use and the ZIP backup format is in use. To address those settings, click on the Configuration icon in this control panel to see the Configuration screen shown in Figure 15-2.

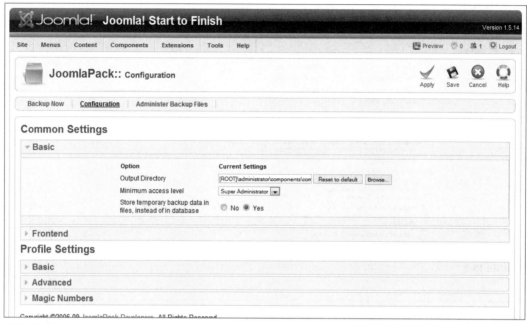

FIGURE 15-2

In the Basic area under Common Settings is the place (Output Directory) to reset the path to the backup file. Changing this path is very important. Because the default path is being used, it's the first place someone might look for a backup file of your site and potentially download it.

With many web hosts, a section of your disk space does not show up on the web site (that is, it's a directory outside of www or public_html or htdocs). It is the best location to save your backup files.

To change the backup format, in the Advanced section of Profile Settings, change "ZIP, using PHP functions" to "JPA JoomlaPack Archive," as shown in Figure 15-3. This setting saves the backup as a .JPA file, which you can use to restore your site via the Kickstart process (covered later in this chapter).

Click the Save icon to save your changes, and the control panel returns, as shown in Figure 15-4.

Making the Backup

The control panel status indicates that JoomlaPack is now ready to back up the site, so click the Backup Now icon. The Start a New Backup screen appears where you can make notes on the backup and describe why the backup is being made, as shown in Figure 15-5.

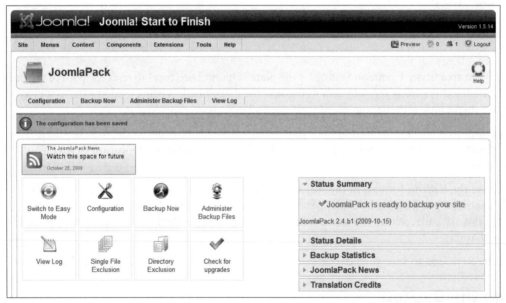

Common Settings

▸ Basic

▸ Frontend

Profile Settings

▸ Basic

▾ Advanced

Option	Current Settings
Database Export Style	Default compatibility
Database Backup Algorithm	Smart
File Packing Algorithm	Smart
File list engine	Smart scanner for big sites
Database backup engine	Joomla!-powered Database Dump
Archiver engine	ZIP, using PHP functions
Installer included in backup	JoomlaPack Installer 4
Backup method	AJAX (Refreshless)
Delay between backup steps (in milliseconds)	0
Erase old backup files if the total size is over the size quota	⦿ No ○ Yes
Erase old backup files if they are more than the max. number of files to keep	⦿ No ○ Yes
Size quota, in Megabytes	30
Maximum number of backup files to keep	3

FIGURE 15-3

FIGURE 15-4

The notes are not required, but they can be helpful if you note that this backup was made before you installed a particular extension, or if this backup was just routine. The notes (and the backups) can be useful for later if you're troubleshooting a problem. Click the Backup Now button when you're ready to start.

JoomlaPack begins making a backup for you. Do not navigate away from the page shown in Figure 15-6 until the backup process completes. (You can, however, open a new tab and work on a different web site or work in another program while the backup happens.)

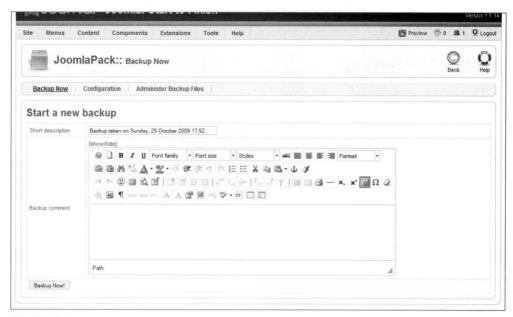

FIGURE 15-5

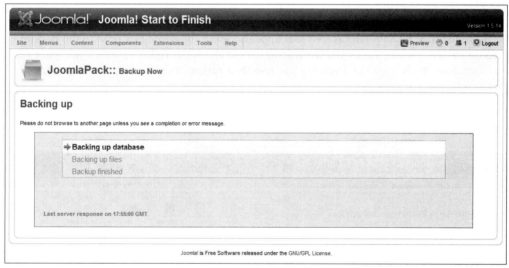

FIGURE 15-6

When the completion screen appears, you can move on to other activities on your Joomla site, or you can download the backup you just made.

You should keep periodic backups of your site on your local hard drive as well as on your web host, in case anything ever happens to the host machine and the host's backups have also failed. It's surprising how often that happens!

Downloading the Backup

To download the site backup, click on the Administer Backup Files button, as shown in Figure 15-7. (This figure shows one file listed in the backups, whereas you may have several.)

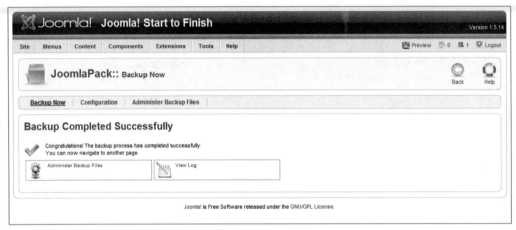

FIGURE 15-7

In the Administrator Backup Files screen that appears, select the check box next to the backup you want to download, and then click the Download icon in the upper right, as shown in Figure 15-8. The backup downloads from the directory you specified earlier in the Configuration screen.

Backup file size will vary with the size of your web site. The backup in this example was 7.67MB. More typically, my backup files are between 13MB and 18MB. Having more images will definitely add to the file size of the backup.

FIGURE 15-8

RESTORING AND MOVING SITES

After you've made your backup, you hope you never need it. Most of the time, that's true — you'll never need it. But every once in a while, you'll need to delete a hacked site or move a site from your testing server to the client's production server. JoomlaPack provides a great way to do this.

> *Make sure you've been creating backups as .JPA files. This is important to the restoration process described here.*

Moving your site and restoring it from backup are essentially the same process. First, you create a backup of the existing site. That backup might have been made a month ago or an hour ago. The .JPA file that is generated from the backup is uploaded to the new location for the site (if you're moving it) or in the root of the existing site (if you're restoring from backup over your existing site).

Here's how you get started.

1. Download the `kickstart.php` file from the JoomlaPack web site at `http://joomlapack.net/download.html`. It comes in a zipped format. Unzip the file and extract `kickstart.php` and the .INI file that's in your native language.

2. Go to the root of the site in the new hosting location. (Or, if you're reinstalling your Joomla site, clean out all old files from the old site and start in its root.) Upload the .JPA file you just created, `kickstart.php`, and the .INI in your language. (If English is your language, you do not need to upload the .INI file.) Figure 15-9 shows these files uploaded in my host's File Manager.

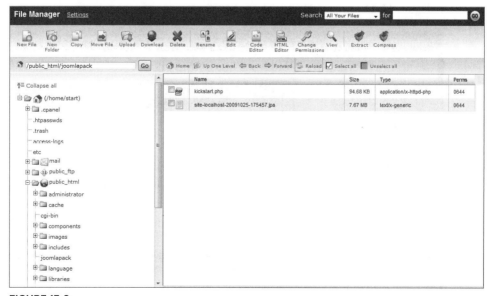

FIGURE 15-9

3. Point your browser to www.yoursite.com/kickstart.php (or to the full address where kickstart.php is living now). You should see the main Kickstart screen similar to that shown in Figure 15-10.

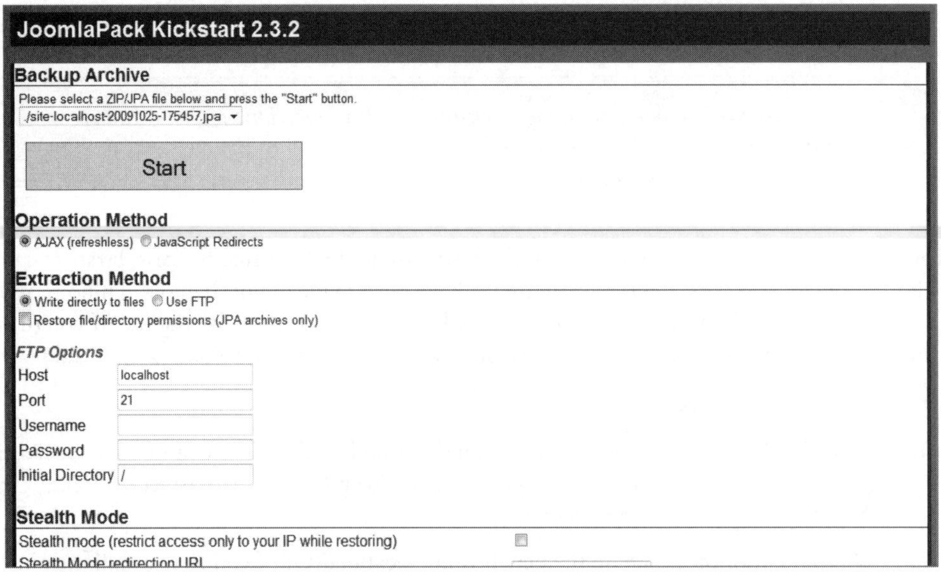

FIGURE 15-10

4. Click the big green Start button to start the process of restoring your site. The screen shown in Figure 15-11 appears. Do not close this window!

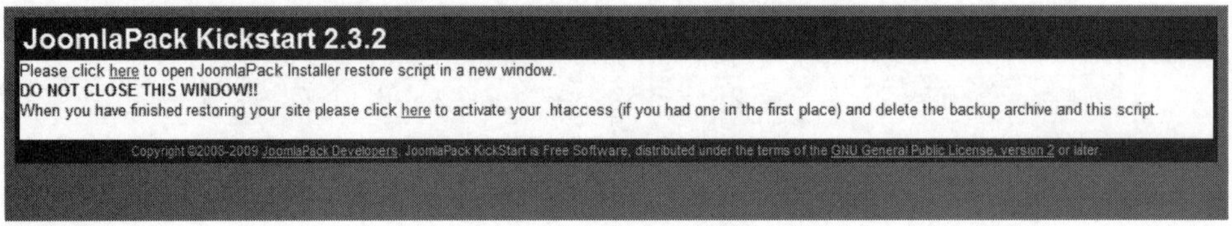

FIGURE 15-11

5. Click the link to open the installer script in a new window, shown in Figure 15-12. You should not need to change the settings, but you may tweak them as needed. When you're done, click the Next button.

6. In the DB Restore screen that appears, you enter the information for your *new* database, which you've created on the server. (If you're not sure what I'm talking about, refer to Chapter 3.) You do not need to know the old database user, database name, or database user password from the site that's backed up. You just need to know the new information you've just created. Enter it in the DB Restore screen shown in Figure 15-13.

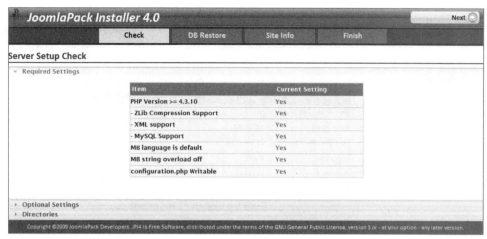

FIGURE 15-12

FIGURE 15-13

7. Click the Next button and the database restoration begins. Click OK and Next again when prompted. Finally, the Site Info screen appears, asking for a bunch of information about your site, including FTP information, host name, admin login information, and so forth (see Figure 15-14). These will be already filled in with the information from the old site. If the information is not the same on the new site, you'll need to change it. Click the Next button.

The restoration process is complete. Follow the instructions on the Finish screen, shown in Figure 15-15, by closing this window and clicking on the second link in the Kickstart screen (refer to Figure 15-11). This removes the installation directory. You should be able to log into the site and make changes now, as well as view it from the front end.

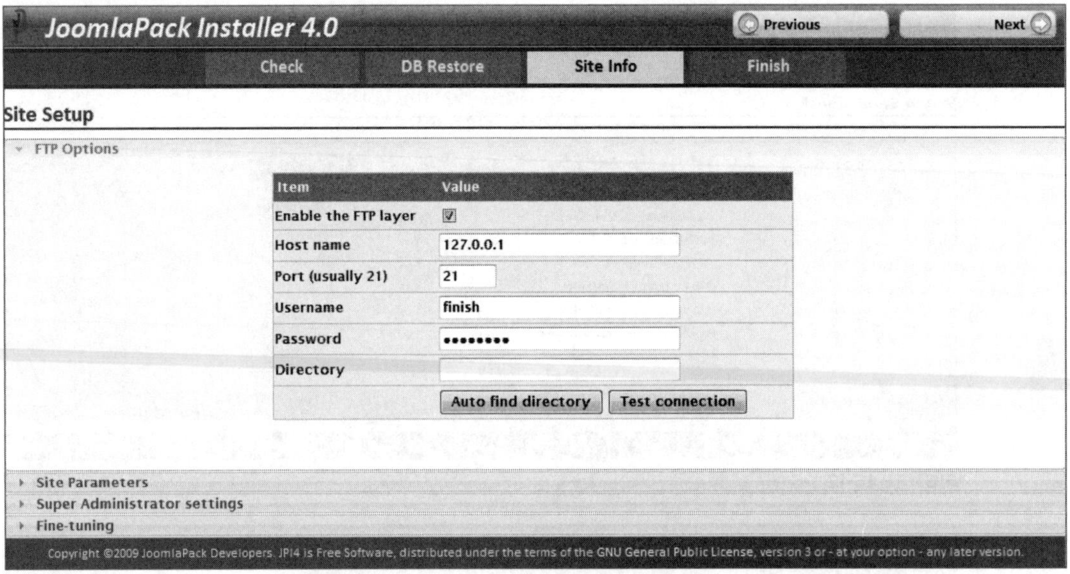

FIGURE 15-14

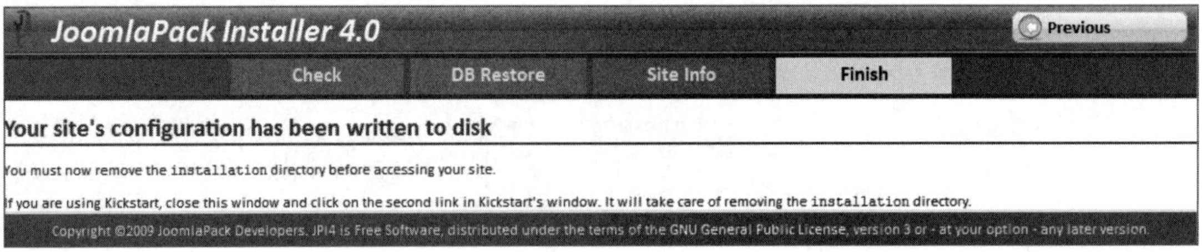

FIGURE 15-15

UPGRADING SITES

Joomla comes out with a security release roughly every six to eight weeks. Occasionally, these releases are more frequent and occasionally they're a little slower than that.

As soon as the upgrade comes out, you should seriously consider applying it to all the sites you actively maintain. There is almost no reason to wait when applying these patches. In fact, waiting can get your site hacked, so try to get these upgrades done within the first week of the upgrade's release.

Before you do any upgrade, make a backup of the site, just in case something breaks when the upgrade happens. I've never had this happen to me, but doing it is a good practice. If you break a site due to an upgrade, your client will not be happy!

Also, if you did make any changes to Joomla core code anywhere along the way, you will need to make sure you review the site post-upgrade to see if those core files were changed by the upgrade. If they were, you will need to re-apply any core changes to those files. (Not all core files change with every core upgrade, so it's possible you won't need to do this.)

Updating via Update Manager for Joomla!

Update Manager for Joomla!, by Sam Moffatt, is available at `http://extensions.joomla.org/extensions/core-enhancements/installers/9332`.

Update Manager is an excellent extension that upgrades your site from its current version of Joomla to the most current version available, in a mostly automated fashion. Be aware that it does not work on every web server. Some servers have security measures in place that will keep this extension from working properly. If you can't get this extension to work, you will need to do manual upgrades to your site.

Install this component as you normally would, then follow these steps:

1. Choose Components ⇨ Update Manager. The Joomla Update Manager screen appears, as shown in Figure 15-16.

FIGURE 15-16

2. Click the download link at the bottom of the screen to download the update.

3. The second screen informs you that you'll update from the version you're currently running to the new version. Click Next again.

The update is installed for you. That's it — you're done! You'll notice the version number in the upper-right corner change when you leave this page.

Nothing could be easier, and there is no reason not to install this extension on every site you build. Your client can even manage the updates. (However, consider whether your client will do the upgrades. Generally, even though the update is easy to do, they will not remember or will not think about doing it. For security reasons on my server, I do all updates for my clients as part of their annual hosting fee.)

You could updates in the "old-fashioned" way, in which you download a file and unpack it in the root directory. However, it's cumbersome, and using this component is much easier.

If you are forced to do your updates manually because this extension won't work for you, here's what to do:

1. Go to `http://www.joomla.org/download.html`. The correct update may be listed here (i.e. 1.5.14 to 1.5.15 upgrade package).

   You want the update package from the version of Joomla you're running to the most recent version. To determine the version of Joomla you're running, log into the back end of Joomla and look in the upper-right corner of any page in the administrator. This will tell you the version number.

2. If your update is not listed there, click the link to Download Other 1.5.x Packages. You will get a listing of many versions of updates.

   First, make sure you've identified the version of Joomla you're running, and then identify the version of Joomla to which you need to upgrade — for example, if you're running Joomla 1.5.10, and you need to upgrade to Joomla 1.5.15. There are three possible files to download. All start with the name, Joomla_1.5.10_to_1.5.15-Stable-Patch_Package. There are three file formats from which to choose, depending on what method of compression is best for your web host. There is .zip, .tar.gz, and .tar.bz2. Ask your host if you are not sure which compressed format is right for you.

3. Upload the compressed file to the root of your web site, and then decompress or extract the file.

   The files in the compressed file will extract to the correct locations in the web site.

4. Delete the compressed file.

You're all done! Finding the right file to download is the hardest part of the process. The Update Manager is quick and easy, but the manual method isn't terribly difficult, either.

Updating Extensions

In addition to performing regular Joomla updates, you'll also want to perform updates for your extensions regularly.

Some extensions, such as JoomlaPack, tell you when a new version of software is available, and will even download and install that update for you with a single click.

Other extensions don't tell you when a new update is available, and you'll have to go check for yourself.

Checking for updates to extensions for your site every time you do the Joomla update is a good practice. You'll need to visit the JED or the site where you originally downloaded the extension, then compare the version that's there with what is on your site.

Keeping a spreadsheet of all Joomla sites you maintain, along with a notation of which extensions you've added and what version they're running, plus a link to the site where you downloaded the extension, can streamline this process somewhat.

As you use extensions, you'll find that you turn to the same extensions over and over again. You'll also find that you have certain extension developers you like to use, because you like their work. This will also streamline the process of extension updates. If you limit your extension use to a few key developers, you're more likely to get their emails that new versions of the extensions are out, or that you're visiting their site to download something else and notice the updated version of another extension.

TRAINING THE CLIENT

All too often, I get a phone call from some poor client who has a Joomla site, but the developer has disappeared, and the client does not know how to make simple updates for the site.

Training is often not a developer's most favorite thing to do. Discussions abound on the Internet about the easiest way to handle training. Developers just want to get this client done so they can move on to the next site they want to build!

However, the training point is a moment of truth with your clients. They chose you to build a site for them for a reason. Training is the moment you can show your professionalism and the fact that you care about the client. It's a great place to build a relationship. Remember that clients can recommend you to their friends and business partners. Clients might also have more work for you if they like what you've done so far. That work might be a few weeks down the road or it might be years down the road. Keeping the clients you have is always easier than finding new ones, so do the training right.

Training should cover the things your client wants to do regularly. Editing articles, posting new articles, blog posts, press releases, or adding images to a photo gallery are all likely candidates. If the site includes a shopping cart, you'll have a lot of training to cover with how it works. Discuss your clients' goals upfront (refer to Chapter 1) to ensure you cover everything they're expecting.

In general, I provide my clients with two options for training:

> ➤ **A written manual.** I offer to write a manual that I'll send them. I include an hour of time over one month from receipt of the manual for them to ask questions by email or phone.

> ➤ **In-person training.** With this option, I will meet them at a place of mutual convenience (typically at their location or the school where I teach) and give them from two to four hours of training for up to four people. I find that attention spans wander after two hours, so generally the session doesn't go much longer than that. The client takes notes while I go through the processes needed for maintaining the site.

Some clients will choose both options for training, which is a good way to generate extra revenue, and it also gives the client the opportunity to feel very comfortable with working with their new Joomla web site.

If you write documentation, walk through the processes yourself while you describe them. Take a lot of screenshots. SnagIt (www.techsmith.com) is a great tool for capturing screenshots quickly and easily. ScreenSteps (www.screensteps.com) is a great documentation tool that enables you to take screenshots and annotate them easily. You might also build up a series of documents describing how to complete common Joomla tasks. Over time, assembling the documentation for your clients becomes quick and easy, since you'll eventually have all of the standard Joomla tasks (like creating and editing articles, creating and editing menu items, etc) documented.

WHAT'S NEXT?

The site is completed, debugged, and the client is all trained. What's next?

I recommend immediate discussions with your client about what comes next.

Don't abandon your client by saying, "It's been fun, gotta run, enjoy your site!" Your client likes to know a safety net is nearby in case something goes wrong. Make sure you make it clear to your clients that they can call or email with questions and concerns. You might also make it clear that beyond some period of time, those questions and concerns are not free. I generally give my clients a month after launch to ask questions as needed. After that, I charge them my hourly rate, in 15-minute increments.

Maintenance plans are a great thing to discuss at this point. Some clients want regular, ongoing contact and training. Maybe you're doing search engine optimization work. Maybe you're helping with writing blog posts. In these cases, some clients will want to contract with you for a fixed number of hours each month. You might give them a discounted price on your hourly rate for this ongoing contract, because you don't need to hunt for work and you can count on their regular check. Generally speaking, if they don't use the time in a given month, it might not carry over to the next month. Sometimes it does. You will want to negotiate with your client.

Other clients won't want the ongoing fee, but they'll want to know you're available if they need you. In this case, you charge your standard hourly rate as required. You need to tell the client how quickly you will respond to their requests and what happens if you're out of town.

Sometimes clients want 24/7 support for their site. If you're a freelancer, this support is tough to provide, no matter how hard you try. You might want to look into a support service if this type of support is required. Open Source Support Desk (www.opensourcesupportdesk.com), based in the Netherlands, specializes in providing ongoing Joomla support and training at an hourly rate. This option might be good for those sorts of clients, either outside of your regular business hours, or even all the time.

Finally, do not hesitate to approach your clients if you find an addition that might work well on their site. Be a partner to your clients, not just the person who clicks buttons on the web site. You helped discover the site strategy and goals, the target audience, and you shaped the site map. You should have a good sense of additions to the site that would work well. By having a continuing relationship with clients, you can bring these suggestions to their attention, resulting in more work for you. You can also tell them when the time has come to do a site redesign.

Above all, remember that each client is a relationship for you. Each client can recommend you to the next person, who recommends you to the next person, and so forth. You will build a reputation in your local area or in the Joomla community. Over time, work will start to come to you without a huge amount of effort on your part. Treat your clients well and take good care of them, and they will ultimately take great care of you, too.

APPENDIX

Jen's Favorite Joomla! Extensions

All Joomla developers eventually compile a list of favorite extensions, as well as favorite extension developers. I've listed some of these in this appendix, with a link to the developer's web site.

In the course of evaluating extensions, my longtime engineer and friend, Bill Tomczak, and I have developed *Bill and Jen's Coding Theorem*. This theorem says that if the HTML and CSS are of good quality, the PHP is also of good quality. We have yet to find an exception to this rule in all of our years of looking at web sites and extensions.

The extensions in this appendix have made both of us either mostly happy or completely happy when using them. I hope you will find them useful as well.

ABSOLUTELY ESSENTIAL EXTENSIONS FOR ANY JOOMLA! WEB SITE

This section describes two extensions I always install as soon as I'm done installing Joomla: JoomlaPack and JCE. And I install Mass Content on 90% of the sites I build.

JoomlaPack

JoomlaPack, described extensively in Chapter 15, is a must-have for any Joomla site. It enables you to create a backup of all Joomla files (including images) plus your Joomla database. It also features an easy way to restore sites from backup. This restoration process is useful for moving a site from one server (usually a development server) to the final production server.

www.joomlapack.net

JCE

Chapter 2 covers JCE, the Joomla Content Editor.

Joomla comes with TinyMCE as its editor. The editor is the box you type in when entering content. Unfortunately, TinyMCE has a number of really bad usability problems, notably that browsing to a page on your web site to make a link is impossible (you must know the URL), there's no way to paste in content from Word, and there's no easy way to link to a PDF or other document. JCE addresses all of these usability issues nicely, in an interface that's easy to understand. Furthermore, it comes with an HTML code view, which is useful for me.

`www.joomlacontenteditor.net`

Mass Content

Significantly less well known than JoomlaPack and JCE, Mass Content makes my life so much easier.

How many hours of your life have you wasted creating sections, then categories, then pages and pages of placeholder content pages? If you're working on a slow Internet connection or a slow server, the process is absolutely mind-numbingly boring and takes forever.

Enter Mass Content, another extension I could not survive without. Mass Content lets you create up to 10 sections, categories, or articles in a single screen. (When you create categories, they must pertain to the same section. When you create articles, they must pertain to the same section and category.)

Mass Content can copy my Lorem Ipsum placeholder content from one article to the other quickly and easily — I do not have to copy and paste the content several times.

Mass Content shaves hours off of the creation of pages for big sites. After pages are created, Mass Content is no longer required, so you might want to remove it from your client's site so that he or she doesn't get confused by it.

`http://extensions.joomla.org/extensions/news-production/content-management/2514`

OTHER GREAT EXTENSIONS

I don't install the following extensions on every site, but I do use them on many sites.

XMap

I install XMap, a site-mapping tool, on roughly 90% of the sites I build. This simple tool provides a complete site map of your site by menu. You can exclude certain menus from XMap if you want. It can display your site map in multiple columns or a single column. It can also display an icon to flag links that go offsite.

Site maps are valuable tools for those looking for an overview of the web site. They're particularly valuable for search engines, because all links are clearly mapped out and accessible from a single page.

`http://joomla.vargas.co.cr/`

Azrul.com

Azrul Rahim is one of my favorite extension developers. Azrul has written MyBlog, JomComment, and JomSocial, and greatly extended Joomla in doing so.

➤   **MyBlog** is the extension I use when a client asks for blogging functionality. Building a blog with Joomla's core functionality is totally possible. After all, several different blog views and possibilities exist (see Chapter 6). However, Joomla's blog functionality doesn't have the greatest usability when you're trying to create a blog post from the front end of the web site.

   MyBlog has a Wordpress-like interface. It's a great solution for creating and editing blog posts from the front end of the web site. It supports multiple bloggers, so a given blogger does not have access to another blogger's post from the front end of the site (even if both bloggers have super admin access). The tagging of posts is also supported. The downside is that the editor for MyBlog is rather limited. This may not be a bad thing for clients, but I would prefer a more full-featured editor.

➤   **JomComment** is commenting software designed to seamlessly integrate with MyBlog. You can configure JomComment to permit commenting on all pages of the web site or just specific sections of the web site. Commenting has anti-spam technology included.

➤   **JomSocial** is an excellent new extension enabling you to easily add community features to your Joomla site. It's easier to set up and configure than Community Builder (the previous reigning Joomla champion in this category). JomSocial is one of the most expensive Joomla extensions on the market today, but it will save you hours of configuration time, as compared to Community Builder.

   www.azrul.com

JoomlaWorks

I am a huge fan of the extensions from JoomlaWorks. Without exception, every extension I have used from this developer has had great HTML and CSS (and Bill tells me they have great PHP as well).

➤   **FrontPage SlideShow** is what introduced me to JoomlaWorks. This extension rotates photos by fading them in and out. You can include writing on top of the images or on the side. Several template layouts come with the extension. Clients can add their own photos or rotate photos out, as they want.

➤   **Simple Image Gallery** and **Simple Image Gallery Pro** are simple photo galleries that live directly in an article. They are actually plug-ins that you call from within your article. Point Simple Image Gallery to a specific folder in your media manager, and it will generate thumbnails which, when clicked, will show a full-size version of the photo in a lightbox. Simple Image Gallery Pro does everything Simple Image Gallery does, but it also allows captions for photos.

➤   **Ultimate Content Display** is an extremely useful module that displays your articles in module format, either by rotating them (fade in, fade out) or by showing a list of headlines.

➤   **AllVideos** allows for easy embedding of videos from YouTube, Vimeo, and more.

➤   **K2** allows for nested categories, tagged articles, and even some user controls. It's fabulous for larger web sites.

    www.joomlaworks.gr

RSForm!Pro

RSForm!Pro, as you might expect, enables you to create forms for your Joomla web site. The forms are very straightforward to create, and you do not need to know HTML to use the extension. (However, as always, I think you can do more with configuration if you do know HTML.)

RSForm!Pro sends a completed form to the e-mail address(es) of your choice. It also records the form in a database, which you can later download as a CSV file (comma-separated value, which Microsoft Excel or Access can open).

You can use RSForm!Pro as a registration form for free seminars, for online surveys, for customized contact forms, and much more. Bill likes the way RSForm!Pro lets him create seemingly unlimited integrations with other extensions, regardless of whether they're from RSJoomla!. He can also customize the inner workings of the form.

www.rsjoomla.com

Grumpy Contacts

Finally, one of my favorite extensions is Grumpy Contacts, written by Bill Tomczak of Grumpy Engineering, LLC.

In the early days of Joomla, an extension was available called PeopleBook that Bill and I used on a bunch of sites. It allowed creating individual profiles of people for a web site, including their name, title, address, e-mail, phone, bio, photo, and a way of creating custom fields.

Unfortunately, extension support was short-lived, and it disappeared from the JED before long. Bill and I wanted PeopleBook for Joomla 1.5, so Bill decided to write it for us.

The extension is great for providing a list of staff members, their titles and contact information, and any background information. There's also an e-mail form on their page so you can contact them directly.

Bill has also added a Zip code locator function to Grumpy Contacts. Bill and I used this extension at www.byo.com to show lists of home brew suppliers within a certain radius of a given Zip code. We also used it on an insurance company web site to provide lists of agents in a given Zip code.

www.grumpyengineering.com

INDEX